Contents at a Glance

Table of Contents

Introduction

. . . .

So you wanna play guitar, huh? And why wouldn't you?

You may as well face it: In the music world, guitars set the standard for *cool* (and we're not *just* being biased here). Since the 1950s, many of the greatest stars in rock 'n' roll, blues, and country have played the guitar. Think of Chuck Berry doing his one-legged hop (the "duck walk") across the stage while belting out "Johnny B. Goode"; Jimi Hendrix wailing on his upside-down, right-handed (and sometimes flaming) Stratocaster; Bonnie Raitt slinkily playing her slide guitar; Garth Brooks with his acoustic guitar and Western shirts; B.B. King's authoritative bending and expressive vibrato on his guitar "Lucille"; or Jim Hall's mellow jazz guitar stylings. (Even Elvis Presley, whose guitar prowess may not have exceeded five chords, still used the guitar effectively onstage as a prop.) The list goes on.

Playing electric guitar can put you out in front of a band, where you're free to roam, sing, and connect with your adoring fans. Playing acoustic guitar can make you the star of the vacation campfire sing-along. And playing any kind of guitar can bring out the music in your soul and become a cherished lifetime hobby.

About This Book

Guitar For Dummies, 4th Edition, delivers everything the beginning to intermediate guitarist needs: From buying a guitar to tuning the guitar to playing the guitar to caring for the guitar — this book has it all!

Believe it or not, many would-be guitarists never really get into playing because they have the wrong guitar. Or maybe the strings are too difficult to press down (causing a great deal of pain). *Guitar For Dummies,* 4th Edition, unlike *some* other books we could mention, doesn't assume that you already have the right guitar — or even any guitar at all, for that matter. In this book, you find everything you need to know (from a buyer's guide to buying strategies, to guitars and accessories for particular styles) to match yourself with the guitar and equipment that fit your needs and budget.

Most guitar books want you to practice the guitar in the same way that you practice the piano. First, you learn where the notes fall on the staff; then you learn about the length of time that you're supposed to hold the notes; then you move on to practicing scales; and the big payoff is to practice song after unrecognizable song that you probably don't care about playing anyway. If you're looking for this kind of ho-hum guitar book, you've definitely come to the wrong place. But don't worry, you'll find no shortage of that kind of book.

The truth is that many great guitarists don't know how to read music, and many who *can* read music learned to do so after they learned to play the guitar. Repeat after us: *You don't need to read music to play the guitar.* Chant this mantra until you believe it, because this principle is central to the design of *Guitar For Dummies,* 4th Edition.

One of the coolest things about the guitar is that, even though you can devote your lifetime to perfecting your skills, you can start faking it rather quickly. We assume that, instead of concentrating on what the 3/4 time signature means, you want to play music — real music (or at least recognizable music). We want you to play music, too, because that's what keeps you motivated and practicing.

So how does *Guitar For Dummies,* 4th Edition, deliver? Glad you asked. The following list tells you how this book starts you playing and developing real guitar skills quickly:

- ✔ **Look at the photos.** Fingerings you need to know appear in photos in the book. Just form your hands the way we show you in the photos. Simple.

- ✔ **Read guitar tablature.** Guitar *tablature* is a guitar-specific shorthand for reading music that actually shows you what strings to strike and what frets to hold down on the guitar to create the sound that's called for. *Tab* (as it's known to its friends and admirers) goes a long way toward enabling you to *play* music without *reading* music. Don't try this stuff on the piano!

- ✔ **View videos and listen to audio tracks.** More than 80 short videos enable you to see how key selected techniques are executed. You can also listen to all the songs and exercises in the book performed on nearly 100 audio tracks. Doing so is important for a couple of reasons: You can figure out the rhythm of the song as well as how long to hold notes by listening instead of reading. We could tell you all sorts of really cool things about the audio tracks, such as how they have the featured guitar on one channel and the accompaniment on the other (so you can switch back and forth by using the balance control on your stereo), but, aw shucks, we don't want to brag on ourselves too much.

✔ **Look at the music staff as you improve.** To those who would charge that *Guitar For Dummies,* 4th Edition, rejects the idea of reading music, we respond: "Not so, Fret Breath!" The music for all the exercises and songs appears above the tab. So you get the best of both worlds: You can associate the music notation with the sound you're making after you already know how to make the sound. Pretty cool, huh?

A serious guitar is a serious investment, and, as with any other serious investment, you need to maintain it. *Guitar For Dummies,* 4th Edition, provides the information you need to correctly store, maintain, and care for your six-string, including how to change strings and what little extras to keep stashed away in your guitar case.

Foolish Assumptions

We really don't make many assumptions about you. We don't assume that you already own a guitar. We don't assume that you have a particular preference for acoustic or electric guitars or that you favor a particular style. Gee, this is a pretty equal-opportunity book!

Okay, we do assume some things. We assume that you want to play a *guitar,* not a banjo, Dobro, or mandolin, and we concentrate on the six-string variety. We assume you're relatively new to the guitar world. And we assume that you want to start playing the guitar quickly, without a lot of messing around with reading notes, clefs, and time signatures. You can find all that music-reading stuff in the book, but that's not our main focus. Our main focus is helping you make cool, sweet music on your six-string.

Icons Used in This Book

In the margins of this book, you find several helpful little icons that can make your journey a little easier:

Expert advice that can hasten your journey to guitar excellence.

Skip to a real song for some instant guitar gratification. Go to www.dummies. com/go/guitar for videos and audio clips.

Something to write down on a cocktail napkin and store in your guitar case.

 Watch out, or you could cause damage to your guitar or someone's ears.

 The whys and wherefores behind what you play. The theoretical and, perhaps at times, obscure stuff that you can skip at the time, if you so desire, but that you may return to at a later time for a deeper understanding of these concepts and techniques.

Beyond the Book

Guitar For Dummies, 4th Edition, provides text, photos, and diagrams to help you get your head around — and your hands on — the guitar. But membership in the *Guitar For Dummies* club also gets you something else of great value: access to the online assets that help you stay connected even when your eyes aren't focused somewhere between the book's covers.

To begin with, we have an electronic version of a Cheat Sheet that gives you quick, at-a-glance guidance to several aspects of the guitar that help your playing. The eCheat Sheet is divided into four sections, dealing with such diverse topics as notation explanations, common chords for various music styles, and recommended tools and accessories to have on hand for your guitar playing sessions. Check it out at www.dummies.com/cheatsheet/guitar.

You can find several free pieces of information online at www.dummies.com/extras/guitar.

You also can find online video and audio files at www.dummies.com/go/guitar that demonstrate exactly what the exercises and songs sound like and how they should be played. As a bonus, we include two printable documents (in the form of PDFs): a page of blank chord diagrams that you can fill in with the chord forms of your choice and a page of blank music paper, containing a treble clef staff and a tab staff. We encourage you to print these documents and fill them with song excerpts or exercises that you're focusing on. Be sure to check out Appendix C for a full explanation of and guide to the online files.

Where to Go from Here

Guitar For Dummies, 4th Edition, has been carefully crafted so you can find what you want or need to know about the guitar and no more. Because each chapter is self-contained, you can skip information that you've already mastered and not feel lost. Yet, at the same time, you can also follow along from front to back and practice the guitar in a way that builds step by step on your previous knowledge.

To find the information you need, you can simply look through the table of contents to find the area that you're interested in, or you can look for particular information in the index at the back of the book.

If you're a beginner and are ready to start playing right away, you can skip Chapter 1 and go straight to Chapter 2, where you get your guitar in tune. Then browse through Chapter 3 on developing the skills you need to play and dive straight in to Chapter 4. Although you can skip around somewhat in the playing chapters, if you're a beginner, we urge you to take the chapters in order, one at a time. Moreover, you should stick to Chapter 4 until you start to form calluses on your fingers, which really help you to make the chords sound right without buzzing.

If you don't yet have a guitar, you should start in Part V, the shopper's guide, and look for what you need in a basic practice guitar. After you buy your ax, you can get on with playing, which is the real fun after all, right?

Above all, remember that a hallmark of any *For Dummies* book is that it's non-linear. You can start reading from the beginning of any chapter in any Part of the book, and the text will make sense to you. We encourage you to skip around among the introduction chapters, the instruction chapters, the style chapters, and the shopping and maintenance chapters. And don't forget to top off a reading session with a Part of Tens chapter or two. Those chapters give you plenty of info to impress even the most jaded guest at a cocktail party. And if you do decide to read the book straight through, in a linear fashion, even though you don't have to, well, we think that's just fine, too.

Part I
Getting Started with Guitar

Head to www.dummies.com for supplemental information to help you in your guitar-playing endeavors.

In this part . . .

- ✔ Know how to identify the different parts of acoustic and electric guitars and what makes them unique.

- ✔ Understand how the guitar works to appreciate how it can produce sweet sounds.

- ✔ Discover how to tune your guitar so you can make in-tune music and prevent the local dogs from howling.

- ✔ Grasp how to position your body and hands correctly before you play.

- ✔ Comprehend how to read guitar notation to increase the ways you can absorb guitar music.

- ✔ Play a chord step-by-step to get your fingers in place for making real music.

Chapter 1

Guitar Basics: The Parts of a Guitar and How It Makes Music

●●

In This Chapter

▶ Identifying the different parts of the guitar

▶ Understanding how the guitar works

▶ Access the audio tracks and video clips at www.dummies.com/go/guitar

●●

All guitars — whether painted purple with airbrushed skulls and lightning bolts or finished in a natural-wood pattern with a fine French lacquer — share certain physical characteristics that make them behave like guitars and not violins or tubas. If you're confused about the difference between a headstock and a pickup or you're wondering which end of the guitar to hold under your chin, this chapter is for you.

We describe the differences among the various parts of the guitar and tell you what those parts do. We also tell you how to hold the instrument and why the guitar sounds the way it does. And, in case you took us seriously, you *don't* hold the guitar under your chin — unless, of course, you're Jimi Hendrix.

The Parts and Workings of a Guitar

Guitars come in two basic flavors: *acoustic* and *electric*. From a hardware standpoint, electric guitars have more components and doohickeys than acoustic guitars. Guitar makers generally agree, however, that making an acoustic guitar is harder than making an electric guitar. That's why, pound for pound, acoustic guitars cost just as much or more than their electric counterparts. (When you're ready to go guitar or guitar accessory shopping, you can check out Chapters 16 or 17, respectively.) But both types follow the same basic approach to such principles as neck construction and string tension. That's why both acoustic and electric guitars have similar shapes and features, despite a sometimes radical difference in tone production (unless, of course, you think that Segovia and Metallica are indistinguishable). Figures 1-1 and 1-2 show the various parts of acoustic and electric guitars.

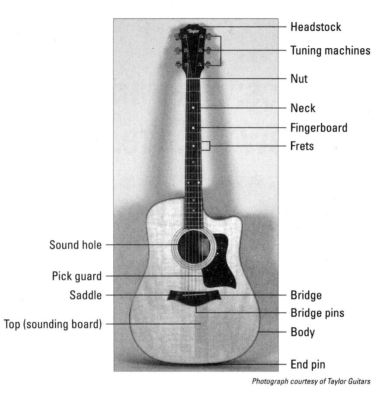

Photograph courtesy of Taylor Guitars

Figure 1-1:
Typical acoustic guitar with its major parts labeled.

The following list tells you the functions of the various parts of a guitar:

- **Back (acoustic only):** The part of the body that holds the sides in place; made of two or three pieces of wood.

- **Bar (electric only):** On some models, a metal rod attached to the bridge that varies the string tension by tilting the bridge back and forth. Also called the tremolo bar, whammy bar, vibrato bar, and wang bar.

- **Body:** The box that provides an anchor for the neck and bridge and creates the playing surface for the right hand. On an acoustic, the body includes the amplifying sound chamber that produces the guitar's tone. On an electric, it consists of the housing for the bridge assembly and electronics (pickups as well as volume and tone controls).

- **Bridge:** The metal (electric) or wooden (acoustic) plate that anchors the strings to the body.

- **Bridge pins (acoustic only):** Plastic or wooden dowels that insert through bridge holes and hold the strings securely to the bridge.

- **End pin:** A post where the rear end of the strap connects. On *acoustic-electrics* (acoustic guitars with built-in pickups and electronics), the pin often doubles as the *output jack* where you plug in.

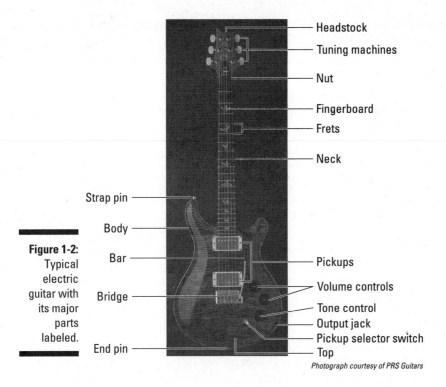

Headstock

Tuning machines

Nut

Fingerboard

Frets

Neck

Strap pin

Body

Figure 1-2:
Typical
electric
guitar with
its major
parts
labeled.

Bar

Bridge

End pin

Pickups

Volume controls

Tone control

Output jack

Pickup selector switch

Top

Photograph courtesy of PRS Guitars

- ✔ **Fingerboard:** A flat, planklike piece of wood that sits atop the neck, where you place your left-hand fingers to produce notes and chords. The fingerboard is also known as the *fretboard,* because the frets are embedded in it.

- ✔ **Frets:** (1) Thin metal wires or bars running perpendicular to the strings that shorten the effective vibrating length of a string, enabling it to produce different pitches. (2) A verb describing worry, as in "He frets about how many little parts are on his guitar."

- ✔ **Headstock:** The section that holds the tuning machines (hardware assembly) and provides a place for the manufacturer to display its logo. Not to be confused with "Woodstock," the section of New York that provided a place for the '60s generation to display its music.

- ✔ **Neck:** The long, clublike wooden piece that connects the headstock to the body.

- ✔ **Nut:** A grooved sliver of stiff nylon or other synthetic substance that stops the strings from vibrating beyond the neck. The strings pass through the grooves on their way to the tuning machines in the headstock. The nut is one of the two points at which the vibrating area of the string ends. (The other is the bridge.)

- ✔ **Output jack (electric only):** The insertion point for the cord that connects the guitar to an amplifier or other electronic device.

- ✔ **Pickup selector (electric only):** A switch that determines which pickups are currently active.

- ✔ **Pickups (electric only):** Barlike magnets that create the electrical current, which the amplifier converts into musical sound.

- ✔ **Saddle:** For acoustic, a thin plastic strip that sits inside a slot in the bridge; for electric, separate metal pieces that provide the contact point for the strings and the bridge.

- ✔ **Sides (acoustic only):** Separate curved wooden pieces on the body that join the top to the back.

- ✔ **Strap pin:** Metal post where the front, or top, end of the strap connects. (*Note:* Not all acoustics have a strap pin. If the guitar is missing one, tie the top of the strap around the headstock.)

- ✔ **Strings:** The six metal (for electric and steel-string acoustic guitars) or nylon (for classical guitars) wires that, drawn taut, produce the notes of the guitar. Although not strictly part of the actual guitar (you attach and remove them at will on top of the guitar), strings are an integral part of the whole system, and a guitar's entire design and structure revolves around making the strings ring out with a joyful noise. (See Chapter 18 for info on changing strings.)

- ✔ **Top:** The face of the guitar. On an acoustic, this piece is also the *sounding board,* which produces almost all the guitar's acoustic qualities. On an electric, the top is merely a cosmetic or decorative cap that overlays the rest of the body material.

- ✔ **Tuning machines:** Geared mechanisms that raise and lower the tension of the strings, drawing them to different pitches. The string wraps tightly around a post that sticks out through the top, or face, of the headstock. The post passes through to the back of the headstock, where gears connect it to a tuning key. Also known as tuners, tuning pegs, tuning keys, and tuning gears.

- ✔ **Volume and tone controls (electric only):** Knobs that vary the loudness of the guitar's sound and its bass and treble frequencies.

How Guitars Make Sound

After you can recognize the basic parts of the guitar (see the preceding section for help), you may also want to understand how those parts work together to make sound (in case you happen to choose the *Parts of a Guitar* category in *Jeopardy!* or get into a heavy argument with another guitarist about string vibration and string length). We present this information in the following sections just so you know why your guitar sounds the way it does, instead of like a kazoo or an accordion. The important thing to remember is that a guitar makes the sound, but you make the music.

Strings doing their thing

Any instrument must have some part of it moving in a regular, repeated motion to produce musical sound (a sustained tone, or pitch). In a guitar, this part is the vibrating string. A string that you bring to a certain tension and then set in motion (by a plucking action) produces a predictable sound — for example, the note A. If you tune a string of your guitar to different tensions, you get different tones. The greater the tension of a string, the higher the pitch.

You couldn't do very much with a guitar, however, if the only way to change pitches was to frantically adjust the tension on the strings every time you pluck a string. So guitarists resort to the other way to change a string's pitch — by shortening its effective vibrating length. They do so by fretting — pacing back and forth and mumbling to themselves. (Just kidding; guitarists never do *that* kind of fretting unless they haven't held their guitars for a couple of days.) In guitar-speak, *fretting* refers to pushing the string against the fretboard so the string vibrates only between the fingered fret (metal wire) and the bridge. This way, by moving the left hand up and down the neck (toward the bridge and the nut, respectively), you can change pitches comfortably and easily.

The fact that smaller instruments, such as mandolins and violins, are higher in pitch than are cellos and basses (and guitars, for that matter) is no accident. Their pitch is higher because their strings are shorter. The string tension of all these instruments may be closely related, making them feel somewhat consistent in response to the hands and fingers, but the drastic difference in string lengths is what results in the wide differences of pitch among them. This principle holds true in animals, too. A Chihuahua has a higher-pitched bark than a St. Bernard because its strings — er, vocal cords — are much shorter.

Using left and right hands together

The guitar normally requires two hands working together to create music. If you want to play, say, middle C on the piano, all you do is take your index finger, position it above the appropriate white key under the piano's logo, and drop it down: *donnnng*. A preschooler can sound just like Elton John if playing only middle C, because just one finger of one hand, pressing one key, makes the sound.

The guitar is somewhat different. To play middle C on the guitar, you must take your left-hand index finger and fret the 2nd string (that is, press it down to the fingerboard) at the 1st fret. This action, however, doesn't itself produce a sound. You must then strike or pluck that 2nd string with your right hand to actually produce the note middle C audibly. *Music readers take note:* The guitar sounds an octave lower than its written notes. For example, playing a written, third-space C on the guitar actually produces a middle C.

Notes on the neck: Half steps and frets

The smallest *interval* (unit of musical distance in pitch) of the musical scale is the *half step.* On the piano, the alternating white and black keys represent this interval (as do the places where you find two adjacent white keys with no black key in between). To proceed by half steps on a keyboard instrument, you move your finger up or down to the next available key, white or black. On the guitar, *frets* — the horizontal metal wires (or bars) that you see embedded in the fretboard, running perpendicular to the strings — represent these half steps. To go up or down by half steps on a guitar means to move your left hand one fret at a time, higher or lower on the neck.

Comparing how acoustics and electrics generate sound

Vibrating strings produce the different tones on a guitar. But you must be able to *hear* those tones, or you face one of those if-a-tree-falls-in-a-forest questions. For an acoustic guitar, that's no problem, because an acoustic instrument provides its own amplifier in the form of the hollow sound chamber that boosts its sound . . . well, acoustically.

But an electric guitar makes virtually no acoustic sound at all. (Well, a tiny bit, like a buzzing mosquito, but nowhere near enough to fill a stadium or anger your next-door neighbors.) An electric instrument creates its tones entirely through electronic means. The vibrating string is still the source of the sound, but a hollow wood chamber isn't what makes those vibrations audible. Instead, the vibrations disturb, or *modulate,* the magnetic field that the *pickups* — wire-wrapped magnets positioned underneath the strings — produce. As the vibrations of the strings modulate the pickup's magnetic field, the pickup produces a tiny electric current that exactly reflects that modulation.

Guitars, therefore, make sound by amplifying string vibrations either acoustically (by passing the sound waves through a hollow chamber) or electronically (by amplifying and outputting a current through a speaker). That's the physical process anyway. How a guitar produces *different* sounds — and the ones that you want it to make — is up to you and how you control the pitches that those strings produce. Left-hand fretting is what changes these pitches. Your right-hand motions not only help produce the sound by setting the string in motion, but they also determine the *rhythm* (the beat or pulse), *tempo* (the speed of the music), and *feel* (interpretation, style, spin, magic, mojo, *je ne sais quoi,* whatever) of those pitches. Put both hand motions together, and they spell music — make that *guitar* music.

Chapter 2

How to Tune Your Guitar

*T*uning is to guitarists what parallel parking is to city drivers: an everyday and necessary activity that can be vexingly difficult to master. Unlike the piano, which a professional tunes and you never need to adjust until the next time the professional tuner comes to visit, the guitar is normally tuned by its owner — and it needs constant adjusting.

One of the great injustices of life is that before you can even play music on the guitar, you must endure the painstaking process of getting your instrument in tune. Fortunately for guitarists, you have only six strings to tune as opposed to the couple hundred strings in a piano. Also encouraging is the fact that you can use several different methods to get your guitar in tune, as this chapter describes.

Before You Begin: Strings and Frets by the Numbers

We're going to start from square one, or in this case, string one. Before you can tune your guitar, you need to know how to refer to the two main players — strings and frets.

✔ **Strings:** Strings are numbered consecutively 1 through 6. The 1st string is the skinniest, located closest to the floor (when you hold the guitar in playing position). Working your way up, the 6th string is the fattest, closest to the ceiling.

We recommend that you memorize the letter names of the open strings (E, A, D, G, B, E, from 6th to 1st) so you're not limited to referring to them by number. An easy way to memorize the open strings in order is to remember the phrase *Eddie Ate Dynamite; Good Bye, Eddie.*

✔ **Frets:** *Fret* can refer to either the space where you put your left-hand finger or to the thin metal bar running across the fingerboard. Whenever you deal with guitar fingering, *fret* means the space in between the metal bars — where you can comfortably fit a left-hand finger. (We introduce frets and other important parts of the guitar in Chapter 1.)

The 1st fret is the region between the *nut* (the thin, grooved strip that separates the headstock from the neck) and the first metal bar. The 5th fret, then, is the fifth square up from the nut — technically, the region between the fourth and fifth metal fret bars.

Most guitars have a marker on the 5th fret, either a decorative design embedded in the fingerboard or a dot on the side of the neck, or both.

One more point of business to square away. You'll come across the terms *open strings* and *fretted strings* from this point on in this book. Here's what those terms mean:

✔ **Open string:** A string you play without pressing down on it with a left-hand finger.

✔ **Fretted string:** A string you play while pressing down on it at a particular fret.

Tuning Your Guitar to Itself with the 5th-Fret Method

Relative tuning is so named because you don't need any outside reference to which you tune the instrument. As long as the strings are in tune in a certain relationship with each other, you can create sonorous and harmonious tones. Those same tones may turn into sounds resembling those of a catfight if you try to play along with another instrument, however; but as long as you tune the strings relative to one another, the guitar is in tune with itself.

To tune a guitar by using the relative method, choose one string — say, the 6th string — as the starting point. Leave the pitch of that string as is; then tune all the other strings relative to that 6th string.

The *5th-fret method* derives its name from the fact that you almost always play a string at the 5th fret and then compare the sound of that note to that of the next open string. You need to be careful, though, because the 4th fret (the 5th fret's jealous understudy) puts in a cameo appearance toward the end of the process.

Here's how to get your guitar in tune by using the 5th-fret method (check out the diagram in Figure 2-1 that outlines all five steps):

1. **Play the 5th fret of the 6th (low E) string (the fattest one, closest to the ceiling) and then play the open 5th (A) string (the one next to it).**

   Let both notes ring together (in other words, allow the 6th string to continue vibrating while you play the 5th string). Their pitches should match exactly. If they don't seem quite right, determine whether the 5th string is lower or higher than the fretted 6th string.

   - If the 5th string seems lower, or _flat,_ turn its tuning key with your left hand (in a counterclockwise direction as you look directly at the tuning key) to raise the pitch.

   - If the 5th string seems _sharp,_ or higher sounding, use its tuning key to lower the pitch (by turning it in a clockwise direction as you look directly at the tuning key).

    You may go too far with the tuning key if you're not careful; if so, you need to reverse your motions. In fact, if you _can't_ tell whether the 5th string is higher or lower, tune it flat intentionally (that is, tune it too low) and then come back to the desired pitch.

2. **Play the 5th fret of the 5th (A) string and then play the open 4th (D) string.**

   Let both of these notes ring together. If the 4th string seems flat or sharp relative to the fretted 5th string, use the tuning key of the 4th string to adjust its pitch accordingly. Again, if you're not sure whether the 4th string is higher or lower, overtune it in one direction — flat, or lower, is better — and then come back.

3. **Play the 5th fret of the 4th (D) string and then play the open 3rd (G) string.**

   Let both notes ring together again. If the 3rd string seems flat or sharp relative to the fretted 4th string, use the tuning key of the 3rd string to adjust the pitch accordingly.

4. **Play the 4th (_not_ the 5th!) fret of the 3rd (G) string and then play the open 2nd (B) string.**

   Let both strings ring together. If the 2nd string seems flat or sharp, use its tuning key to adjust the pitch accordingly.

5. **Play the 5th (yes, back to the 5th for this one) fret of the 2nd (B) string and then play the open 1st (high E) string.**

   Let both notes ring together. If the 1st string seems flat or sharp, use its tuning key to adjust the pitch accordingly. If you're satisfied that both strings produce the same pitch, you've now tuned the upper (that is, _upper_ as in higher-pitched) five strings of the guitar relative to the fixed (untuned) 6th string. Your guitar's now in tune with itself.

You may want to go back and repeat the process, because some strings may have slipped out of tune. To get the hang of the 5th-fret tuning method and matching fretted strings against open ones, check out Video Clip 1.

Figure 2-1:
Place your fingers on the frets as shown and match the pitch to the next open string.

Video Clip 1

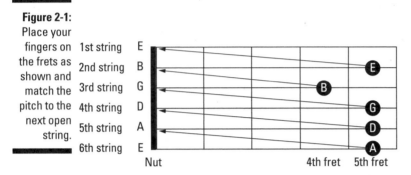

© John Wiley & Sons, Inc.

When you tune in the normal way, you use your left hand to turn the tuning peg. But after you remove your finger from the string that you're fretting, it stops ringing; therefore, you can no longer hear the string you're trying to tune to (the fretted string) as you adjust the open string. However, you can tune the open string while keeping your left-hand finger on the fretted string. Simply use your right hand! After you strike the two strings in succession (the fretted string and the open string), take your right hand and reach over your left hand (which remains stationary as you fret the string) and turn the tuning peg of the appropriate string until both strings sound exactly the same.

Tuning Your Guitar to an External Source

Getting the guitar in tune with itself through the 5th-fret method in the preceding section is good for your ear but isn't very practical if you need to play with other instruments or voices that are accustomed to standard tuning references (see the section "Getting a taste of the tuning fork," a little later in this chapter). If you want to bring your guitar into the world of other people or instruments, you need to know how to tune to a fixed source, such as a piano, pitch pipe, tuning fork, or electronic tuner. Using such a source ensures that everyone is playing by the same tuning rules. Besides, your guitar and strings are built for optimal tone production if you tune to standard pitch.

The following sections describe some typical ways to tune your guitar by using fixed references. These methods enable you to not only get in tune but also make nice with all the other instruments in the neighborhood.

Keying in to the piano

Because it holds its pitch so well (needing only biannual or annual tunings, depending on conditions), a piano is a great tool to use for tuning a guitar. Assuming that you have an electronic keyboard or a well-tuned piano around, all you need to do is match the open strings of the guitar to the appropriate keys on the piano. Figure 2-2 shows a piano keyboard and the corresponding open guitar strings.

Putting that pitch pipe to work

Obviously, if you're off to the beach with your guitar, you're not going to want to put a piano in the back of your car, even if you're really fussy about tuning. So you need a smaller and more practical device that supplies standard-tuning reference pitches. Enter the pitch pipe. The *pitch pipe* evokes images of stern, matronly chorus leaders who purse their prunelike lips around a circular harmonica to deliver an anemic squeak that instantly marshals together the reluctant voices of the choir. Yet pitch pipes serve their purpose.

For guitarists, special pitch pipes exist consisting of pipes that play only the notes of the open strings of the guitar (but sounding in a higher range) and none of the in-between notes. The advantage of a pitch pipe is that you can hold it firmly in your mouth while blowing, keeping your hands free for tuning. The disadvantage to a pitch pipe is that you sometimes take a while getting used to hearing a wind-produced pitch against a struck-string pitch. But with practice, you can tune with a pitch pipe as easily as you can with a piano. And a pitch pipe fits much more easily into your shirt pocket than a piano does!

Getting a taste of the tuning fork

After you get good enough at discerning pitches, you need only one single-pitched tuning reference to get your whole guitar in tune. The tuning fork offers only one pitch, and it usually comes in only one flavor: A (the one above middle C, which vibrates at 440 cycles per second, commonly known as *A-440*). But that note's really all you need. If you tune your open 5th string

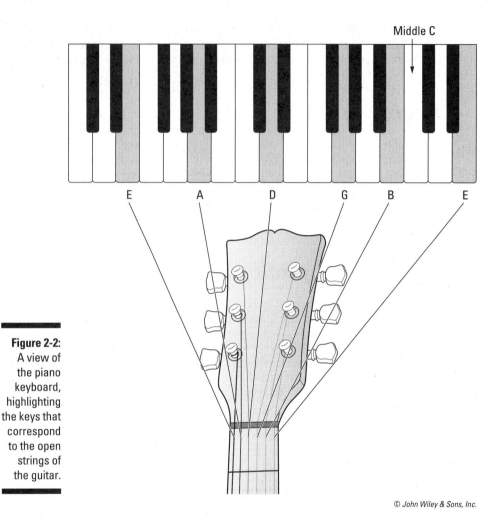

Middle C

E   A   D   G   B   E

Figure 2-2:
A view of
the piano
keyboard,
highlighting
the keys that
correspond
to the open
strings of
the guitar.

© John Wiley & Sons, Inc.

(A) to the tuning fork's A (although the guitar's A sounds in a lower range), you can tune every other string to that string by using the relative tuning method that we discuss in the section "Tuning Your Guitar to Itself with the 5th-Fret Method" earlier in this chapter.

Using a tuning fork requires a little finesse. You must strike the fork against something firm, such as a tabletop or kneecap, and then hold it close to your ear or place the stem (or handle) — and *not* the tines (or fork prongs) — against something that resonates. This resonator can be the tabletop again or the top of the guitar. (You can even hold it between your teeth, which leaves your hands free! It really works, too!) At the same time, you must somehow play an A and tune it to the fork's tone. The process is kind of like pulling your house keys out of your pocket while you're loaded down with an armful of groceries. The task may not be easy, but if you do it enough, you eventually become an expert.

Electing to employ the electronic tuner

The quickest and most accurate way to get in tune is to employ an *electronic tuner*. This handy device seems to possess witchcraft-like powers. Newer electronic tuners made especially for guitars can usually sense what string you're playing, tell you what pitch you're nearest, and indicate whether you're flat (too low) or sharp (too high). About the only thing these devices don't do is turn the tuning keys for you (although we hear they're working on that). Some older, graph-type tuners feature a switch that selects which string you want to tune. Figure 2-3 shows a typical electronic tuner.

Figure 2-3: An electronic tuner makes tuning a snap.

Photograph courtesy of KORG USA, Inc.

You can either plug your guitar into the tuner (if you're using an electric instrument) or you can use the tuner's built-in microphone to tune an acoustic. In both types of tuners — the ones where you select the strings and the ones that automatically sense the string — the display indicates two things: what note you're closest to (E, A, D, G, B, E) and whether you're flat or sharp of that note.

Nine-volt batteries or two AAs that can last for a year with regular usage (up to two or even three years with only occasional usage) usually power electronic tuners. Many electronic tuners are inexpensive (as low as $20 or so) and are well worth the money. You can also find tuners in the form of apps on smartphones and other handheld devices and on the web. (For more on tuners, see Chapter 17.)

Using the audio tracks

Lest we forget, you have at your disposal one more fixed source as a tuning reference: your *Guitar For Dummies* audio tracks.

For your tuning convenience, we play the open strings on Track 1. Listen to the tone of each open string as it sounds slowly, one at a time (1st to the 6th, or skinniest to fattest) and tune your guitar's open strings to those on the audio track. Go back to the beginning of Track 1 to repeat the tuning notes as often as necessary to get your strings exactly in tune with the strings on the audio track.

The benefit of using Track 1 to help you tune is that it always plays back the exact pitch and never goes sharp or flat, not even a little bit. So you can use Track 1 at any time to get perfectly tuned notes.

Chapter 3

Preparing to Play: Holding the Guitar and Reading Guitar Notation

....

In This Chapter

▶ Positioning your body and hands before you play

▶ Reading chord diagrams, tablature, and rhythm slashes

▶ Playing a chord

▶ Access the audio tracks and video clips at `www.dummies.com/go/guitar`

....

Guitars are user-friendly instruments. They fit comfortably into the arms of most humans, and the way your two hands fall on the strings naturally is pretty much the position from which you should play. In this chapter, we tell you all about good posture techniques and how to hold your hands — just as if you were a young socialite at a finishing school.

We jest because we care. But you really do need to remember that good posture and position, at the very least, prevent strain and fatigue and, at best, help develop good concentration habits and tone. After we get you positioned correctly with the guitar, we go over some basic music-deciphering skills and show you how to play a chord.

Assuming the Positions

You can either sit or stand while playing the guitar, and the position you choose makes virtually no difference whatsoever to your tone or technique. Most people prefer to sit while practicing but stand while performing publicly. (**Note:** The one exception to the sit or stand option is the classical guitar, which you normally play in a sitting position. The orthodox practice is to play in a seated position only. This practice doesn't mean that you *can't* play a classical-style guitar or classical music while standing, but the serious pursuit of the classical guitar requires that you sit while playing. See Chapter 14 for full details.)

In the following sections, we describe sitting and standing postures for playing the guitar, and we show you how to position both of your hands.

Sitting down and playing a spell

To hold the guitar in a sitting position, rest the *waist* of the guitar on your right leg. (The waist is the indented part between the guitar's upper and lower *bouts,* which are the protruding curved parts that look like shoulders and hips.) Place your feet slightly apart. Balance the guitar by lightly resting your right forearm on the bass bout, as shown in Figure 3-1. Don't use the left hand to support the neck. You should be able to take your left hand completely off the fretboard without the guitar dipping toward the floor.

Classical-guitar technique, on the other hand, requires you to hold the instrument on your *left* leg, not on your right. This position puts the center of the guitar closer to the center of your body, making the instrument easier to play, especially with the left hand, because you can better execute the difficult fingerings of the classical-guitar music in that position. Chapter 14 shows the classical-guitar sitting position.

Figure 3-1:
Typical
sitting
position.

Photograph courtesy of Cherry Lane Music

You must also elevate the classical guitar, which you can do either by raising the left leg with a specially made *guitar foot stool* (the traditional way) or by using a *support arm,* which goes between your left thigh and the guitar's lower side (the modern way). This device enables your left foot to remain on the floor and instead pushes the guitar up in the air.

Standing up and delivering

To stand and play the guitar, you need to securely fasten (or tie) a strap to both strap pins on the guitar. Then, you can stand in a normal way and check out how cool you look in the mirror with that guitar slung over your shoulders. You may need to adjust the strap to get the guitar at a comfortable playing height.

If your strap slips off a pin while you're playing in a standing position, you have about a 50-50 chance of catching your guitar before it hits the floor (and that's if you're quick and experienced with slipping guitars). So don't risk damaging your guitar by using an old or worn strap or one with holes that are too large for the pins to hold securely. Guitars aren't built to bounce, as the Who have demonstrated so many times.

Your body makes a natural adjustment in going from a sitting position to a standing position. So don't try to overanalyze where your arms fall, relative to your sitting position. Just stay relaxed and, above all, *look cool.* (You're a guitar player now! Looking cool is just as important as knowing how to play . . . well, *almost* as important.) Figure 3-2 shows a typical standing position.

Fretting with your left hand

To get an idea of correct left-hand positioning on the guitar, extend your left hand, palm up, and make a loose fist, placing your thumb roughly between your 1st and 2nd fingers. All your knuckles should be bent. Your hand should look about the same after you stick a guitar neck in there. The thumb glides along the back of the neck, straighter than if you were making a fist but not rigid. The finger knuckles stay bent whether they're fretting or relaxed. Again, the left hand should fall in place very naturally on the guitar neck — as if you're picking up a specially made tool that you've been using all your life.

To *fret* a note, press the tip of your finger down on a string, keeping your knuckles bent. Try to get the fingertip to come down vertically on the string rather than at an angle. This position exerts the greatest pressure on the string and also prevents the sides of the finger from touching adjacent strings — which may cause either buzzing or *muting* (deadening the string or preventing it from ringing). Use your thumb from its position underneath the neck to help *squeeze* the fingerboard for a tighter grip. Video Clip 2 shows you how to apply your left-hand fingers to the fingerboard to fret correctly.

Figure 3-2:
Typical
standing
position.

Photograph courtesy of Cherry Lane Music

When playing a particular fret, keep in mind that you don't place your finger directly on the metal fret wire but in between the two frets (or between the nut and 1st fret wire). For example, if you're playing the 5th fret, place your finger in the square between the 4th and 5th fret wires. Place it not in the center of the square (midway between the fret wires), but closer to the higher fret wire. This technique gives you the clearest sound and prevents buzzing.

Left-hand fretting requires strength, but don't be tempted to try speeding up the process of strengthening your hands through artificial means. Building up the strength in your left hand takes time. You may see advertisements for hand-strengthening devices and believe that these products may expedite your left-hand endurance. Although we can't declare that these devices never work (and the same goes for the home-grown method of squeezing a racquet ball or tennis ball), one thing's for sure: Nothing helps you build your left-hand fretting strength better or faster than simply playing guitar.

Because of the strength your left hand exerts while fretting, other parts of your body may tense up to compensate. At periodic intervals, make sure you relax your left shoulder, which has a tendency to rise as you work on your fretting. Take frequent "drop-shoulder" breaks. You want to keep your upper arm and forearm parallel to the side of your body. Relax your elbow so it stays at your side.

To maintain a good left-hand position, you need to keep it comfortable and natural. If your hand starts to hurt or ache, *stop playing and take a rest.* As with any other activity that requires muscular development, resting enables your body to catch up.

In the following sections, we give you additional, specific details on left-hand fretting for electric and classical guitars.

Electric endeavors

Electric necks are both narrower (from the 1st string to the 6th) and shallower (from the fingerboard to the back of the neck) than acoustic necks. Electric guitars, therefore, are easier to fret. But the space between each string is smaller, so you're more likely to touch and deaden an adjacent string with your fretting finger. The biggest difference, however, between fretting on an electric and on a nylon- or steel-string acoustic is the action.

A guitar's *action* refers to how high above the frets the strings ride and, to a lesser extent, how easy the strings are to fret. On an electric guitar, fretting strings is like passing a hot knife through butter. The easier action of an electric enables you to use a more relaxed left-hand position than you normally would on an acoustic, with the palm of the left hand facing slightly outward. Figure 3-3 shows a photo of the left hand resting on the fingerboard of an electric guitar, fretting a string.

Figure 3-3: The electric guitar neck lies comfortably between the thumb and the 1st finger as the 1st finger frets a note.

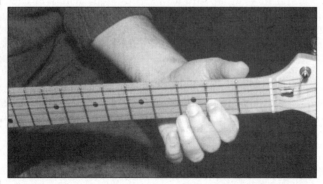

Photograph courtesy of Cherry Lane Music

Classical conditions

Because nylon-string guitars have a wide fingerboard and are the model of choice for classical music, their necks require a slightly more (ahem) formal left-hand approach. Try to get the palm-side of your knuckles (the ones that connect your fingers to your hand) to stay close to and parallel to the side of the neck so the fingers run perpendicular to the strings and all the fingers are the same distance away from the neck. (If your hand isn't perfectly parallel, the little finger "falls away" or is farther from the neck than your index finger.) Figure 3-4 shows the correct left-hand position for nylon-string guitars.

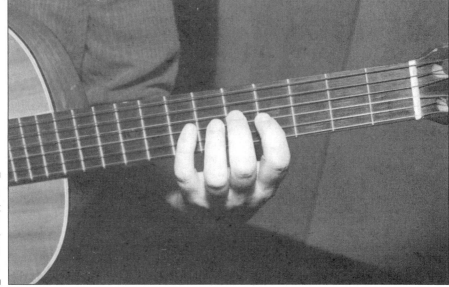

Photograph courtesy of Cherry Lane Music

Figure 3-4:
Correct
left-hand
position for
a classical
guitar.

Picking with your right hand

If you hold a guitar in your lap and drape your right arm over the upper bout, your right hand, held loosely outstretched, crosses the strings at about a 60 degree angle. This position is good for playing with a pick. For fingerstyle playing, you want to turn your right hand more perpendicular to the strings. For classical guitar, you want to keep the right hand as close to a 90 degree angle as possible.

In the following sections, we provide guidelines on right-hand picking with a pick and with your fingers. Refer to Video Clip 3 to double-check that you're picking correctly.

If you're using a pick

You do almost all your electric guitar playing with a pick, whether you're belting out rock 'n' roll, blues, jazz, country, or pop. On acoustic, you can play either with a pick or with your fingers. On both electric and acoustic, you play most *rhythm* (chord-based accompaniment) and virtually all *lead* (single-note melodies) by holding the pick, or *plectrum* (the old-fashioned term), between the thumb and index finger. Figure 3-5 shows the correct way to hold a pick — with just the tip sticking out, perpendicular to the thumb.

If you're *strumming* (playing rhythm), you strike the strings with the pick by using wrist and elbow motion. The more vigorous the strum, the more elbow you must put into the mix. For playing lead, you use only the more economical wrist motion. Don't grip the pick too tightly as you play — and plan on dropping it a lot for the first few weeks that you use it.

Figure 3-5:
Correct pick-holding technique.

Photograph courtesy of Cherry Lane Music

Picks come in various *gauges.* A pick's gauge indicates how stiff, or thick, it is.

- ✔ Thinner picks are easier to manage for the beginner.

- ✔ Medium picks are the most popular, because they're flexible enough for comfortable rhythm playing yet stiff enough for leads.

- ✔ Heavy-gauge picks may seem unwieldy at first, but they're the choice for pros, and eventually all skilled instrumentalists graduate to them (although a few famous holdouts exist — Neil Young being a prime example).

If you're using your fingers

If you eschew such paraphernalia as picks and want to go au naturel with your right hand, you're fingerpicking (although you can fingerpick with special individual, wraparound picks that attach to your fingers — called, confusingly enough, *fingerpicks*). *Fingerpicking* means that you play the guitar by plucking the strings with the individual right-hand fingers. The thumb plays the *bass,* or low, strings, and the fingers play the *treble,* or high, strings. In fingerpicking, you use the tips of the fingers to play the strings, positioning the hand over the sound hole (if you're playing acoustic) and keeping the wrist stationary but not rigid. Maintaining a slight arch in the wrist so the fingers come down more vertically on the strings also helps. Chapter 13 contains more information on fingerpicking style, including figures showing proper hand position.

Because of the special right-hand strokes that you use in playing classical guitar (the *free stroke* and the *rest stroke*), you must hold your fingers almost perfectly perpendicular to the strings to execute the correct technique. A perpendicular approach enables your fingers to draw against the strings with maximum strength. See Chapter 14 for more information on the rest stroke and free stroke.

Getting Your Head around Guitar Notation

Although you don't need to read music to play the guitar, musicians have developed a few simple tricks through the years that aid in communicating such basic ideas as song structure, chord construction, chord progressions, and important rhythmic figures. Pick up on the shorthand devices for *chord diagrams, tablature,* and *rhythm slashes* (which we describe in the following sections), and you're sure to start coppin' licks faster than Vince Gill pickin' after three cups of coffee.

We promise that you don't need to read music to play the guitar. With the help of the chord diagrams, tablature, and rhythm slashes that we explain in this section, plus hearing what all this stuff sounds like through the magic of audio tracks and video clips, you can pick up on everything you need to understand and play the guitar. Beginning in Chapter 4, listen closely to the audio tracks and video clips, and follow the corresponding written examples to make sure you understand how the two relate.

Understanding chord diagrams

Don't worry — reading a chord diagram is *not* like reading music; it's far simpler. All you need to do is understand where to put your fingers to form a chord. A *chord* is defined as the simultaneous sounding of three or more notes.

Figure 3-6 shows the anatomy of a chord chart, and the following list briefly explains what the different parts of the diagram mean:

> ✔ *The grid of six vertical lines and five horizontal ones* represents the guitar fretboard, as if you stood the guitar up on the floor or chair and looked straight at the upper part of the neck from the front.

✔ The *vertical lines* represent the guitar strings. The vertical line at the far left is the low 6th string, and the right-most vertical line is the high 1st string.

✔ The *horizontal lines* represent frets. The thick horizontal line at the top is the *nut* of the guitar, where the fretboard ends. So the 1st fret is actually the second vertical line from the top. (Don't let the words here confuse you; just look at the guitar.)

✔ The *dots* that appear on vertical string lines between horizontal fret lines represent notes that you fret.

✔ The *numerals* directly below each string line (just below the last fret line) indicate which left-hand finger you use to fret that note. On the left hand, 1 = index finger; 2 = middle finger; 3 = ring finger; and 4 = little finger. You don't use the thumb to fret, except in certain unusual circumstances.

✔ The *X* or *O* symbols directly above some string lines indicate strings that you leave open (unfretted) or that you don't play. An *X* (not shown in Figure 3-6) above a string means that you don't pick or strike that string with your right hand. An *O* indicates an open string that you do play.

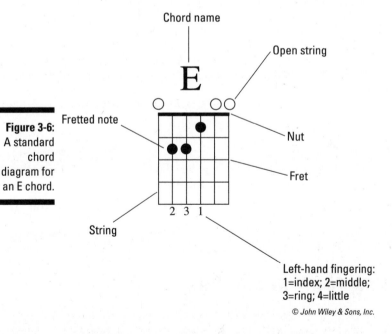

Figure 3-6: A standard chord diagram for an E chord.

Chord name

Open string

E

Fretted note

Nut

Fret

String

2 3 1

Left-hand fingering: 1=index; 2=middle; 3=ring; 4=little

© John Wiley & Sons, Inc.

REMEMBER

If a chord starts on a fret *other* than the 1st fret (which you can see in Chapters 11 and 12), a numeral appears to the right of the diagram, next to the top fret line, to indicate in which fret you actually start. (In such cases, the top line is *not* the nut.) In most cases, however, you deal primarily with chords that fall within only the first four frets of the guitar. Chords that fall within the first four frets typically use open strings, so they're referred to as *open* chords.

Taking in tablature

Tablature (or just *tab,* for short) is a notation system that graphically represents the frets and strings of the guitar. Whereas chord diagrams do so in a static way, tablature shows how you play music over a period of time. For all the musical examples that appear in this book, you see a *tablature staff* (or *tab staff,* for short) beneath the standard notation staff. This second staff reflects exactly what's going on in the regular musical staff above it but in *guitar language.* Tab is guitar-specific — in fact, many call it simply *guitar tab.* Tab doesn't tell you what *note* to play (such as C or F♯ or E♭). It does, however, tell you what *string* to fret and where exactly on the fingerboard to *fret* that string.

Figure 3-7 shows you the tab staff and some sample notes and a chord. The top line of the tab staff represents the 1st string of the guitar — high E. The bottom line of the tab corresponds to the 6th string on the guitar, low E. The other lines represent the other four strings in between — the second line from the bottom is the 5th string, and so on. A number appearing on any given line tells you to fret that string in that numbered fret. For example, if you see the numeral 2 on the second line from the top, you need to press down the 2nd string in the 2nd fret above the nut (actually, the space between the 1st and 2nd metal frets). A 0 on a line means that you play the open string.

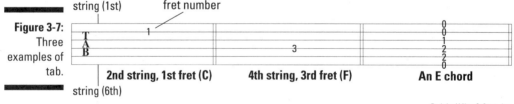

Figure 3-7: Three examples of tab.

string (1st)

fret number

2nd string, 1st fret (C)   4th string, 3rd fret (F)   An E chord

string (6th)

© *John Wiley & Sons, Inc.*

Reading rhythm slashes

Musicians use a variety of shorthand tricks to indicate certain musical directions. They use this shorthand because, although a particular musical concept itself is often simple enough, to notate that idea in standard written music form may prove unduly complicated and cumbersome. So musicians use a road map that gets the point across yet avoids the issue of reading (or writing) music.

Rhythm slashes are slash marks (/) that simply tell you *how* to play rhythmically but not *what* to play. The chord in your left hand determines what you play. Say, for example, that you see the diagram shown in Figure 3-8.

Figure 3-8:
One
measure of
an E chord.

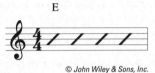

© John Wiley & Sons, Inc.

If you see such a chord symbol with four slashes beneath it, as shown in the figure, you know to finger an E chord and strike it four times. What you don't see, however, is a number of differently pitched notes clinging to various lines of a music staff, including several hole-in-the-center half notes and a slew of solid quarter notes — in short, any of that junk that you needed to memorize in grade school just to play "Mary Had a Little Lamb" on the recorder. All you need to remember on seeing this particular diagram is to "play an E chord four times." Simple, isn't it?

Discovering How to Play a Chord

Chords are the basic building blocks of songs. You can play a chord (the simultaneous sounding of three or more notes) several ways on the guitar — by *strumming* (dragging a pick or the back of your fingernails across the strings in a single, quick motion), *plucking* (with the individual right-hand fingers), or even smacking the strings with your open hand or fist. (Okay, that's rare, unless you're in a heavy metal band.) But you can't just strike *any* group of notes; you must play a group of notes organized in some musically meaningful arrangement. For the guitarist, that means learning some left-hand chord forms.

After you think you understand (somewhat) the guitar notation we describe in the preceding sections, your best bet is to jump right in and play your first chord. We suggest that you start with E major, because it's a particularly guitar-friendly chord and one that you use a lot.

After you get the hang of playing chords, you eventually find that you can move several fingers into position simultaneously. For now, however, just place your fingers one at a time on the frets and strings, as the following instructions indicate (you can also refer to Figure 3-6):

1. **Place your 1st (index) finger on the 3rd string, 1st fret (actually between the nut and 1st fret wire but closer to the fret wire).**

   Don't press down hard until you have your other fingers in place. Apply just enough pressure to keep your finger from moving off the string.

2. **Place your 2nd (middle) finger on the 5th string, 2nd fret.**

   Again, apply just enough pressure to keep your fingers in place. You now have two fingers on the guitar, on the 3rd and 5th strings, with an as-yet unfretted string (the 4th) in between.

3. **Place your 3rd (ring) finger on the 4th string, 2nd fret.**

   You may need to wriggle your ring finger a bit to get it to fit in there between the 1st and 2nd fingers and below the fret wire.

Figure 3-9 shows a photo of how your E chord should look after all your fingers are positioned correctly. Now that your fingers are in position, strike all six strings with your right hand to hear your first chord, E. To see how to form an E chord step-by-step, check out Video Clip 4.

Figure 3-9:
Notice how the fingers curve and the knuckles bend on an E chord.

Photograph courtesy of Jon Chappell

One of the hardest things to do in playing chords is to avoid *buzzing*. Buzzing results if you're not pressing down quite hard enough when you fret. A buzz can also result if a fretting finger accidentally comes in contact with an adjacent string, preventing that string from ringing freely. Without removing your fingers from the frets, try "rocking and rolling" your fingers around on their tips to eliminate any buzzes when you strum the chord.

Part II
Ready to Play: The Basics

Top five ways to master new chords

- ✔ Search the Internet by entering any chord name followed by the phrase "guitar chord diagrams."

- ✔ Ask a friend. Playing guitar is more fun when done with a friend, and friends help each other. So have your guitar-playing friends show you the chords they know so that you can add them to your arsenal.

- ✔ Acquire as much sheet music and as many songbooks of your favorite music as you can. Published sheet music often includes guitar chord diagrams.

- ✔ Check out popular video instruction sites, like YouTube, for fellow guitarists sharing their knowledge on chords, songs, and playing techniques.

- ✔ Even if you ignore the instructional content of this book (at least for the moment), you can still get tons of chords just by looking at the chord diagrams within the pages (including Appendix B, which offers 96 common chords).

web extras

Go online to www.dummies.com/cheatsheet/guitar to view or print a Cheat Sheet containing valuable info and helpful tips and tricks to make your guitar-playing sessions more fun and productive.

In this part . . .

- ✔ Check out basic major and minor chords in the A, D, G, and C families to prepare you to play a wide range of songs.

- ✔ Understand how to read tablature in order to play melodies and riffs without reading music.

- ✔ Focus on playing a song's melody, instead of strumming its chords, which gets you ready for playing riffs and solos.

- ✔ Add some spice with 7th chords to make your music sound bluesy, funky, or jazzy.

Chapter 4

The Best Way to Begin: Strumming Chords

*A*ccompanying yourself as you sing your favorite songs — or as someone else sings them if your voice is less than melodious — is one of the best ways to pick up basic guitar chords. If you know how to play basic chords, you can play lots of popular songs right away — from "Skip to My Lou" to "Louie Louie."

In this chapter, we organize the major and minor chords into families. A *family of chords* is simply a group of related chords. We say they're *related* because you often use these chords together to play songs. The concept is sort of like color-coordinating your clothing or assembling a group of foods to create a balanced meal. Chords in a family go together like peanut butter and chocolate (except that chords in a family are less messy). Along the way, we help you expand your guitar notation vocabulary as you start to develop your chord-playing and strumming skills.

Think of a family of chords as a plant. If one of the chords — the one that feels like home base in a song (usually the chord you start and end a song with) — is the plant's root, the other chords in the family are the different shoots rising up from that same root. Together, the root and shoots make up the family. Put 'em all together and you have a lush garden . . . er, make that a *song*. By the way, the technical term for a family is *key*. So you can say something like, "This song uses A-family chords" *or* "This song is in the key of A."

Chords in the A Family

The A family is a popular family for playing songs on the guitar because, like other families we present in this chapter, its chords are easy to play. That's because A-family chords contain *open strings* (strings that you play without pressing down any notes). Chords that contain open strings are called *open chords,* or *open-position chords.* Listen to "Fire and Rain," by James Taylor, or "Tears in Heaven," by Eric Clapton, to hear the sound of a song that uses A-family chords.

The basic chords in the A family are A, D, and E. Each of these chords is what's known as a *major* chord. A chord that's named by a letter name alone, such as these (A, D, and E), is always major. (See the nearby sidebar "Checking out chord qualities" for an explanation of different types of chords.) The following sections explain how to finger and strum chords in the A family.

Fingering A-family chords

When fingering chords, you use the "ball" of your fingertip, placing it just behind the fret (on the side toward the tuning pegs). Arch your fingers so the fingertips fall perpendicular to the neck. And make sure your left-hand fingernails are short so they don't prevent you from pressing the strings all the way down to the fingerboard.

Checking out chord qualities

Chords have different qualities, which has nothing to do with whether they're good or bad little chords. You can define *quality* as the *relationship* between the different notes that make up the chord — or simply, what the chord sounds like.

Besides the quality of being major, other chord qualities include *minor, 7th, minor 7th,* and *major 7th.* The following list describes each of these types of chord qualities:

- **Major chords:** These are simple chords that have a stable sound.

- **Minor chords:** These are simple chords that have a soft, sometimes sad sound.

- **7th chords:** These are bluesy, funky-sounding chords.

- **Minor 7th chords:** These chords sound mellow and jazzy.

- **Major 7th chords:** These chords sound bright and jazzy.

Each type of chord, or chord quality, has a different kind of sound, and you can often distinguish the chord type just by hearing it. Listen, for example, to the sound of a major chord by strumming A, D, and E. (For more information on 7th, minor 7th, and major 7th chords, check out Chapter 6.)

Figure 4-1 shows the fingering for the A, D, and E chords — the basic chords in the A family. (If you're unclear about reading the chord diagrams, check out Chapter 3.)

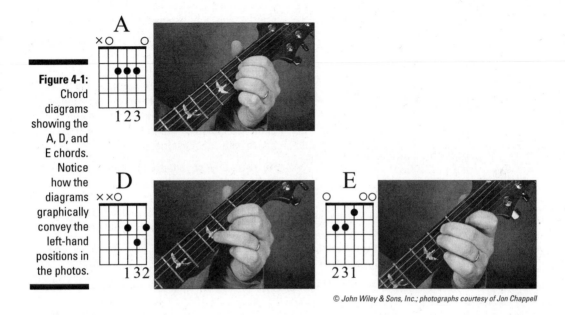

Figure 4-1:
Chord diagrams showing the A, D, and E chords. Notice how the diagrams graphically convey the left-hand positions in the photos.

© John Wiley & Sons, Inc.; photographs courtesy of Jon Chappell

Don't play any strings marked with an *X* (the 6th string on the A chord and the 5th and 6th strings on the D chord, for example). Strike just the top five (5th through 1st) strings in the A chord and the top four (4th through 1st) strings in the D chord. Selectively striking strings may be awkward at first, but keep at it and you'll get the hang of it. If you play a string marked with an *X* and we catch you, we'll revoke your picking privileges on the spot.

Strumming A-family chords

Use your right hand to strum these A-family chords with one of the following:

- ✔ A pick
- ✔ Your thumb
- ✔ The back of your fingernails (in a brushing motion toward the floor)

Start strumming from the lowest-pitched string of the chord (the side of the chord toward the ceiling as you hold the guitar) and strum toward the floor.

Playing callus-ly

Playing chords can be a little painful at first. (We mean for you, not for people within earshot; c'mon, we're not *that* cruel.) No matter how tough you are, if you've never played the guitar before, your left-hand fingertips are *soft*. Fretting a guitar string, therefore, is going to feel to your fingertips almost as if you're hammering a railroad spike with your bare hand. (Ouch!)

In short, *pressing down on the string hurts*. This situation isn't weird at all — in fact, it's quite normal for beginning guitarists. (Well, it's weird if you *enjoy* the pain.) You must develop nice, thick calluses on your fingertips before playing the guitar can ever feel completely comfortable. It may take weeks or even months to build up those protective layers of dead skin, depending on how much and how often you play. But after you finally earn your calluses, you never lose them (completely, anyway). Like a Supreme Court justice, you're a guitar player *for life*.

You can develop your calluses by playing the basic chords in this chapter over and over again. As you progress, you also gain strength in your hands and fingers and become more comfortable in general while playing the guitar. Before you know it's happening, fretting a guitar becomes as natural to you as shaking hands with your best friend.

As with any physical-conditioning routine, make sure you stop and rest if you begin to feel tenderness or soreness in your fingers or hands. Building up those calluses takes *time,* and you can't hurry time (or love, for that matter, as Diana Ross would attest).

A *progression* is simply a series of chords that you play one after the other. Figure 4-2 presents a simple progression in the key of A and instructs you to strum each chord — in the order shown (reading from left to right) — four times. Use all *downstrokes* (dragging your pick across the strings toward the floor) as you play. Listen to the example on Track 2 to hear the rhythm of this progression and try to play along with it. You also can view Video Clip 5 to see and hear Figure 4-2.

Figure 4-2:
A simple chord progression in the key of A (using only chords in the A family).

Track 2, 0:00

Video Clip 5

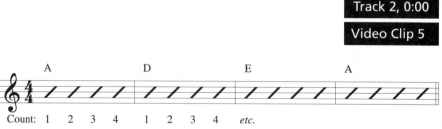

© John Wiley & Sons, Inc.

After strumming each chord four times, you come to a vertical line in the music that follows the four strum symbols. This line is a *bar line*. It's not something that you play. Bar lines visually separate the music into smaller sections known as *measures,* or *bars*. (You can use these terms interchangeably; they both mean the same thing.) Measures make written music easier to grasp, because they break up the music into little, digestible chunks. See Appendix A for more information on bar lines and measures.

Don't hesitate or stop at the bar line. Keep your strumming speed the same throughout, even as you play "between the measures" — that is, in the imaginary "space" from the end of one measure to the beginning of the next that the bar line represents. Start out playing as slowly as necessary to help you keep the beat steady. You can always speed up as you get more confident and proficient in your chord fingering and switching.

By playing a progression over and over, you start to develop left-hand strength and calluses on your fingertips. Try it (and try it . . . and try it . . .).

If you want to play a song right away, you can. Skip to the section "Songs with Basic Major and Minor Chords," later in this chapter. Because you now know the basic open chords in the A family, you can play "Kumbaya." Rock on!

Chords in the D Family

The basic chords that make up the D family are D, Em (*read:* "E minor"), G, and A. The D family, therefore, shares two basic open chords with the A family (D and A) and introduces two new ones: Em and G. Because you already know how to play D and A from the preceding section, you need to work on only two more chords (covered in the following sections) to add the entire D family to your repertoire: Em and G. Listen to "Here Comes the Sun," by the Beatles, or "Who Says," by John Mayer, to hear the sound of a song that uses D-family chords.

Minor describes the quality of a type of chord. A minor chord has a sound that's distinctly different from that of a major chord. You may characterize the sound of a minor chord as *sad, mournful, scary,* or even *ominous.* Note that the relationship of the notes that make up the chord determines a chord's quality. A chord that's named by a capital letter followed by a small *m* is always minor.

Fingering D-family chords

Figure 4-3 shows you how to finger the two basic chords in the D family that aren't in the A family: Em and G. You may notice that none of the strings in either chord diagram displays an *X* symbol, so you get to strike all the strings whenever you play a G or Em chord. If you feel like it, go ahead and celebrate by dragging your pick or right-hand fingers across the strings in a big *keraaaang.*

Practicing and getting good

Saying that the more you practice, the better you'll get may sound obvious, but it's true. However, perhaps even more important is this concept: *The more you practice, the faster you'll get good.* Although there's no set amount of practice time for "getting good," a good rule is to practice a minimum of 30 minutes every day. Also, it's generally agreed that practicing at regular intervals is better than jamming a week's worth of time (say, 3½ hours) all into one practice session.

If at first you find a new technique difficult to master, stick with it, and you'll eventually get the hang of it. To get even better on the guitar, we suggest the following:

✔ Set aside a certain time every day for practicing.

✔ Get together with your guitar-playing friends, and get them to listen to what you're doing.

✔ Create a practice environment where you have privacy, away from distractions (TV, conversations, your mother bugging you to come to dinner, and so on).

✔ Watch videos of guitar players who play the kind of music you like and that you'd like to learn.

Try the following trick to quickly pick up how to play Em and to hear the difference between the major and minor chord qualities: Play E, which is a major chord, and then lift your index finger off the 3rd string. Now you're playing Em, which is the minor-chord version of E. By alternating the two chords, you can easily hear the difference in quality between a major and minor chord.

Notice the alternative fingering for G (2-3-4 instead of 1-2-3). As your hand gains strength and becomes more flexible, you want to switch to the 2-3-4 fingering instead of the initially easier 1-2-3 fingering (the version shown in Figure 4-3). You can switch to other chords with greater ease and efficiency by using the 2-3-4 fingering for G.

Figure 4-3:
The Em and G chords. Notice that all six strings are available for play in each chord.

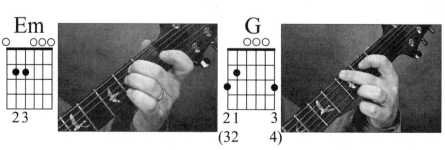

© John Wiley & Sons, Inc.; photographs courtesy of Jon Chappell

Strumming D-family chords

In Figure 4-4, you play a simple chord progression, using D-family chords. Notice the difference in the strum in this figure versus that of Figure 4-2.

- In Figure 4-2, you strum each chord four times per measure. Each strum is one pulse, or beat.

- Figure 4-4 divides the second strum of each measure (or the second beat) into two strums — down and up — both of which together take up the time of one beat, meaning that you must play each strum in beat 2 twice as quickly as you do a regular strum.

Figure 4-4:
This progression contains chords commonly found in the key of D.

Track 2, 0:16

Video Clip 6

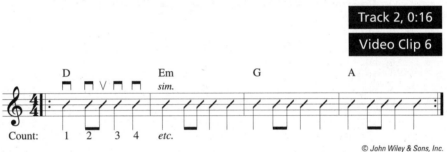

© John Wiley & Sons, Inc.

The additional symbol ⊓ with the strum symbol means that you strum down toward the floor, and V means that you strum up toward the ceiling. (If you play your guitar while hanging in gravity boots, however, you must reverse these last two instructions.) The term *sim.* is an abbreviation of the Italian word *simile,* which instructs you to keep playing in a similar manner — in this case, to keep strumming in a *down, down-up, down, down* pattern. You can see the motion of the downstrokes and upstrokes in Video Clip 6.

If you're using only your fingers for strumming, play upstrokes with the back of your thumbnail whenever you see the symbol V.

Knowing the basic open chords in the D family (D, Em, G, and A) enables you to play a song in the key of D right now. If you skip to the section "Songs with Basic Major and Minor Chords," later in this chapter, you can play the song "Swing Low, Sweet Chariot" right now. Go for it!

Chords in the G Family

By tackling related chord families (as A, D, and G are), you carry over your knowledge from family to family in the form of chords that you already know from earlier families. The basic chords that make up the G family are G, Am, C, D, and Em. If you already know G, D, and Em (which we describe in the preceding sections on the A and D families), you can now try Am and C (covered in the following sections). Listen to "You've Got a Friend," as played by James Taylor, or "Every Rose Has Its Thorn," by Poison, to hear the sound of a song that uses G-family chords.

Fingering G-family chords

In Figure 4-5, you see the fingerings for Am and C, the new chords you need to play in the G family. Notice that the fingering of these two chords is similar: Each has finger 1 on the 2nd string, 1st fret, and finger 2 on the 4th string, 2nd fret. (Only finger 3 must change — adding or removing it — in switching between these two chords.) In moving between these chords, keep these first two fingers in place on the strings. Switching chords is always easier if you don't need to move all your fingers to new positions. The notes that different chords share are known as *common tones.* Notice the X over the 6th string in each of these chords. Don't play that string while strumming either C or Am. (We mean it!)

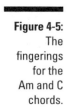

Figure 4-5: The fingerings for the Am and C chords.

© John Wiley & Sons, Inc.; photographs courtesy of Jon Chappell

Strumming G-family chords

Figure 4-6 shows a simple chord progression you can play by using G-family chords. Play this progression over and over to get accustomed to switching chords and to build up those left-hand calluses. It *does* get easier after a while. We promise!

Notice that in each measure, you play beats 2 *and* 3 as "down-up" strums. Listen to Track 2 to hear this sound; check out Video Clip 7 to see the figure played.

Knowing the basic open chords in the G family (G, Am, C, D, and Em) enables you to play a song in the key of G right now. Skip to the section "Songs with Basic Major and Minor Chords," later in this chapter, and you can play "Auld Lang Syne." As the relieved shepherd said after the mother sheep returned to the flock, "Happy, Ewe Near."

Figure 4-6: A chord progression you can play, using only G-family chords.

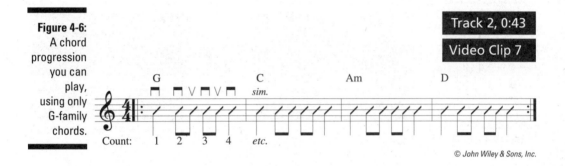

© John Wiley & Sons, Inc.

Chords in the C Family

The last chord family we need to discuss is C. Some people say that C is the easiest key to play in. That's because C uses only the white-key notes of the piano in its musical scale and, as such, is sort of the music theory square one — the point at which everything (and, usually, everyone) begins in music. We chose to place the C family last in this chapter because, heck, it's so easy that it has lots of chords in its family — too many to master all at once.

The basic chords that make up the C family are C, Dm, Em, F, G, and Am. If you practice the preceding sections on the A-, D-, and G-family chords, you know C, Em, G, and Am. (If not, check them out.) So in this section, you need to pick up only two more chords: Dm and F. After you know these two additional chords, you have all the basic major and minor chords we describe in this chapter down pat. Listen to "Dust in the Wind," by Kansas, or "Lucky," by Jason Mraz and Colbie Caillat, to hear the sound of a song that uses C-family chords.

Fingering C-family chords

In Figure 4-7, you see the new chords you need to play in the C family. Notice that both the Dm and F chords have the 2nd finger on the 3rd string, 2nd fret. Hold down this common tone as you switch between these two chords.

Figure 4-7:
The Dm and F chords. Notice the indication (⌒) in the F-chord diagram tells you to fret (or barre) two strings with one finger.

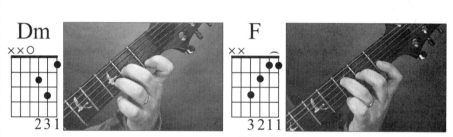

© John Wiley & Sons, Inc.; photographs courtesy of Jon Chappell

Many people find the F chord the most difficult chord to play of all the basic major and minor chords. That's because F uses no open strings, and it also requires a *barre*. A barre is what you're playing whenever you press down two or more strings at once with a single left-hand finger. To play the F chord, for example, you use your 1st finger to press down both the 1st and 2nd strings at the 1st fret simultaneously.

You must exert extra finger pressure to play a barre. At first, you may find that, as you strum the chord (hitting the top four strings only, as the *X*s in the chord diagram indicate), you hear some buzzes or muffled strings. Experiment with various placements of your index finger. Try adjusting the angle of your finger or try rotating your finger slightly on its side. Keep trying until you find a position for the 1st finger that enables all four strings to ring clearly as you strike them.

Strumming C-family chords

Figure 4-8 shows a simple chord progression you can play by using C-family chords. Play the progression over and over to get used to switching among the chords in this family and, of course, to help build up those nasty little calluses. Video Clip 8 shows the right-hand motion for the syncopated figure in the middle of each bar.

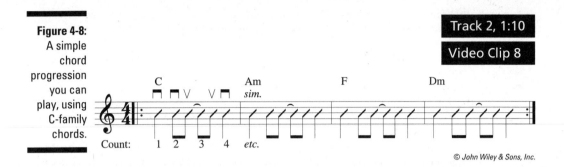

© *John Wiley & Sons, Inc.*

Figure 4-8: A simple chord progression you can play, using C-family chords.

Track 2, 1:10

Video Clip 8

Look at Figure 4-8. Notice the small curved line joining the second half of beat 2 to beat 3. This line is known as a *tie.* A tie tells you not to strike the second note of the two tied notes (in this case, the one on beat 3). Instead, just keep holding the chord on that beat (letting it ring) without restriking it with your right hand.

Listen to Track 2 to hear the sound of this strumming pattern. This slightly jarring rhythmic effect is an example of *syncopation.* In syncopation, the musician either strikes a note (or chord) where you don't expect to hear it or fails to strike a note (or chord) where you do expect to hear it.

You probably usually expect to strike notes on the beats (1, 2, 3, and 4). In the example in Figure 4-8, however, you don't strike a chord on beat 3. That variation in the strumming pattern makes the chord on beat 2½ feel as if it's *accentuated* (or, as musicians say, *accented*). This accentuation interrupts the normal (expected) pulse of the music, resulting in the syncopation of the music. Syncopation breaks up the regular pattern of beats and presents an element of surprise in music. The balance between expectation and surprise in music is what holds a listener's interest. (Well, that and the promise of free hors d'oeuvres at the intermission.)

To play a song that uses C-family chords right now, skip to the song "Michael, Row the Boat Ashore," in the next section. Bon voyage!

Songs with Basic Major and Minor Chords

This section is where the *real music* happens — you know, *songs.* If the titles here hearken back to those bygone campfire days in the distant recesses of your youth, fear not, young-at-heart campers. These songs, although seemingly simple, illustrate universal principles that carry over into the — shall we say it? — *hipper* musical genres. Pick up on these songs first, and you're certain to be playing the music of your choice in no time — we promise!

You may notice that all the strumming examples we provide earlier in this chapter are only four measures long. Must all your exercises be limited this way, you may ask? No, but songwriters do very commonly write music in four-measure phrases. So the length of these exercises prepares you for actual passages in real songs. You may also notice that each strumming example is in 4/4 time, which means that each measure contains four beats. Any reason? Most popular songs contain four beats per measure, so the 4/4 time signature in the exercises also prepares you to play actual songs. (See Appendix A for more information on time signatures.)

In the examples you find in earlier sections of this chapter, you play each chord for one full measure. But in this section of actual songs, you sometimes play a single chord for more than a measure, and sometimes you change chords within a single measure. Listen to the audio track for each song to hear the rhythm of the chord change as you follow the beat numbers (1, 2, 3, and 4) that appear below the guitar staff.

After you can comfortably play your way through these songs, try to memo-rize them. That way, you don't need to stare into a book as you're trying to develop your rhythm.

If you get bored with these songs — or with the way *you* play these songs — show the music to a guitar-playing friend and ask him to play the same songs by using the strumming patterns and chord positions we indicate. Listening to someone else play helps you hear the songs objectively, and if your friend has a little flair, you may pick up a cool little trick or two. Work on infusing a bit of *personality* into all your playing, even if you're just strumming a simple folk song.

Here's some special information to help you play the songs in this section:

> ✔ **Kumbaya:** To play "Kumbaya" (the ultimate campfire song), you need to know how to play A, D, and E chords (see the section "Fingering A-family chords," earlier in this chapter); how to strum by using all downstrokes; and how to start a fire by using only two sticks and some dried leaves.

> The first measure in this song is known as a *pickup* measure, which is incomplete; it starts the song with one or more beats missing — in this case, the first two. During the pickup measure, the guitar part shows a *rest,* or a musical silence. Don't play during the rest; begin playing on

the syllable *ya* on beat 1. Notice, too, that the last bar is missing two beats — beats 3 and 4. The missing beats in the last measure enable you to repeat the pickup measure in repeated playings of the song, and to make that measure, combined with the first incomplete measure, total the requisite four beats.

✔ **Swing Low, Sweet Chariot:** To play "Swing Low, Sweet Chariot," you need to know how to play D, Em, G, and A chords (see the section "Fingering D-family chords," earlier in this chapter); how to play down and down-up strums; and how to sing like James Earl Jones.

This song starts with a one-beat pickup, and the guitar rests for that beat. Notice that beat 2 of measures 2, 4, and 6 has two strums instead of one. Strum those beats down and then up (2 and 4) with each strum twice as fast as a regular strum.

✔ **Auld Lang Syne:** To play "Auld Lang Syne," you need to know how to play G, Am, C, D, and Em chords (see the section "Fingering G-family chords," earlier in this chapter); how to play down and down-up strums; and what *auld lang syne* means in the first place.

Measure 8 is a little tricky, because you play three different chords in the same measure (Em, Am, and D). In the second half of the measure, you change chords on each beat — one stroke per chord. Practice playing only measure 8 slowly, over and over. Then play the song.

In changing between G and C (bars 4 to 6 and 12 to 14), fingering G with fingers 2, 3, and 4 instead of 1, 2, and 3 makes the chord switch easier. If you finger the chord that way, the 2nd and 3rd fingers form a shape that simply moves over one string.

✔ **Michael, Row the Boat Ashore:** To play "Michael, Row the Boat Ashore," you need to know how to play C, Dm, Em, F, and G chords (see the section "Fingering C-family chords," earlier in this chapter); how to play a syncopated eighth-note strum (see the section "Strumming C-family chords," earlier in this chapter); and the meaning of the word *hootenanny.*

The strumming pattern here is *syncopated.* The strum that normally occurs on beat 3 is *anticipated,* meaning that it actually comes half a beat early. This kind of syncopation gives the song a Latin feel. Listen to Track 6 to hear the strumming rhythm.

On the Dm and F chords, you don't strum the lowest two strings (the 6th and 5th). For the C chord, don't strum the bottom string (the 6th).

Kumbaya

Track 3

Video Clips 9

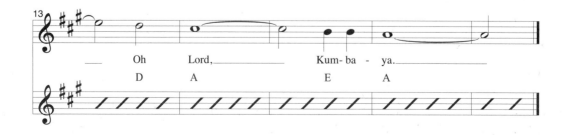

Swing Low, Sweet Chariot

Auld Lang Syne

Track 5

Video Clips 11

Michael, Row the Boat Ashore

Track 7

Video Clips 12

Fun with Basic Major and Minor Chords: The "Oldies" Progression

As we promise in the introduction to this chapter, you can play lots of popu-lar songs right away if you know the basic major and minor chords. One cool thing that you can do right now is play *oldies* — songs from the late '50s and early '60s, such as "Earth Angel" and "Duke of Earl." These songs are based on what's sometimes called the *oldies progression*. The oldies progression is a series of four chords; they're repeated over and over to form the accompaniment for a song.

You can play the oldies progression in any key, but the best guitar keys for the oldies progression are C and G. In the key of C, the four chords that make up the progression are C-Am-F-G. And in the key of G, the chords are G-Em-C-D. Try strumming the progression in each key by playing four downstrums per chord. Play the four chords over and over, in the sequence given. If you need help with the fingerings for these chords, check out the sections "Chords in the C Family" and "Chords in the G Family," earlier in this chapter.

The fun begins as you sing oldies while accompanying yourself with the oldies progression. As you sing a particular song, you find that one of the keys (C or G) better suits your vocal range, so use that key. Playing oldies can become addicting, but the good news is that, if you can't stop, you build up your calluses very quickly.

For some songs, you play four one-beat strums per chord; for others, you play eight or two. Here, we list some songs you can play with the oldies progression right now. Next to each, we show you how many times you strum each chord. Don't forget to sing. Have fun!

- **All I Have to Do Is Dream:** Two strums per chord
- **Breaking Up Is Hard to Do:** Two strums per chord
- **Denise:** Two strums per chord
- **Duke of Earl:** Four strums per chord
- **Earth Angel:** Two strums per chord
- **Hey Paula:** Two strums per chord
- **A Hundred Pounds of Clay:** Four strums per chord
- **In the Still of the Night** (the one by the Five Satins, not the Cole Porter one): Four strums per chord
- **Little Darlin':** Eight strums per chord
- **Please, Mr. Postman:** Eight strums per chord
- **Runaround Sue:** Eight strums per chord
- **Sherry:** Two strums per chord
- **Silhouettes:** Two strums per chord
- **Take Good Care of My Baby:** Four strums per chord
- **Tears on My Pillow:** Two strums per chord
- **Teenager in Love:** Four strums per chord
- **There's a Moon Out Tonight:** Two strums per chord
- **You Send Me:** Two strums per chord

Chapter 5

Playing Melodies — without Reading Music!

In This Chapter

▶ Understanding how to read tablature

▶ Figuring out the correct left-hand fingering

▶ Trying alternate picking

▶ Putting it all together on a few songs with single notes

▶ Access the audio tracks and video clips at `www.dummies.com/go/guitar`

Most guitar books present melodies as a way to teach you to read music. In fact, the primary goal of most guitar books isn't to teach you to play guitar in the real world but to teach music reading through the guitar. The difference is significant.

If you pick up guitar playing through a book, you can eventually play nursery-rhyme ditties in perfect quarter and half notes. But if you learn to play as most guitar players do — through friends showing you licks or by using your ear — you can come away playing "Smoke on the Water," "Sunshine of Your Love," "Blackbird," and the entire repertoire of Neil Young. All of which means that you *don't need to read music to play guitar.*

Okay, so maybe reading music is a valuable skill. But the purpose of this chapter isn't to teach you to read; it's to get you to play. If we need to show you a lick, we use *tablature* — a special notation system designed especially for showing *how you play the guitar.* Or we refer you to the audio tracks and video clips so you can hear the lick. Or both.

We offer melodies in this chapter primarily so you can accustom your hands to playing single notes. That way, whenever you decide that you want to play like a *real* guitarist — someone who combines chords, melodies, riffs, and licks into an integrated whole — you're ready to rock.

Note: By the way, a *lick* is a short, melodic phrase, often made up on the spot and played only once. A *riff* is a short melodic phrase, often composed to be the main accompaniment figure in a song (as in "Can you play the 'Day Tripper' riff?").

Reading Tablature

Numbers on the tablature (or *tab*) staff tell you which frets on which strings to finger with your left hand. A 0 indicates an open string. By listening to the audio tracks or watching the video clips, you can hear when to play these notes. And just to be safe, thorough, and completely redundant, we also include the standard notation for:

- People who read music already

- People who plan to read Appendix A (on how to read music) and apply what they read there

- People who want to gradually pick up the skill of music reading (at least by osmosis if not rigorous study) by listening to the audio tracks or watching the video clips and following along with the rhythm notation

- Us, the authors, who get paid by the page

In the following sections, we provide details on how to read tablature from top to bottom and from left to right.

Starting from the top

The music in this book contains a double staff: standard music notation on the top, tab on the bottom.

- The top staff is for music readers or for people interested in standard notation.

- The bottom staff shows the same info (minus the rhythm) but in tab numbers.

Here's how the tab staff works:

- The top line of the tab staff represents the *top* string of the guitar (high E). This positioning of the strings in the tab staff may momentarily confuse you, because the top string in the tab staff — the 1st — is actually the string closest to the floor as you hold the guitar in playing position.

But trust us, the setup's more intuitive this way, and after you make the adjustment, you never think about it again.

By the way, if you hold the guitar flat on your lap, with the neck facing the ceiling, the *1st* string is farthest away from you, just as the *top* line is when you see the tab staff on the page.

✔ Moving on, the second tab line from the top represents the 2nd string (B) and so on down to the bottom tab line, which represents the 6th (low E) string on the guitar.

✔ In guitar tab, lines represent strings and numbers represent frets. However, tab doesn't tell you which left-hand fingers to use. (Neither does standard notation, for that matter.) But more on fingering later.

Looking from left to right

Just as in reading text or music, you start from the left and proceed to the right in reading tab. Using Figure 5-1 as your example, begin with the first note, which you play at the 1st fret of the 2nd string. The placement of the tab number on the second line from the top tells you to play the B string — the one next to high E — and the number 1 tells you to place your finger at the 1st fret. Go ahead and play that note and then proceed to the next note, which is also on the 2nd string, 1st fret. Keep moving right, playing the notes in order, until you reach the end. (Don't worry about the symbols above the numbers for now; we explain them in the section "Using Alternate Picking," later in this chapter.)

The vertical lines that appear on the staff after every few notes are *bar lines*. They divide the staff into small units of time, called *bars* or *measures*. Measures help you count beats and break up the music into smaller, more manageable units. In Figure 5-1, you see four measures of four beats each; Video Clip 13 shows how to play the figure. See Appendix A for more information on beats and measures.

After you understand the concepts of top versus bottom and left to right in the tab staff and also understand that the lines indicate strings and the numbers on the lines indicate fret position, you can listen to the audio tracks, watch the video clips, and easily follow (and play) the tab. If you didn't realize it yet, you're picking up guitar the multimedia way. (Mail us your proof-of-purchase, and we'll even send you a secret decoder ring and virtual-reality goggles! Just kidding!)

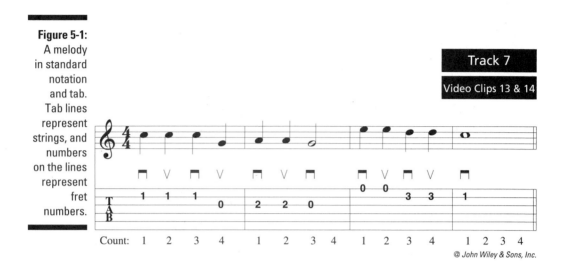

© John Wiley & Sons, Inc.

Figure 5-1:
A melody in standard notation and tab. Tab lines represent strings, and numbers on the lines represent fret numbers.

Getting a Grip on Left-Hand Fingering

After you figure out how to read guitar tablature (see the preceding section), you know what frets to press down, but you still may have no idea which fingers to use to press down the frets. Well, we can clear that up pretty quickly. Usually, you don't need any notation to alert you to which fingers to use, because you most often play in position. Stick with us for a moment.

A *position* on the guitar is a group of four consecutive frets; for example, frets 1, 2, 3, 4 or 5, 6, 7, 8. The first fret in a series of four marks the beginning of a new position; for example, frets 2, 3, 4, and 5, frets 3, 4, 5, and 6, and so on, are positions as well. But the easiest way to play melodies on the guitar is to play them in *1st* or *2nd position* — that is, using frets 1 through 4 or frets 2 through 5 — because these positions are close to the nut, allowing you to easily and smoothly utilize the open strings as well as the fretted notes in playing a melody.

Open position itself consists of the combination of all the open strings plus the notes in the 1st or 2nd position — just as the chords you play low on the neck, using open strings (A, D, Em, and so on), are known as *open chords*. (For more information on open chords, check out Chapter 4.)

In any position, each finger plays the notes of a specific fret — and only that fret. The index finger always plays the notes of the lowest fret in that position (*lowest* meaning toward the nut), with the other fingers covering the other frets in sequential order. In 1st position, for example, the fret numbers correspond to the fingers — the 1st finger (the index finger) plays the notes in the 1st fret; the 2nd finger (middle finger) plays the notes in the 2nd fret; and so on. Using one finger per fret enables you to switch between notes quickly.

As you play the open-position melodies in this chapter, make sure you press your left-hand fingers down correctly, as follows:

✔ Press down on the string with the tip of your finger just *before* the metal fret wire (toward the nut).

✔ Keep the last joint of the finger perpendicular (or as close to perpendicular as possible) to the fretboard.

Using Alternate Picking

As you play a song, you use both hands at the same time. After you figure out which notes to press with the left hand, you need to know how to strike the strings with the right.

You can use either a pick or the right-hand fingers to strike single notes; for now, use the pick, holding it firmly between the thumb and index finger (perpendicular to the thumb with just the tip sticking out). Check out Chapter 3 for more information on holding the pick. (We discuss playing with the fingers in Chapters 13 and 14.)

Alternate picking is the right-hand picking technique that uses both *downstrokes* (toward the floor) and *upstrokes* (toward the ceiling). The advantage of alternate picking is that you can play rapid, successive notes in a smooth, flowing manner. Single notes that you need to play relatively fast almost always require alternate picking.

Try the following experiment:

1. **Hold the pick between your thumb and index finger of your right hand.**

   Again, see Chapter 3 for more info on holding the pick.

2. **Using only downstrokes, pick the open 1st string repeatedly as fast as possible (down-down-down-down, and so on).**

   Try to play as smoothly and evenly as possible.

3. **Now try the same thing but alternating downstrokes and upstrokes (down-up-down-up, and so on).**

   This alternating motion feels much quicker and smoother, doesn't it?

The reason you can play faster with alternate picking is clear. To play two successive downstrokes, you'd need to bring the pick back up above the E string *anyway*. But by actually striking the string with the pick on the way back up (using an upstroke) instead of avoiding the string, you can greatly increase your speed.

Check to make sure you understand the concept of alternate picking by following the next two sets of steps. The symbols for a downstroke and upstroke are the same ones used for strumming in Chapter 4.

To play a downstroke (the ⊓ symbol above the tab), follow these steps:

1. Start with the pick slightly above the string (on the "ceiling" side).

2. Strike the string in a downward motion (toward the floor).

To play an upstroke (the V symbol above the tab), follow these steps:

1. Start with the pick below the string (on the "floor" side).

2. Strike the string in an upward motion (toward the ceiling).

The melody in the tab staff example we show you earlier in Figure 5-1 is actually that of "Old MacDonald Had a Farm." Try playing that melody to see how it sounds. First, play the tune slowly, using only downstrokes. Then play it faster by using alternating picking, as the symbols above the tab staff indicate. Check your pick work against the performance in Video Clip 14. Here a pick, there a pick, everywhere a pick-pick. . . .

Playing Songs with Simple Melodies

In Chapter 4, all the songs you play are in 4/4 time. The songs in this chapter, on the other hand, are in various meters. (The *meter* indicates the number of beats per measure: 4, 3, 2, and so on; see Appendix A for more information on beats and measures.) You play all these songs in open position. (See the section "Getting a Grip on Left-Hand Fingering," earlier in this chapter.)

You've probably known the songs in this chapter all your life but never thought about them in a musical sense — what meter they're in and what rhythms they use — and you almost certainly never thought of "E-I-E-I-O" as alternating downstrokes and upstrokes.

The fact that a bunch of supposedly simple folk songs — tunes you've never thought twice about before — now make you feel slow and clumsy as you try to play them may seem a bit deflating. But playing the guitar is a cumulative endeavor. Every technique you pick up, even if you practice it in "Little Brown Jug," applies to *all* songs that use those same techniques, from Van Morrison to Beethoven, from "Moondance" to the "Moonlight Sonata." Hang in there with the technical stuff and the rest follows.

Here's some useful information about the songs to help you along:

- **Little Brown Jug:** To play this song, you need to know how to count two beats per measure (see Appendix A); how to finger notes in 1st position (see the section "Getting a Grip on Left-Hand Fingering," earlier in this chapter); and how to make a song about getting drunk sound suitable for small children.

  The time signature (2/4) tells you that this song has only two beats per measure (not four). Play all the fretted notes in the 1st position by using the same-numbered left-hand fingers as the fret numbers — that is, use the 1st finger for the 1st fret, the 2nd finger for the 2nd fret, and so on. Follow the ⊓ and ∨ indications above the tab numbers for downstrokes and upstrokes. The *sim.* means to continue in the same style for the rest of the song.

- **On Top of Old Smoky:** To play this song, you need to know how to count three beats per measure (see Appendix A); how to finger notes in 1st position (see the section "Getting a Grip on Left-Hand Fingering," earlier in this chapter); and how to make a song about infidelity sound childlike and whimsical.

  This old favorite has three beats per measure, as the time signature (3/4) indicates. This song is in open position — the one that combines 1st position with the open strings. Use the same finger numbers for fretting as the indicated fret number. We don't indicate any symbols for up and down picking for you in this song; use your own judgment and pick out the notes of the song in the way that feels most natural to you. Some of these notes you can play by using either upstrokes or downstrokes.

- **Swanee River:** To play this song, you need to know how to count four beats per measure (see Appendix A); how to finger notes in 2nd position (see the section "Getting a Grip on Left-Hand Fingering," earlier in this chapter); and how to sound politically correct while playing a song about the old plantation.

  This old tune of the South has four beats per measure, as its 4/4 time signature indicates. Play the song by using the open position that combines the *2nd position* with the open strings — that is, your 1st finger plays the notes on the 2nd fret; your 2nd finger plays the notes on the 3rd fret; and your 3rd finger plays the notes on the 4th fret.

  You can also play the song by using the *1st position* with open strings, but playing it that way is a lot harder. (Fingers 1 and 3 are stronger than 2 and 4.) Try it if you don't believe us. See — we told you! (Oh, and see the section "Getting a Grip on Left-Hand Fingering," earlier in this chapter, for more information about playing in position.)

Notice the symbols for up and down picking above the tab staff. Play downstrokes (⊓) for the notes that fall on the beats and upstrokes (∨) for the notes that fall between the beats. Again, *sim.* means keep playing in the same style to the end.

By the way, this song's actual title is "Old Folks at Home," but most people call it "Swanee River." (It's the song that stumped Ralph Kramden on the game show *The $99,000 Answer* on an old *Honeymooners* episode. The tune was written by Stephen Foster — not Ed Norton!)

Little Brown Jug

Track 8

Video Clip 15

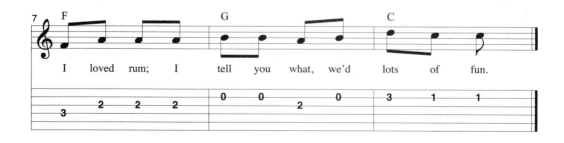

On Top of Old Smoky

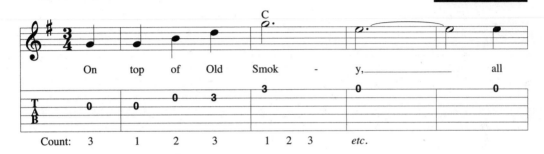

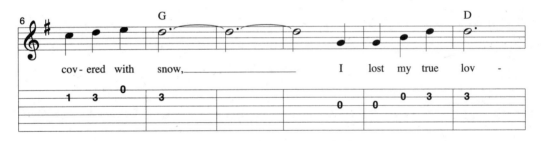

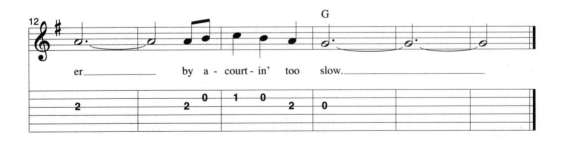

Swanee River (Old Folks at Home)

Chapter 6

Adding Some Spice with 7th Chords

In This Chapter

▶ Playing dominant, minor, and major 7th chords

▶ Trying songs that use 7th chords

▶ Having fun with 7th chords

▶ Access the audio tracks and video clips at `www.dummies.com/go/guitar`

In this chapter, we show you how to play what are known as open-position 7th chords. Seventh chords are no more difficult to play than are the simple major or minor chords we describe in Chapter 4, but their sound is more complex than that of major and minor chords (because they're made up of four different notes instead of three), and their usage in music is a little more specialized.

The situation is kind of like that of the knives in your kitchen. Any big, sharp knife can cut both a pizza and a pineapple, but if you spend a lot of time doing either, you figure out that you need to use the circular-bladed gizmo for the pizza and a cleaver for the pineapple. These utensils may not be as versatile or as popular as your general-purpose knives, but if you're making Hawaiian-style pizza, nothing beats 'em. The more your culinary skills develop, the more you appreciate specialized cutlery. Likewise, the more your ear skills develop, the more you understand where to substitute 7th chords for the more ordinary major and minor chords. The different 7th chords can make the blues sound *bluesy* and jazz sound *jazzy*.

Seventh chords come in several varieties, and each type has a different sound, or quality. In this chapter, we introduce you to the three most important types of 7th chords you encounter in playing the guitar — dominant 7th, minor 7th, and major 7th.

Dominant 7th Chords

Dominant seems a funny, technical name for a chord that's called a plain "seven" if you group it with a letter-name chord symbol. If you say just C7 or A7, for example, you're referring to a dominant 7th chord.

Actually, the term *dominant* refers to the 5th degree of a major scale — but you don't need to worry about the music theory.

The important thing is that you call the chords in the following sections "dominant 7ths" merely to distinguish them from other types of 7th chords (minor 7ths and major 7ths, which we discuss later in this chapter). Note, too, that *dominant* has nothing whatsoever to do with leather and studded collars. You can hear the sound of dominant 7ths in such songs as Sam the Sham and the Pharaohs' "Wooly Bully," the Beatles' "I Saw Her Standing There," and Oasis's "Roll with It."

D7, G7, and C7

The D7, G7, and C7 chords are among the most common of the open dominant 7ths. (For more on open chords, see Chapter 4.) Figure 6-1 shows you diagrams of these three chords that guitarists often use together to play songs.

Video Clip 18

D7
× × ○
213

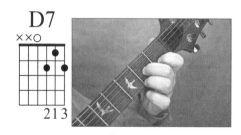

Figure 6-1:
Chord
diagrams for
D7, G7,
and C7.

G7
○ ○ ○
32   1

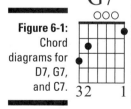

C7
×   ○
3 2 4 1

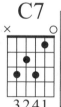

© *John Wiley & Sons, Inc.; photographs courtesy of Jon Chappell*

If you already know how to play C (which we introduce in Chapter 4), you can form C7 by simply adding your pinky on the 3rd string at the 3rd fret.

Notice the *X*s above the 5th and 6th strings on the D7 chord. Don't play those strings as you strum. Similarly, for the C7 chord, don't play the 6th string as you strum. Check out the right-hand motion in Video Clip 18 to see what your right hand should look like.

Practice strumming D7, G7, and C7. You don't need written music for this exercise, so you're on the honor system to do it. Try strumming D7 four times, G7 four times, and then C7 four times. You want to accustom your left hand to the feel of the chords themselves and to switching among them.

If you want to play a song right now with these new chords, skip to the section "Songs with 7th Chords," later in this chapter. You can play "Home on the Range" with the chords you know right now.

E7 (the two-finger version) and A7

Two more 7th chords you often use together to play songs are the E7 and A7 chords. Figure 6-2 shows how you play these two open 7th chords.

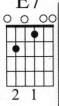   

Figure 6-2:
Chord diagrams for E7 and A7.

© John Wiley & Sons, Inc.; photographs courtesy of Jon Chappell

If you know how to play E (check out Chapter 4), you can form E7 by simply removing your 3rd finger from the 4th string.

This version of the E7 chord, as Figure 6-2 shows, uses only two fingers. You can also play an open position E7 chord with four fingers (as we describe in the following section). For now, however, play the two-finger version, because it's easier to fret quickly, especially if you're just starting out.

Practice E7 and A7 by strumming each chord four times, switching back and forth between them. Be sure to avoid striking the 6th string on the A7 chord.

If you want to play a song that uses these two open 7th chords right now, skip to the section "Songs with 7th Chords," later in this chapter, and play "All Through the Night."

E7 (the four-finger version) and B7

Two more popular open-position 7th chords are the four-finger version of E7 and the B7 chord. Figure 6-3 shows you how to finger the four-finger E7 and the B7 chords. Most people think that this E7 has a better *voicing* (vertical arrangement of notes) than does the two-finger E7. You often use the B7 chord along with E7 to play certain songs. Be sure to avoid striking the 6th string on the B7 chord.

Figure 6-3:
Chord
diagrams
for E7 (the
four-finger
version)
and B7.

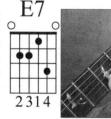  

© John Wiley & Sons, Inc.; photographs courtesy of Jon Chappell

If you already know how to play E (see Chapter 4), you can form this E7 by simply adding your pinky on the 2nd string at the 3rd fret.

Practice these chords by strumming each one four times, switching back and forth. As you do so, notice that your 2nd finger plays the same note at the same fret in each chord — the one at the 2nd fret of the 5th string. This note is a *common tone* (that is, it's common to both chords). In switching back and forth between the two chords, keep this finger down on the 5th string — doing so makes switching easier.

Always hold down common tones whenever you're switching chords. They provide an anchor of stability for your left hand.

To use these chords in a song right now, skip to the section "Songs with 7th Chords," later in this chapter, and play "Over the River and through the Woods."

Minor 7th Chords — Dm7, Em7, and Am7

Minor 7th chords differ from dominant 7th chords in that their character is a little softer and jazzier. Minor 7th chords are the chords you hear in "Moondance," by Van Morrison, the verses of "Light My Fire," by the Doors, and "Box Set," by Barenaked Ladies.

Figure 6-4 shows diagrams for the three open-position minor 7th (m7) chords: Dm7, Em7, and Am7. (See Chapter 9 and Appendix B for more minor 7th chords.)

Video Clip19

Figure 6-4: Chord diagrams for Dm7, Em7, and Am7.

 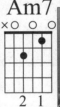 

© John Wiley & Sons, Inc.; photographs courtesy of Jon Chappell

Notice that the Dm7 uses a two-string *barre* — that is, you press down two strings with a single finger (the 1st finger, in this case) at the 1st fret. Angling your finger slightly or rotating it on its side may help you fret those notes firmly and eliminate any buzzes as you play the chord. Also, the 6th and 5th strings have *X*s above them. Don't strike those strings while strumming.

You finger the Am7 chord much like you do the C chord that we show you in Chapter 4; just lift your 3rd finger off a C chord — and you have Am7. In switching between C and Am7 chords, be sure to hold down the two common tones with your 1st and 2nd fingers. This way, you can switch between the

chords much more quickly. And if you know how to play an F chord (see Chapter 4), you can form Dm7 simply by removing your 3rd finger.

Major 7th Chords — Cmaj7, Fmaj7, Amaj7, and Dmaj7

Major 7th chords differ from dominant 7th chords and minor 7th chords in that their character is bright and jazzy. You can hear this kind of chord at the beginning of "Ventura Highway," by America, "Don't Let the Sun Catch You Crying," by Gerry and the Pacemakers, and "Hard Shoulder," by Mark Knopfler.

Figure 6-5 shows four open-position major 7th (maj7) chords: Cmaj7, Fmaj7, Amaj7, and Dmaj7. (For more major 7th chords, check out Chapter 9 and Appendix B.)

Video Clip 20

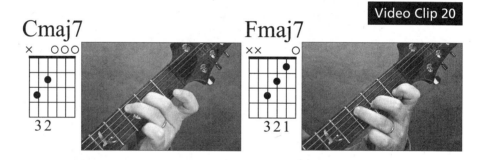

Figure 6-5: Chord diagrams for Cmaj7, Fmaj7, Amaj7, and Dmaj7 chords.

© John Wiley & Sons, Inc.; photographs courtesy of Jon Chappell

Notice that the Dmaj7 uses a three-string barre with the 1st finger. Rotating the 1st finger slightly on its side helps make the chord easier to play. Refer to Video Clip 20 to make sure your 1st finger position resembles the one in the video. Don't play the 6th or 5th strings as you strike the Dmaj7 or Fmaj7 (see the *X*s in the diagrams in Figure 6-5). And don't play the 6th string on the Amaj7 or Cmaj7.

In moving between Cmaj7 and Fmaj7, notice that the 2nd and 3rd fingers move as a fixed shape across the strings. You don't fret any string in a Cmaj7 chord with your 1st finger, but keep it curled and poised above the 1st fret of the 2nd string so you can bring it down quickly for the switch to Fmaj7.

Practice moving back and forth (strumming four times each) between Cmaj7 and Fmaj7 and between Amaj7 and Dmaj7.

To use these chords in a song right now, check out the next section and play "It's Raining, It's Pouring" and "Oh, Susanna."

Songs with 7th Chords

Listen to the audio tracks to hear the rhythm of the strums of these songs as you follow the slash notation in the guitar part (flip to Chapter 3 to find out more about rhythm slashes). Don't try to play the vocal line. It's there only as a reference.

Here's some useful information about the songs to help you along:

✔ **Home on the Range:** To play "Home on the Range," you need to know how to play C, C7, F, D7, and G7 chords (see Chapter 4 for the C and F chords and the section "Dominant 7th Chords," earlier in this chapter, for the others); how to play a bass-strum-strum pattern; and how to wail like a coyote.

In the music, you see the words *bass strum strum* over the rhythm slashes. Instead of simply strumming the chord for three beats, play only the lowest note of the chord on the first beat and then strum the remaining notes of the chord on beats 2 and 3. The *sim.* means to keep on playing this pattern throughout.

✔ **All through the Night:** To play "All Through the Night," you need to know how to play D, E7 (use the two-finger version for this song), A7, and G chords (see Chapter 4 for the D and G chords and the section earlier in this chapter on the E7 and A7 chords); how to read repeat signs; and how to stay awake during this intensely somnolent ditty.

In the music, you see *repeat signs,* which tell you to play certain measures twice (in this case, you play measures 1, 2, 3, 4, and then measures 1, 2, 3, 5). A repeat sign consists of a thick vertical line and a thin vertical line (through the staff) with two dots next to them. A repeat sign that marks the *beginning* of a section to be repeated has its dots to the *right* of the vertical lines. You see this at the beginning of measure 1. A repeat sign that marks the *end* of a section to be repeated has its dots to the *left* of the vertical lines, as at the end of measure 4. See Appendix A for more information on repeat signs.

✔ **Over the River and through the Woods:** To play "Over the River and through the Woods," you need to know how to play A, D, E7 (use the four-finger version), and B7 chords (see Chapter 4 for the A and D chords and the section on the four-finger version of E7 and B7, earlier in this chapter); how to strum in 6/8 time; and the way to Grandma's house (in case your horse stumbles and you need to shoot it).

The 6/8 time signature has a lilting feel to it — sort of as though the music has a gallop or limp. "When Johnny Comes Marching Home Again" is another familiar song that you play in 6/8 time. (See Appendix A for more information on time signatures.) Count only two beats per measure — not six — with each group of three eighth notes sounding like one big beat; otherwise, you'll end up sounding like a rabbit that's had three cups of coffee.

✔ **It's Raining, It's Pouring:** To play "It's Raining, It's Pouring," you need to know how to play Amaj7 and Dmaj7 chords (see the section, "Major 7th Chords — Cmaj7, Fmaj7, Amaj7, and Dmaj7," earlier in this chapter) and how to sing in a really whiny, annoying voice.

This song is a jazzed-up version of the old nursery rhyme "It's Raining, It's Pouring," also known as the childhood taunt "Billy Is a Sissy" (or whichever personal childhood nemesis you plug in to the title). The major 7th chords you play in this song sound jazzy and give any song a modern sound. Use all downstrokes on the strums.

✔ **Oh, Susanna:** To play "Oh, Susanna," you need to know how to play Cmaj7, Dm7, Em7, Fmaj7, Am7, D7, G7, and C chords (see Chapter 4 for C and various sections earlier in this chapter for the different 7th chords) and how to balance a banjo on your knee while traveling the Southern United States.

This arrangement of "Oh, Susanna" uses three types of 7th chords: dominant 7ths (D7 and G7), minor 7ths (Dm7, Em7, and Am7), and major 7ths (Cmaj7 and Fmaj7). Using minor 7ths and major 7ths gives the song a hip sound. Use all downstrokes on the strums.

Lest you think this attempt to "jazz up" a simple folk song comes from out of the blue, listen to James Taylor's beautiful rendition of "Oh, Susanna" on the 1970 album *Sweet Baby James* to hear a similar approach. He actually says "banjo" without sounding corny.

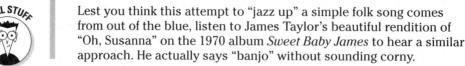

Home on the Range

Track 11

Video Clip 21

All through the Night

Track 12

Video Clip 22

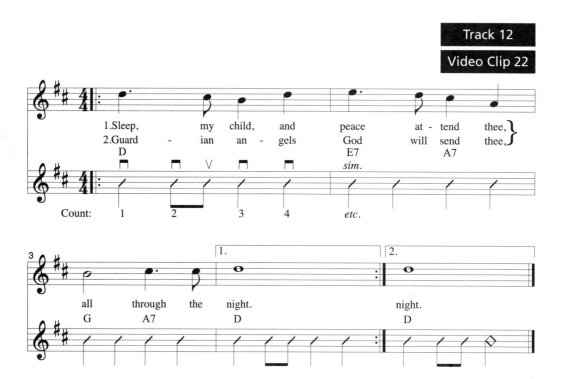

Over the River and through the Woods

Track 13

Video Clip 23

It's Raining, It's Pouring

Track 14

Video Clip 24

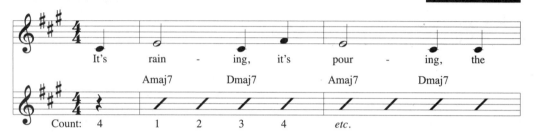

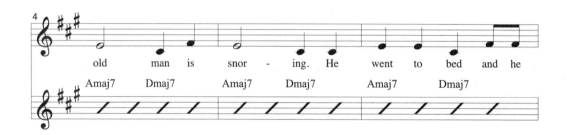

Oh, Susanna

Track 15

Video Clip 25

Fun with 7th Chords: The 12-Bar Blues

Playing the guitar isn't all about folk songs and nursery rhymes, you know. Sometimes you can pick up something really cool. And what's cooler than the blues? By knowing a few dominant 7th chords and being able to strum four beats per measure, you already have the basics down pat for playing 99 percent of all blues songs ever written.

Ninety-nine percent?! That's right! The 12-bar blues follow a simple chord formula, or *progression,* that involves three dominant 7ths. In this progression, you don't need to know any new chords or techniques; you need to know only which three dominant 7th chords to play — and in which order. In the following sections, we explain how to play the 12-bar blues and note the ease with which you can write your own blues song.

Playing the 12-bar blues

The key of E is one of the best guitar keys for playing the blues. Figure 6-6 shows the chord progression to a 12-bar blues in E. Practice this pattern and get familiar with the way chords change in a blues progression. Note that in the pattern in Figure 6-6, you play only three different chords — E7, A7, and B7 — and you play them in a particular order, with each chord lasting a certain number of bars, as follows: E7 (four bars), A7 (two bars), E7 (two bars), B7 (one bar), A7 (one bar), E7 (one bar), B7 (one bar).

Track 16

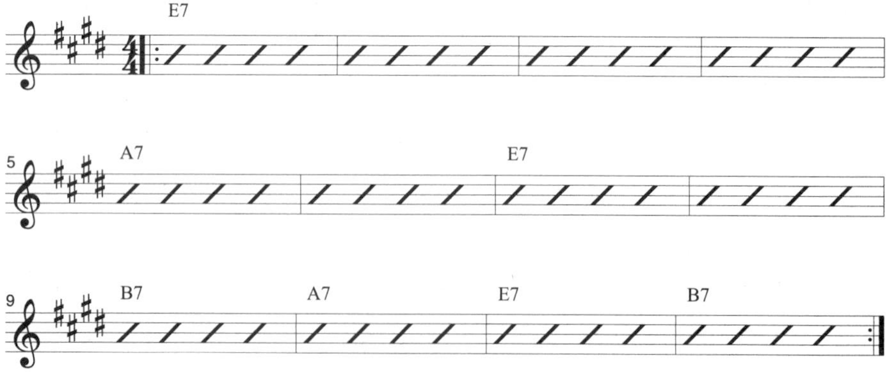

Figure 6-6:
A 12-bar blues progression in E.

© John Wiley & Sons, Inc.

Famous 12-bar blues songs include "Rock Around the Clock," "Blue Suede Shoes," "Roll Over Beethoven," "Long Tall Sally," "Kansas City," "The Twist," "The Peppermint Twist," and "Johnny B. Goode." You can play any of these right now just by singing along and observing the 12-bar scheme in Figure 6-6. (For more information on 12-bar blues, see Chapters 11 and 12.)

Writing your own blues song

Blues songs are simple to write lyrics for. (Just think of any Little Richard song.) Usually you repeat lines and then finish off with a zinger — for example:

> My baby she done left me, and she stole my best friend Joe. My baby she done left me, and she stole my best friend Joe. Now I'm all alone and cryin', 'cause I miss him so.

Try composing some lyrics yourself, improvise a melody, and apply them to the blues progression that we outline here.

As a rule, a good blues song must include the following elements:

✔ A subject dealing with hardship or injustice

✔ A locale or situation conducive to misery

✔ Bad grammar

Use Table 6-1 to find mix-and-match elements for your blues songs.

Table 6-1	Elements for a Good Blues Song	
Song Element	*Good Blues*	*Bad Blues*
Subject	Treachery, infidelity, your mojo	Rising interest rates, an impending market correction, the scarcity of good help
Locale	Memphis, the Bayou, prison	Aspen, Rodeo Drive, Starbucks
Bad grammar	"My baby done me wrong."	"My life-partner has been insensitive to my needs."

Why not compose one yourself? Call it the "Left-Hand Callus Blues" and talk about how them bad ol' strings put a big hurtin' on your fingertips. Then see Chapter 12 for more info on the blues.

Part III
Beyond the Basics: Starting to Sound Cool

Top four articulations to make your playing sound cool

- ✔ Hammer-ons allow you to sound another note without re-striking the string and are powerful tools in building a smooth, legato single-note solo.
- ✔ Pull-offs are the counterpart to hammer-ons, used for descending sequences.
- ✔ Slides are another great way to connect two notes together in a smooth, gliding way.
- ✔ Bends allow you to change pitch by stretching the string and are essential for playing rock and electric blues lead guitar.

 Check out www.dummies.com/extras/guitar for a surefire method for finding barre chords anywhere on the neck.

In this part . . .

✔ Practice scales in position to help you explore the upper regions of the fretboard.

✔ Play songs in position to minimize left-hand movement and produce a smooth sound.

✔ Add meat and flavor to your playing with double-stops.

✔ Understand how movable barre chords allow you to play practically any chord.

✔ Grasp special articulations to make your guitar talk, sing, and cry.

Chapter 7

Making Things Smooth by Playing in Position

In This Chapter

▶ Practicing single notes in position

▶ Playing songs in position

▶ Access the audio tracks and video clips at www.dummies.com/go/guitar

*O*ne of the giveaways of beginning guitar players is that they can play only down the neck, in open position. As you get to know the guitar better, you find you can use the whole neck to express your musical ideas. In this chapter, you venture out of open-position base camp into the higher altitudes of position playing.

Playing Scales and Exercises in Position

As you listen to complicated-sounding guitar music played by virtuoso guitarists, you may imagine their left hands leaping around the fretboard with abandon. But usually, if you watch those guitarists on stage or TV, you discover that their left hands hardly move at all. Those guitarists are playing in position.

Playing in position means that your left hand remains in a fixed location on the neck, with each finger more or less on permanent assignment to a specific fret, and that you fret every note — you don't use any open strings. If you're playing in *5th position,* for example, your 1st finger plays the 5th fret, your 2nd finger plays the 6th fret, your 3rd finger plays the 7th fret, and your 4th finger plays the 8th fret. A *position,* therefore, gets its name from the fret that your 1st finger plays. (What guitarists call *open position* consists of the combination of all the open strings plus the notes in 1st or 2nd position.)

In addition to enabling you to play notes where they feel and sound best on the fingerboard (not just where you can most easily grab available notes, such as the open-string notes in open position), playing in position makes you look cool — like a nonbeginner! Think of it this way: A lay-up and a slam dunk are both worth two points in basketball, but only in the latter case does the announcer scream, "And the crowd goes wild!"

In the following sections, we explain the differences between playing in position and playing with open strings; we also provide plenty of exercises to help you get comfortable with playing in position.

Playing in position versus playing with open strings

Why play in position? Why not use open position and open strings all the time? We can give you two key reasons:

- ✓ **It's easier to play high-note melodies.** Playing in open position allows you to play up to only the 4th or 5th fret. If you want to play higher than that, position playing enables you to play the notes smoothly and economically.

- ✓ **You can instantly transpose any pattern or phrase that you know in position to another key simply by moving your hand to another position.** Because position playing involves no open strings, everything you play in position is *movable*.

People have the idea that playing guitar in lower positions is easier than playing in higher ones. The higher notes actually aren't harder to play; they're just harder to read in standard notation if you don't get too far in a conventional method book (where reading high notes is usually saved for last). But here, you're focusing on guitar playing rather than music reading — so go for the high notes whenever you want.

Playing exercises in position

The major scale (you know, the familiar do-re-me-fa-sol-la-ti-do sound you get by playing the white keys on the piano starting from C) is a good place to start practicing the skills you need to play in position. Figure 7-1 shows a C major scale in 2nd position. Although you can play this scale in open position, play it as the tab staff in the figure indicates, because you want to start practicing your position playing. If you're unfamiliar with playing scales, play along to Video Clip 26.

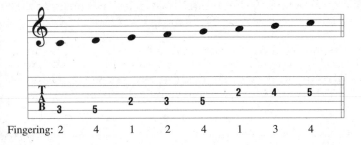

Video Clip 26

Figure 7-1:
A one-
octave
C-major
scale in 2nd
position.

Fingering: 2   4   1   2   4   1   3   4

© John Wiley & Sons, Inc.

The most important thing about playing in position is the location of your left hand — in particular, the position and placement of the fingers of your left hand. The following list contains tips for positioning your left hand and fingers:

✔ **Keep your fingers over the appropriate frets the entire time you're playing.** Because you're in 2nd position for this scale, keep your 1st finger over the 2nd fret, your 2nd finger over the 3rd fret, your 3rd finger over the 4th fret, and your 4th finger over the 5th fret at all times — even if they're not fretting any notes at the moment.

✔ **Keep all your fingers close to the fretboard, ready to play.** At first, your fingers may exhibit a tendency to straighten out and rise away from the fretboard. This tendency is natural, so work to keep them curled and to hold them down near the frets where they belong for the position.

✔ **Relax!** Although you may think that you need to intensely focus all your energy on performing this maneuver correctly or positioning that finger just so, you don't. What you're actually working toward is simply adopting the most natural and relaxed approach to playing the guitar. (You may not think it all that natural right now, but eventually, you'll catch the drift. Honest!) So take things easy, but remain aware of your movements. Is your left shoulder, for example, riding up like Quasimodo's? Check it periodically to make sure it stays tension-free. And be sure to take frequent deep breaths, especially if you feel yourself tightening up.

Look at Figure 7-1 and notice that the score indicates left-hand fingerings under the tab numbers. These indicators aren't essential because the position itself dictates these fingerings. But if you want, you can read the finger numbers (instead of the tab numbers) and play the C scale that way (keeping an eye on the tab staff to check which string you're on). Then, if you memorize the fingerings, you have a *movable pattern* that enables you to play a major scale from any starting note.

Play the *one-octave scale* (one having a range of only eight notes) shown in Figure 7-1 by using both downstrokes and upstrokes — that is, by using alternate (down and up) picking. Try it descending as well (you should practice all scales ascending and descending). (See Chapter 5 for more information on alternate picking.) ***Note:*** This scale is not on an audio track; you already know how it sounds — it's the familiar *do-re-mi-fa-sol-la-ti-do.*

After you practice the one-octave scale for a while, you can move to the next level. Figure 7-2 shows a two-octave C-major scale (one with a range of 15 notes) in the 7th position. Notice that this scale requires you to play on all six strings. Refer to Video Clip 27 to help orient your left hand for playing in 7th position.

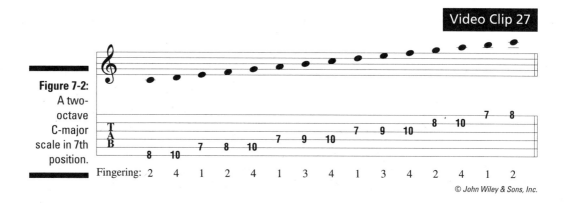

Figure 7-2: A two-octave C-major scale in 7th position.

© John Wiley & Sons, Inc.

To help you remember to hold your fingers over the appropriate frets all the time (even if they're not playing at the moment) and keep your fingers close to the fretboard, we have a twist on an old expression: Keep your friends close, your enemies closer, and your frets even closer.

Practice playing the scale shown in Figure 7-2 up and down the neck, using alternate picking. If you memorize the fingering pattern (shown under the tab numbers), you can play any major scale simply by moving your hand up or down to a different position. Try it. And then challenge the nearest piano player to a *transposing* (key-changing) contest, using the major scale.

Play scales slowly at first to ensure that your notes sound clean and smooth, and then gradually increase your speed.

Shifting positions

Music isn't so simple that you can play it all in one position, and life would be pretty static if you could. In real-world situations, you must often play an uninterrupted passage that takes you through different positions. To do so successfully, you need to master the *position shift* with the aplomb of an old politician.

Andrés Segovia, legend of the classical guitar, devised fingerings for all 12 major and minor scales. (See Chapter 20 for more information on Segovia.) Figure 7-3 shows how Segovia played the two-octave C-major scale. It differs from the two scales in the preceding section in that it requires a position shift in the middle of the scale. Watch and listen to Video Clip 28 to hear the imperceptible movement of the left hand during the shift.

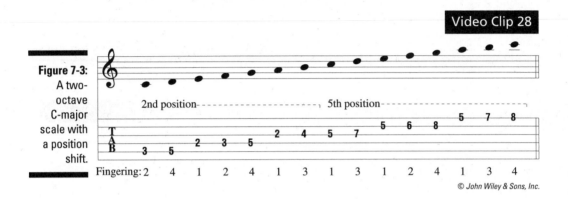

Figure 7-3: A two-octave C-major scale with a position shift.

© John Wiley & Sons, Inc.

Play the first seven notes in 2nd position and then shift up to 5th position by smoothly gliding your 1st finger up to the 5th fret (3rd string). As you play the scale downward, play the first eight notes in 5th position, and then shift to 2nd position by smoothly gliding your 3rd finger down to the 4th fret (3rd string). The important thing is that the position shift sound seamless. Someone listening shouldn't be able to tell that you shift positions. The trick is in the smooth gliding of the 1st (while ascending) or 3rd (while descending) finger.

You must practice this smooth glide to make it sound uninterrupted and seamless. Isolate just the two notes involved (3rd string, 4th fret, and 3rd string, 5th fret) and play them over and over as shown in the scale until you can make them sound as if you're making no position shift at all.

Creating your own exercises to build strength and dexterity

Some people do all sorts of exercises to develop their position playing. They buy books that contain nothing but position-playing exercises. Some of these books aim to develop sight-reading skills, and others aim to develop left-hand finger strength and dexterity. But you don't really need such books. You can make up your own exercises to build finger strength and dexterity. (And sight reading doesn't concern you now anyway, because you're reading tab numbers.)

To create your own exercises, just take the two-octave major scale shown earlier in Figure 7-2 and number the 15 notes of the scale as 1 through 15. Then make up a few simple mathematical combinations that you can practice playing. Following are some examples:

- 1-2-3-1, 2-3-4-2, 3-4-5-3, 4-5-6-4, and so on. (See Figure 7-4a.)
- 1-3-2-4, 3-5-4-6, 5-7-6-8, 7-9-8-10, and so on. (See Figure 7-4b.)
- 15-14-13, 14-13-12, 13-12-11, 12-11-10, and so on. (See Figure 7-4c.)

Figure 7-4 shows how these numbers look in music and tab. Remember, these notes are just suggested patterns to memorize and help build dexterity.

Track 17, 0:00

Track 17, 0:10

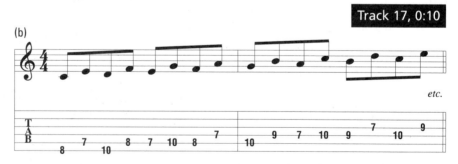

Track 17, 0:20

Figure 7-4: Three examples of patterns to help build up the left hand.

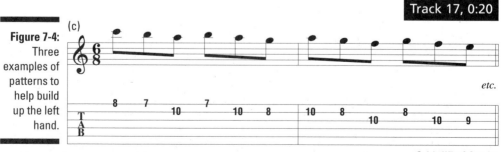

© John Wiley & Sons, Inc.

You get the idea. You can make up literally hundreds of permutations and practice them endlessly — or until you get bored. Piano students have a book called *Hanon* that contains lots of scale permutations to help develop strength and independence of the fingers. You can check out that book for permutation ideas, but making up your own is probably just as easy.

Practicing Songs in Position

Certain keys fall comfortably into certain positions on the guitar. Songs are based in keys, so if you play a song in a particular key, the song will also fall comfortably into a certain position. You can see the importance of position playing in crystal clarity in Part IV. Rock, jazz, blues, and country lead playing all demand certain positions in order to render an authentic sound.

Telling you that the melody of a song sounds best if you play it in one position rather than another may seem a bit arbitrary to you. But trust us on this one — playing a Chuck Berry lick in A is almost impossible in anything *but* 5th position. Country licks that you play in A, on the other hand, fall most comfortably in 2nd position, and trying to play them anywhere else is just making things hard on yourself.

That's one of the great things about the guitar: The best position for a certain style not only sounds best to your ears, but also feels best to your hands. And that's what makes playing the guitar so much fun.

Play these songs by reading the tab numbers and listening to the audio tracks; notice how cool playing up the neck feels instead of playing way down in open position, where those beginners play.

Whenever you're playing in position, be sure to keep your left hand in a fixed position, perpendicular to the neck, with your 1st finger at a given fret and the other fingers following in order, one per fret. Hold the fingers over the appropriate frets, very close to the fretboard, even if they're not fretting notes at the moment.

Here is some useful information to help you play the songs:

- **Simple Gifts:** To play this song, you need to know how to play in 4th position (see the section "Playing Scales and Exercises in Position," earlier in this chapter) and what *'tis* and *'twill* mean.

    This song is in the key of A, making 4th position ideal, because you find all the notes between the 4th and 7th frets. Because you play no open strings in this song, memorize the fingering and then try playing the same melody in other positions and keys. The fingering is the same in every position, even though the tab numbers change. Go on — try it.

✔ **Turkey in the Straw:** To play this song, you need to know how to play in 7th position (see the section "Playing Scales and Exercises in Position," earlier in this chapter) and what saying "day-day to the wagon tongue" means.

When you play this song, you see that the key of G sits nicely in 7th position (with the notes of the song all falling between the 7th and 10th frets). As with "Simple Gifts" (or any song played without open strings), if you memorize the fingering pattern, you can transpose the song to different keys simply by moving the pattern to a higher or lower starting fret.

Simple Gifts

Track 18

Video Clip 29

Turkey in the Straw

Track 19

Video Clip 30

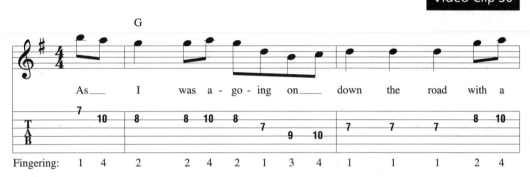

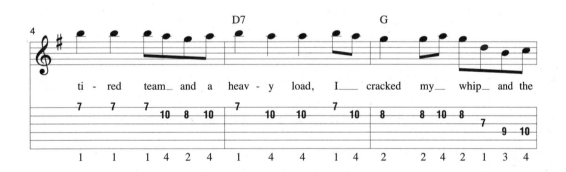

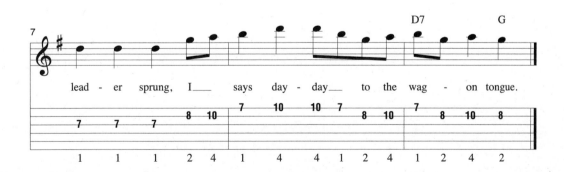

Chapter 8

Doubling Up with Double-Stops

In This Chapter

▶ Playing double-stops up, down, and across the neck

▶ Practicing songs in double-stops

▶ Access the audio tracks and video clips at www.dummies.com/go/guitar

The term *double-stop* doesn't refer to going back to the store because you forgot the milk. Double-stop is guitar lingo for playing two notes at the same time — something the guitar can do with relative ease but that's impossible on woodwinds and only marginally successful on bowed string instruments. (Actually, guitarists lifted the term from violin playing but quickly made double-stops truly their own.) This chapter gives you the scoop on how to play double-stops.

By the way, you do nothing special in fretting double-stops. Fret them the same way you would chords or single notes.

Beginning with the Basics of Double-Stops

You experience the guitar's capability to play more than one note simultaneously as you strum a chord, but you can also play more than one note in a melodic context. Playing double-stops is a great way to play in harmony with yourself. So adept is the guitar at playing double-stops, in fact, that some musical forms — such as '50s rock 'n' roll, country, and Mariachi music (you know, the music that Mexican street bands play) — use double-stops as a hallmark of their styles.

In the following sections, we define double-stops and help you get comfortable with them by providing a few exercises.

Defining double-stops

A double-stop is nothing more than two notes that you play at the same time. It falls somewhere between a single note (one note) and a chord (three or more notes). You can play a double-stop on adjacent strings or on nonadjacent strings (by skipping strings). The examples and songs that you find in this chapter, however, involve only adjacent-string double-stops, because they're the easiest to play.

If you play a melody in double-stops, it sounds sweeter and richer, fuller and prettier than if you play it by using only single notes. And if you play a *riff* in double-stops, it sounds gutsier and fuller — the double-stops just create a bigger sound. Check out some Chuck Berry riffs — "Johnny B. Goode," for example — and you can hear that he uses double-stops all the time.

Trying exercises in double-stops

You can play double-stops in two general ways: by using only *one* pair of strings (the first two strings, for example) — moving the double-stops up and down the neck — or in one area of the neck by using *different* string pairs and moving the double-stops across the neck (first playing the 5th and 4th strings, for example, and then the 4th and 3rd, and so on).

Playing double-stops up and down the neck

Start with a C-major scale that you play in double-stop *3rds* (notes that are two letter names apart, such as C-E, D-F, and so on), exclusively on the first two strings, moving up the neck. This type of double-stop pattern appears in Figure 8-1. The left-hand fingering doesn't appear below the tab numbers in this score, but that's not difficult to figure out. Start with your 1st finger for the first double-stop. (You need only one finger to fret this first double-stop because the 1st string is open.) Then, for all the other double-stops in the scale, use fingers 1 and 3 if the notes are two frets apart (the second and third double-stops, for example) and use fingers 1 and 2 if the notes are one fret apart (the fourth and fifth double-stops, for example). With your right hand, strike only the 1st and 2nd strings. View Video Clip 31 to see the ascending motion of the left hand and the correct fingerings.

Figure 8-1:
A C-major scale that you play in double-stops, moving up the neck on one pair of strings.

© John Wiley & Sons, Inc.

Track 20, 0:00

Video Clip 31

Playing double-stops across the neck

Playing double-stops across the neck is probably more common than playing up and down the neck on a string pair. Figure 8-2 shows a C-major scale that you play in 3rds in open position, moving across the neck; Video Clip 32 shows you how it's done. Again, the example doesn't show the fingerings for each double-stop, but you can use fingers 1 and 2 if the notes are one fret apart (the first double-stop, for example) and fingers 1 and 3 if the notes are two frets apart (the second double-stop, for example).

Figure 8-2:
A C-major scale that you play in double-stops, moving across the neck in open position.

© John Wiley & Sons, Inc.

Track 20, 0:11

Video Clip 32

What's especially common in rock and blues songs is playing double-stops across the neck where the two notes that make up the double-stop are on the same fret (which you play as a two-string barre). Check out Chapters 11 and 12 for more info on rock and blues.

To hear double-stops in action, listen to the opening of Jimmy Buffett's "Margaritaville," Leo Kottke's version of the Allman Brothers' "Little Martha," Van Morrison's "Brown Eyed Girl," Chuck Berry's "Johnny B. Goode," the intros to Simon and Garfunkel's "Homeward Bound" and "Bookends," and the intro to Jason Mraz's "I Won't Give Up."

Playing Songs in Double-Stops

Double-stops can make your playing sound very cool (as when Chuck Berry rocks out on "Johnny B. Goode"), or they can make your melodic passages sound extra sweet (as when two singers harmonize with each other). In the songs that follow, you get to sound both cool ("Double-Stop Rock") and sweet ("Aura Lee" and "The Streets of Laredo").

So get your fingers ready to form lots of little *two-note chords* (double-stops, that is) on these goodies. As we said, to keep things nice and easy, we place all the double-stops on adjacent strings (no muting of "in between" strings necessary!). And here's a tip to make things especially easy: When the two notes of a double-stop fall on the same fret (which happens a lot in the Chuck Berry–inspired "Double-Stop Rock"), play them as a small barre (with a single finger).

Here's some useful information to help you play the songs:

🖊 **Aura Lee:** To play this song — made famous by Elvis Presley as "Love Me Tender" — you need to know how to play double-stops up and down the neck on the 1st and 2nd strings (see the aptly titled section "Playing double-stops up and down the neck," earlier in this chapter) and how to gyrate your pelvis while raising one side of your upper lip.

You play this arrangement of "Aura Lee" exclusively on the first two strings, moving up and down the neck. In the double-stop scales that you practice in Figures 8-1 and 8-2, the two notes of the double-stop move up or down together. In "Aura Lee," the two notes of the double-stop sometimes move in the same direction and sometimes in opposite directions. Other times, one of the notes moves up or down while the other remains stationary. Mixing directions makes an arrangement more interesting. Play and listen to "Aura Lee" and you see what we mean.

Notice that the left-hand fingerings appear under the tab numbers. If the same finger plays successive notes but at different frets, a slanted line indicates the position shift (as in measures 5 and 9). For your right-hand picking, use all downstrokes. Remember to repeat the first four bars (as the repeat signs around them indicate) before continuing to bar 5. (Check out Appendix A for more information on repeat signs.) And make the song tender, just as Elvis did. Uh-thank yew verrah much.

✔ **The Streets of Laredo:** To play this song, you need to know how to play double-stops across the neck (see the section "Playing double-stops across the neck," earlier in this chapter) and how to sound light-hearted while playing a song about a conversation with a corpse.

In this arrangement, you play double-stops across the strings, near the bottom of the neck. The double-stops give the song a sweet, pretty sound — just the thing for a tête-à-tête between a passerby and a mummified cowboy. The tab doesn't indicate fingering, but you can use fingers 1 and 2 for double-stops that are one fret apart and 1 and 3 for double-stops that are two frets apart. For right-hand picking, use all downstrokes.

✔ **Double-Stop Rock:** To play this song, you don't have to know how to do the "duck walk," but you do have to be able to play double-stops with a Chuck Berry rock 'n' roll attitude.

In this arrangement, you play double-stops across the neck, mostly in 5th position (see the section "Playing double-stops across the neck," earlier in this chapter). Using only three one-measure phrases, repeated at various times, you play a 12-bar blues in the key of A (see Chapter 6 for more on the 12-bar blues). Note that the fingering for the phrase played against the E7 chord (measure 9) is the same as that of the phrase played against the D7 chord (measure 5); in fact, the two phrases are the same, albeit two frets apart.

Aura Lee

Track 21

Video Clip 33

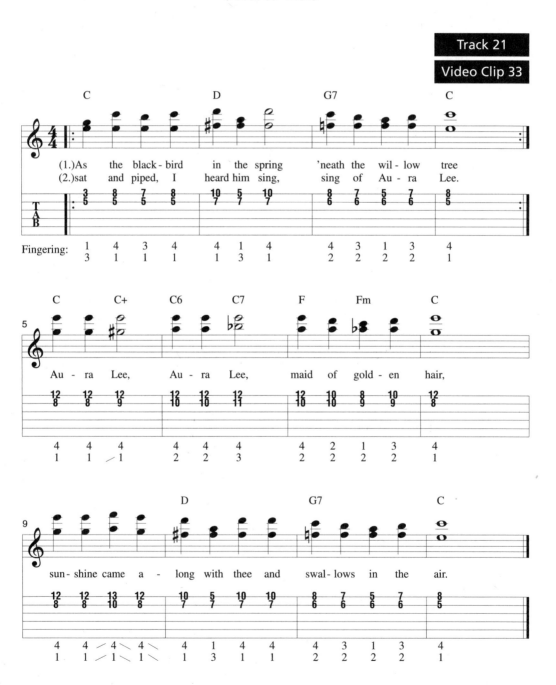

The Streets of Laredo

Track 22

Video Clip 34

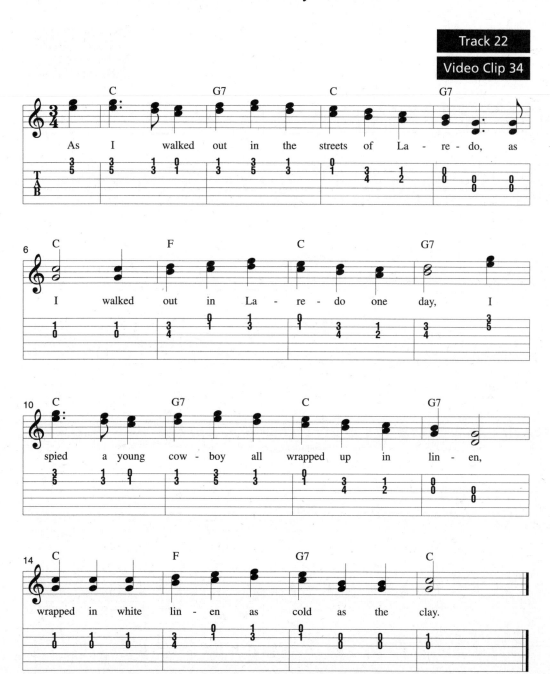

Double-Stop Rock

Chapter 9

Stretching Out: Barre Chords

*I*n this chapter, we show you how to play chords that you can move all around the neck. Unlike open-position chords, which can be played only in one place, *movable chords* can be played at any fret. In most of these movable chords, you play what's called a *barre* (pronounced "bar").

As you play a barre, one of your left-hand fingers (usually the index) presses down all or most of the strings at a certain fret, enabling the remaining fingers to play a chord form immediately above (toward the body of the guitar) the barre finger. Think of your barre finger as a sort of movable nut or capo and your remaining fingers as playing certain open-position chord forms directly above it. (See Chapter 13 if you're not sure how a capo works.) A movable barre chord contains no open strings — only fretted notes. You can slide these fretted notes up or down the neck to different positions to produce other chords of the same quality.

Movable barre chords are either E-based, getting their names from the notes you play on the 6th (low E) string, or A-based, getting their names from the notes you play on the 5th (A) string. We cover both of these types of chords in this chapter. We also give you a quick lesson on *power chords,* which are chords that are neither major nor minor and are usually made up of just the lowest two or three strings of a barre chord or open-position chord.

Major Barre Chords Based on E

One of the most useful movable barre chords is the one based on the open E chord. (See Chapter 4 if you're not sure how to finger an open E chord.) In the following sections, you start working on barre chords with an open-position E chord, discover how to find the correct fret for any major chord, and practice some progressions.

Beginning with an open-position E chord

The best way to get a grip on major barre chords based on E is to start out with an open-position E chord. Follow these steps (as shown in Figure 9-1), and refer to Video Clip 36, if necessary:

1. **Play an open E chord, but instead of using the normal 2-3-1 left-hand fingering, use fingers 3-4-2.**

   This fingering leaves your 1st (index) finger free, hovering above the strings.

2. **Lay your 1st finger down across all six strings on the other side of the nut (the side toward the tuning pegs).**

   Placing your index finger across the strings at this location doesn't affect the sound of the chord because the strings don't vibrate on that side of the nut. Extending your first finger across the width of the strings, however, helps you get the "feel" of a barre chord position. Don't press too hard with any of your fingers, because you're going to move the chord.

3. **Take the entire left-hand shape from Step 2 and slide it up (toward the body of the guitar) one fret so your 1st finger is barring the 1st fret and your E-chord fingers have all advanced up a fret as well.**

   You're now in an F-chord position (because F is one fret higher than E), and you can press down across all the strings with your index finger.

4. **Try playing the notes of the chord one string at a time (from the 6th string to the 1st) to see whether all the notes ring out clearly.**

   The first few times you try this chord, the chances are pretty good that some of the notes aren't going to ring clearly and that your left-hand fingers are going to hurt.

You can use this "sliding up from an open-position chord" technique to form all the barre chords in this chapter. (But we also provide you with another approach in later sections.)

Figure 9-1:
The F barre
chord.

Photograph courtesy of Jon Chappell

Having difficulty at first in creating a barre F is normal (discouraging maybe, but normal). So before you give up on the guitar and take up the sousaphone, here are some tips to help you nail this vexing chord:

✔ Make sure you line up your left-hand thumb on the back of the guitar neck under the spot between your 1st and 2nd fingers. This position gives you maximum leverage while exerting pressure.

✔ Instead of holding your 1st finger totally flat, rotate it a little onto its side.

✔ Move the elbow of your left arm in close to your body, even to the point that it's touching your body at the waist. As you play open-position chords, you find that you usually hold your elbow slightly away from your body. Not so with full barre chords.

✔ If you hear muffled strings, check to see that your left-hand fingers are touching only the appropriate strings and not preventing adjacent ones from ringing. Try exerting more pressure with the fingers and make sure to play on the very tips for extra clearance. Calluses and experience help you get a clear sound from a barre chord.

You need to exert more pressure to fret at the bottom of the neck (at the 1st fret) than you do at, say, the 5th fret. Try moving your F chord up and down the neck to different frets on the guitar to prove to yourself that playing the chord gets easier as you move up the neck. Keep in mind that the essence of this chord form is that it's *movable.* Unlike what your elementary school teachers may have told you, don't sit so still! Move around already!

Playing barre chords on an electric guitar is easier than playing them on an acoustic guitar. The *string gauges* (the thickness of the strings) are lighter on an electric guitar and the *action* (distance of the strings to the fretboard) is lower than on an acoustic. If you're using an acoustic and you're having trouble with barre chords, try playing them on an electric (but not one of those el-cheapo ones from the pawn shop) and take note of the difference. Doing so may inspire you to keep at it.

Finding the right fret for every major E-based barre chord

Because you can play an F chord as a barre chord, you can now, through the miracle of movable chords, play *every major chord* — all 12 of them — simply by moving up the neck. To determine the name of each chord, you simply have to know what note name you're playing on the 6th (low E) string — because all E-based barre chords get their name from the 6th string (just as the open E chord does).

Each fret is a half step away from each adjacent fret. So if a 1st-fret barre chord is F, the 2nd-fret barre chord is F♯; the 3rd-fret chord is G; the 4th fret is G♯; and so on. Check out Appendix A for a listing of the names of the notes on the low E string.

After you reach the 12th fret, the notes — and thus, the barre chords that you play at those frets — repeat: The 13th-fret barre chord is the same as the 1st (F); the 14th is the same as the 2nd (F♯); and so on. The frets work sort of like a clock: 13 equals 1, 14 equals 2, and so on.

Playing progressions using major barre chords based on E

A good way to build your comfort and confidence in playing barre chords is by practicing a *progression,* which is a series of chords. Listen to Track 24 to hear what a four-measure progression using E-based major barre chords sounds like. Figure 9-2 shows the exercise. Below the staff, you see the correct 1st-finger fret for each chord. Video Clip 37 illustrates how the left hand moves around the neck.

Track 24, 0:00

Video Clip 37

Figure 9-2: A progression using E-based major barre chords.

C | A | G | F

Fret: 8 — 5 — 3 — 1

© John Wiley & Sons, Inc.

Use only barre chords for this exercise (and for all the exercises in this chapter), even if you know how to play these chords as open-position chords. Play the C chord, for example, by barring at the 8th fret. Then play A at the 5th fret, G at the 3rd fret, and F at the 1st fret. Use the F-chord fingering for all these chords.

Trying to make all six strings ring out clearly on each chord can get a little tiring. You can give your left-hand fingers a break by releasing pressure as you slide from one chord to the next. This action of *flexing and releasing* can help you develop a little finesse and keep you from tiring so easily. You don't need to keep a Vulcan Death Grip on the neck all the time — only while you're strumming the chord.

Although you can stop altogether if your hand starts to cramp, try to keep at it; as with any physical endeavor, you eventually build up your strength and stamina. Without question, barre chords are the triathlon of guitar playing, so strap on your best Ironman regalia and feel the burn.

To demonstrate the versatility of barre-chord progressions, here's an example that has a syncopated strum and sounds a little like the music of the Kinks. In syncopation, you either strike a chord (or note) where you don't expect to hear it or fail to strike a chord (or note) where you do expect to hear it. (The Kinks, in case you don't recall, were *the* English proto-punk band of the '60s, who gave us such classic hits as "You Really Got Me," "So Tired," and "Lola.") Figure 9-3 shows you how to play this progression by using major barre chords; again, use the F-chord fingering for both of these chords (play G at the 3rd fret and A at the 5th fret). Because the two chords move back and forth so quickly, the *release time* (the period during which you can relax your fingers) is very short. Check out Track 24 to hear how this exercise should sound before you get ready to sub for Ray Davies on a world tour.

Figure 9-3:
A syn-
copated
progression
using
E-based
major barre
chords.

Track 24, 0:13

© *John Wiley & Sons, Inc.*

Minor, Dominant 7th, and Minor 7th Barre Chords Based on E

After you're familiar with the basic feel and movement of the major barre chords described earlier in this chapter, start adding other chord qualities into your *repertoire* (which is a fancy French word for "bag of tricks" that musicians frequently use in discussing their music).

The good news is that everything you know about moving chords around the neck — getting a clear, ringing tone out of the individual notes in the chord (you are practicing, aren't you?) and the flex-and-release action that you use in playing major barre chords — carries over to the other forms of barre chords. Playing a minor, a dominant 7th, or a minor 7th barre form is no more physically difficult than playing a major barre, so as you practice all the various barre chords in the following sections, you should start to notice things getting a little easier. (Flip to Chapter 4 for an introduction to minor chords; we discuss dominant 7th and minor 7th chords in Chapter 6.)

Mastering minor chords

Forming an E-based *minor* barre chord is similar to forming a major barre chord, which we explain in the steps in the section "Beginning with an open-position E chord," earlier in this chapter. You can follow that set of steps, starting with an open Em chord but fingering it with fingers 3 and 4 (instead of how you usually finger the chord, as we describe in Chapter 4). Next, lay your first finger across all the strings on the other side of the nut and then slide the shape up one fret, producing an Fm chord.

As we state earlier in this chapter, you can use this "sliding up from an open-position chord" technique to form all the barre chords in this chapter. But you don't need to go through all that. The following simple steps describe another way to approach the Fm barre chord:

F

1. Play an F major barre chord.

See the section "Beginning with an open-position E chord," earlier in this chapter.

Fm

2. Remove your 2nd finger from the 3rd string.

The 1st-finger barre, which is already pressing down all the strings, now frets the new note on the 3rd string.

That's all you need to do. You instantly change a major barre chord to a minor barre chord by removing just one finger. Now, by using the low-E string chart in Appendix A as the reference, you can play any of the 12 minor chords by moving the Fm chord to the appropriate fret. To play an Am barre chord, for example, you just move the barre to the 5th fret.

If you're not sure whether you're playing a barre chord at the correct fret, try alternating the chord with its open-position form, playing first the barre and then the open form. Play the two versions in rapid succession several times. You can then hear whether the two chords are the same or different.

Try playing the simple progression shown in Figure 9-4, which uses both major and minor barre chords (play C at the 8th fret, Am at the 5th fret, Fm at the 1st fret, and G at the 3rd fret).

Figure 9-4:
A progression using both major and minor barre chords.

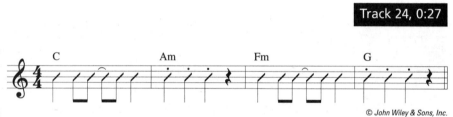

Track 24, 0:27

© John Wiley & Sons, Inc.

The dots above the slashes in bars 2 and 4 of Figure 9-4 are called *staccato* marks. They tell you to cut the notes short. (Instead of playing *daahh-daahh-daahh,* play *di-di-di.*) The best way to cut these notes short is to slightly release your left-hand finger pressure right after you strum the chord. The symbols at the end of the measures 2 and 4 are called *rests.* Don't play during a rest.

Now try playing the progression shown in Figure 9-4 two frets higher than the figure indicates. This two-fret variation gives you a D-Bm-Gm-A progression. You've just *transposed* (changed the key of) the progression quickly and easily — through the magic of movable chords!

Delving into dominant 7th chords

Dominant 7th chords have a sharper, more complex sound than do straight major chords. Switching to a barre dominant 7th chord from a major barre chord, however, is just as easy as switching from a major to a minor barre chord — you just lift a single (although different) finger.

To change an F major barre chord into an F7 barre chord, follow these steps:

1. **Finger an F major barre chord, as we describe in the section "Beginning with an open-position E chord," earlier in this chapter.**

2. **Remove your 4th finger from the 4th string.**

   The 1st-finger barre now frets the chord's new note.

Try playing the simple progression shown in Figure 9-5, using major and dominant 7th barre chords (play G at the 3rd fret, A7 at the 5th fret, C at the 8th fret, and D7 at the 10th fret).

Figure 9-5:
A progression using major and dominant 7th barre chords.

Track 24, 0:40

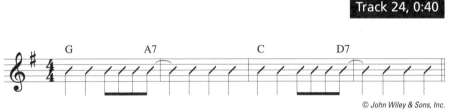

© John Wiley & Sons, Inc.

Playing the progression in Figure 9-5 in different keys is as simple as starting in a location different from the 3rd fret and moving the same relative distance. From wherever you start, simply move up two frets for the second chord, up three more frets for the third chord, and then up two more frets for the fourth chord.

Say the names of the chords you play out loud to help you associate their names with their locations. Although movable chords make transposing on the guitar a snap, memorizing just the pattern of the hand movement instead of the actual chord names you're playing is far too easy. So say the names of the chords as you play them. After enough times through, you instinctively come to know that you play, for example, a B7 chord at the 7th fret.

Trying minor 7th chords

Minor 7th chords have a softer, jazzier, and more complex sound than straight minor chords do. You can form a minor 7th E-based barre chord by simply combining the actions you take to change major to minor and major to dominant 7th.

To change an F major barre chord into an Fm7 barre chord, follow these steps:

F

1. **Play an F major barre chord, as we describe in the section "Beginning with an open-position E chord," earlier in this chapter.**

Fm7

2. **Remove your 2nd finger from the 3rd string and your 4th finger from the 4th string.**

   The 1st-finger barre, which is already pressing down all the strings, frets the new notes on the 3rd and 4th strings.

PLAY THIS!

To help you get accustomed to minor 7th barre chords, we put together the exercise shown in Figure 9-6 (play G at the 3rd fret, Bm7 at the 7th fret, and Am7 at the 5th fret). Listen to Track 24 to hear what it sounds like.

Figure 9-6:
A progression using major and minor 7th barre chords.

Track 24, 0:53

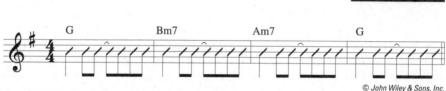

© John Wiley & Sons, Inc.

You can play this progression in different keys simply by starting from chords other than G and moving the same relative number of frets to make the next chord. After the first chord, simply move up four frets for the second chord and then down two for the third chord; then move down another two for the last chord. (You can transpose the other progressions in this section in a similar manner.)

REMEMBER

Say the names of the chords as you play them. Say them out loud. We're not kidding. You want to get so sick of hearing your own voice say the names of these chords at their correct locations that you can *never* forget that you play Am7 — the third chord of this progression — at the 5th fret.

Combining barre chords based on E

What's that we hear? It must be the pitter-patter of little reindeer feet. In the next exercise, as shown in Figure 9-7, you can practice lots of E-based barre chords all over the neck by playing the chord progression to the song "We Wish You a Merry Christmas." To help you out in this exercise, we indicate the fret number your 1st finger barres for each chord.

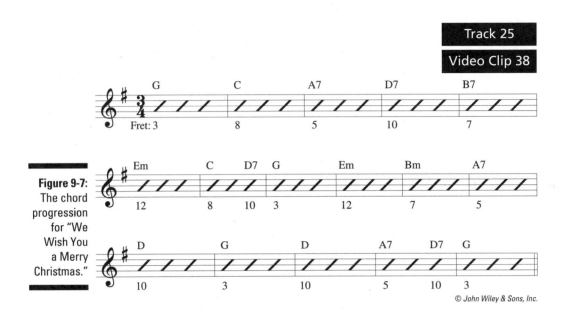

© John Wiley & Sons, Inc.

Figure 9-7: The chord progression for "We Wish You a Merry Christmas."

If you're playing a nylon-string acoustic guitar, you can't play the Em chord at the 12th fret — the body of the guitar gets in the way. (Even on a steel-string acoustic, this chord is almost unplayable.) Substitute an open-position Em chord, but play it with fingers 3 and 4 to keep your hand in the barre formation.

Note: In the section "Songs with Barre Chords and Power Chords," later in this chapter, you can find another version of this song, with melody and lyrics — but don't jump there until after you master your A-based barre chords! (See the following section for the scoop.)

Major Barre Chords Based on A

In the following sections, we introduce another major group of barre chords, the A-based barre chords. The *A-based* major barre chord looks like an open A chord (but with different fingering) and takes its letter name from the fret on the *5th* string at which you place your 1st-finger barre.

The theory seems simple enough, but you may find that this chord is a little more difficult to play than the E-based major barre chord. Don't worry, however, because we have a substitute waiting for you that involves only two fingers. But for now, humor us and create the A-based barre chord according to the directions in the following sections.

Fingering the A-based major barre chord

To finger an A-based major barre chord, follow these steps, and refer to Video Clip 39:

1. **Finger an open A chord, but instead of using the normal fingering of 1-2-3, use 2-3-4.**

   This fingering leaves your 1st (index) finger free and ready to act as the barre finger. (If you're not sure how to finger an open A chord, see Chapter 4.)

2. **Lay your 1st finger down across all six strings, just behind the nut (the side toward the tuning pegs).**

   Because you strum only the top five strings for A-based barre chords, you *could* lay your finger down across just five strings. But most guitarists cover all six strings with the barre because it feels more comfortable and it prevents the open 6th string from accidentally sounding.

   Placing your index finger across the strings at this point doesn't affect the sound of the chord because the strings don't vibrate on this side of the nut. Right now, you're just getting the feel of the chord position. Don't press too hard with any of your fingers because you're going to move the chord.

3. **Take the entire left-hand shape from Step 2 and slide it up one fret so your 1st finger barres the 1st fret, producing a B♭ chord, as shown in Figure 9-8.**

Figure 9-8: The barre B♭ chord.

Photograph courtesy of Jon Chappell

After you finger the B♭ chord, try playing the notes of the chord one string at a time (from the 5th string to the 1st) to see whether all the notes ring out clearly. If you encounter any muffled notes, check to see that your left-hand fingers are touching only the appropriate strings and aren't preventing adjacent ones from ringing. If the sound is still muted, you need to exert more pressure with your fingers.

Finding the right fret for every major A-based barre chord

Because you can play a B♭ chord as a barre chord, you can now play all 12 A-based major barre chords — but only if you know the names of all the notes on the 5th string. All A-based barre chords get their name from the 5th string (just as the open A chord does). Check out Appendix A for the names of the notes on the 5th string.

The notes and frets work sort of like a clock. After you get past 12, they repeat, so the 13th fret is the same as the 1st (B♭); the 14th is the same as the 2nd (B); and so on.

Playing progressions using A-based major barre chords

Before playing any progressions using A-based major barre chords, you need to know that most guitarists don't finger them as we describe earlier (refer to Figure 9-8). Take a look at Figure 9-9 to see another way to finger this chord (using the B♭ chord at the 1st fret as an example). Use your ring finger to barre the three notes at the 3rd fret.

Figure 9-9: Alternative fingering for the A-based major barre chord.

© John Wiley & Sons, Inc.; photograph courtesy of Jon Chappell

The tricky thing about the fingering in Figure 9-9 is that, for the 1st string to ring, you need to engage in a mean contortion with your 3rd finger, elevating the middle knuckle out of the way. Some people can accomplish this position and some can't — it's kind of like wiggling your ears. The people who can't (lift their finger, not wiggle their ears) can use the fingering shown in Figure 9-10.

© John Wiley & Sons, Inc.; photograph courtesy of Jon Chappell

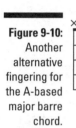

Figure 9-10: Another alternative fingering for the A-based major barre chord.

If you play the B♭ barre chord as shown in Figure 9-10 (with the 1st string not played), make sure the 1st string doesn't accidentally sound. To keep the 1st string quiet, either avoid striking it with your right hand or mute it (deaden it by lightly touching it) with the 3rd finger.

Experiment with all three fingerings and pick the one that feels best for you, but we bet that you decide on the form shown in Figure 9-10.

The exercise shown in Figure 9-11 uses A-based major barre chords and has a light, early rock sound. You can give your left-hand fingers a break by releasing pressure as you slide from one chord to the next. Watch Video Clip 40 to see this pressure release in action. Don't forget that you can (and should) transpose this progression to other keys by moving the entire pattern to a new starting point. Do so for all the exercises in this chapter. Notice, too, the staccato marks in measure 4 (play it *di-di-di*).

Track 26, 0:00

Video Clip 40

Figure 9-11: A progression using A-based major barre chords.

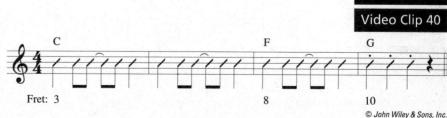

© John Wiley & Sons, Inc.

Minor, Dominant 7th, Minor 7th, and Major 7th Barre Chords Based on A

We admit that the A-based major barre chord is something of an oddball with respect to left-hand fingering. But all the other A-based forms are much more logical and comfortable in terms of left-hand fingering.

For the rest of the A-based forms in the following sections, you don't encounter any weird hand contortions or new techniques. All you do is pick up a variety of different forms to enrich your chord vocabulary.

Minor chords

To form an A-based minor barre chord, you *could* follow steps similar to the ones that we describe in the section "Fingering the A-based major barre chord," earlier in this chapter: Play an open Am chord by using a 3-4-2 fingering instead of 2-3-1 (see Chapter 4 if you need help with the open Am chord); lay your first finger down across all the strings on the other side of the nut; and then slide the shape up one fret and press down firmly, producing a B♭m chord.

But if you want, you can form the B♭m chord by skipping the "sliding up from an open chord" process and just placing your fingers directly on the frets, as indicated by the first chord diagram in Figure 9-12. Check your strings individually to see that they're clear and buzz-free. (Notice that we've gone ahead and also given you the fingerings for B♭7, B♭m7, and B♭maj7 in Figure 9-12. More on these in the following sections.)

The progression in Figure 9-13 is typical of a rock, folk, or country song and uses both major and minor A-based barre chords. Refer to Appendix A if you need the appropriate fret (on the A string) for each chord.

Figure 9-12:
B♭m, B♭7,
B♭m7, and
B♭maj7
barre
chords.

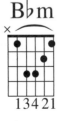
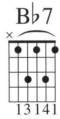
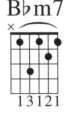

© John Wiley & Sons, Inc.

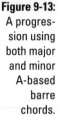

Figure 9-13:
A progression using both major and minor A-based barre chords.

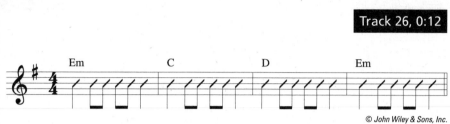

Track 26, 0:12

© John Wiley & Sons, Inc.

Dominant 7th chords

Dominant 7th chords sound bluesy and funky compared to major chords. Refer to Figure 9-12 to see the fingering for the B♭7 barre chord (A-based). Keep in mind that you can "slide up" to this chord from a two-finger, open-position A7 chord (but only if you use a 3-4 fingering for the A7).

Now, using the A-string chart in Appendix A to find the appropriate fret for any A-based barre chord, try playing the simple progression shown in Figure 9-14, which uses major, minor, and dominant 7th A-based barre chords.

Figure 9-14:
A progression using major, minor, and dominant 7th barre chords.

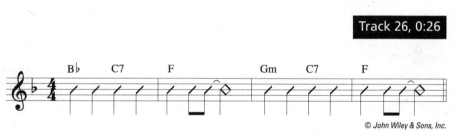

Track 26, 0:26

© John Wiley & Sons, Inc.

Minor 7th chords

Minor 7th chords sound soft and jazzy compared to major chords. You can form the B♭m7 chord by "sliding up" from an open-position Am7 chord (using a 3-2 fingering), or you can refer to the example shown earlier in Figure 9-12 and place your fingers directly on the frets for the B♭m7. (Chapter 6 tells you how to play an open-position Am7 chord.)

The simple progression that Figure 9-15 shows uses A-based minor 7th chords exclusively. If you need to, use Appendix A to find the appropriate fret for each chord.

Figure 9-15:
A progression using minor 7th barre chords.

Track 26, 0:42

© John Wiley & Sons, Inc.

Major 7th chords

Major 7th chords have a bright and jazzy sound compared to major chords. (You may notice that, in the section on E-based barre chords earlier in this chapter, we don't include the major 7th chord. That's because you don't play such chords in a barre form.)

You can form the B♭maj7 chord by "sliding up" from an open-position Amaj7 chord (using a 3-2-4 fingering), or you can refer to the example shown earlier in Figure 9-12 and place your fingers directly on the frets for the barre chord, as the figure shows you. (Chapter 6 tells you how to play an open-position Amaj7 chord.)

The simple progression shown in Figure 9-16 uses A-based minor 7th and major 7th barre chords. Use Appendix A to find the appropriate fret for each chord, if necessary.

Figure 9-16:
A progression using minor 7th and major 7th barre chords.

Track 26, 0:55

© John Wiley & Sons, Inc.

The exercise shown in Figure 9-17 uses the chord progression for the song "We Wish You a Merry Christmas." Play this progression by using only A-based barre chords. To help you out in this exercise, we indicate at which fret to place your 1st-finger barres for each chord. You may notice that the chords are different from those in the earlier "We Wish You a Merry Christmas" example (refer to Figure 9-7), but that's only because we use a different starting chord here.

Track 27, 0:00

Video Clip 41

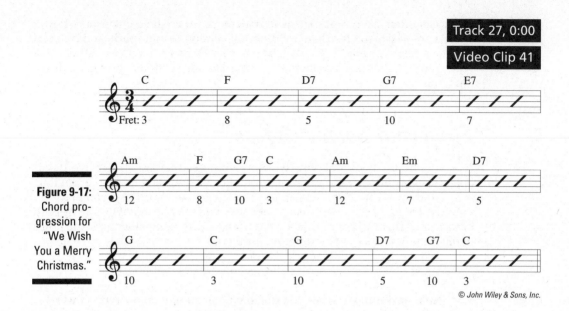

Figure 9-17:
Chord progression for "We Wish You a Merry Christmas."

© John Wiley & Sons, Inc.

If you're playing a nylon-string acoustic guitar, you're going to have trouble playing the Am chord at the 12th fret — the body of the guitar gets in the way. (And playing the chord's no picnic on a steel-string acoustic either.) Substitute an open-position Am chord but use a 3-4-2 fingering to keep your hand in the barre position.

You may notice, in playing the exercises in this chapter — and especially in the "We Wish You a Merry Christmas" exercises — that your left hand leaps around in sudden, jerky movements. That's because you're playing all the required chords by using only one chord form — either the E-based form or the A-based form. If you combine forms, you base your chord selection on economy of movement. The F and B♭ chords are five frets away from each other if you use the same barre form, but they're at the same fret (the 1st) if you use the E-based form of F and the A-based form of B♭. Playing songs actually gets easier as you add additional chords to your arsenal.

To see how much easier playing "We Wish You a Merry Christmas" is if you use A-based barre chords and E-based barre chords together, check it out in the section "Songs with Barre Chords and Power Chords," later in this chapter.

Power Chords

A *power chord* — not to be confused with a power *cord* (the cable that provides electricity to your motorized shoe buffer) — is usually nothing more than the lowest two or three notes of a regular open-position or barre chord.

Guitarists often use power chords in rock music to create a low sound. Power chords are easier to play than are their full-version counterparts and don't contain a major or minor quality to them, so they can stand in for either type of chord. Plus, as you find out in the following sections, they're loads of fun to play!

Fingering power chords

A power chord consists of only two different notes that are always five steps apart, such as A-E or C-G. (Count letter names on your fingers to confirm that A to E and C to G are five steps apart.) But the actual chord that you play may involve more than two strings, because you may be *doubling* one or both of the notes that makes up the power chord — that is, playing the same notes in different octaves (and on different strings).

As do most other chords, power chords come in two varieties:

- ✔ **Open-position:** We show you the most common open-position power chords — E5, A5, and D5 — in Figure 9-18. These chords are merely the two or three lowest notes of the simple open-position E, A, and D chords that we describe in Chapter 4.

- ✔ **Movable:** Movable power chords are simply the two or three lowest notes of the movable barre chords that we describe earlier in this chapter. As is the case with movable barre chords, movable power chords are either E-based, getting their names from the notes you play on the 6th (low E) string, or A-based, getting their names from the notes you play on the 5th (A) string. Figure 9-19 shows the F5 and B♭5 power chords that you play at the 1st fret, but you can move these chords to any fret, determining their names from the charts in Appendix A on the low-E string and A string. Or, better yet, you can determine the power-chord names by memorizing the names of the notes on the 6th and 5th strings — and then you don't need to resort to Appendix A at all! (Hint, hint.)

For the most part, the two- and three-string power chords are interchangeable. For some situations, such as in playing the Chuck Berry–style figures that we present in Chapter 11, the two-string version is preferable.

Knowing when to use power chords

In straight-ahead rock music (and even in some pop music), guitarists often substitute power chords for full chords to give the accompaniment (specifically, the rhythm guitar part) a sparser, leaner sound than what you can get with full chords. This course is sometimes taken to enable the vocal part

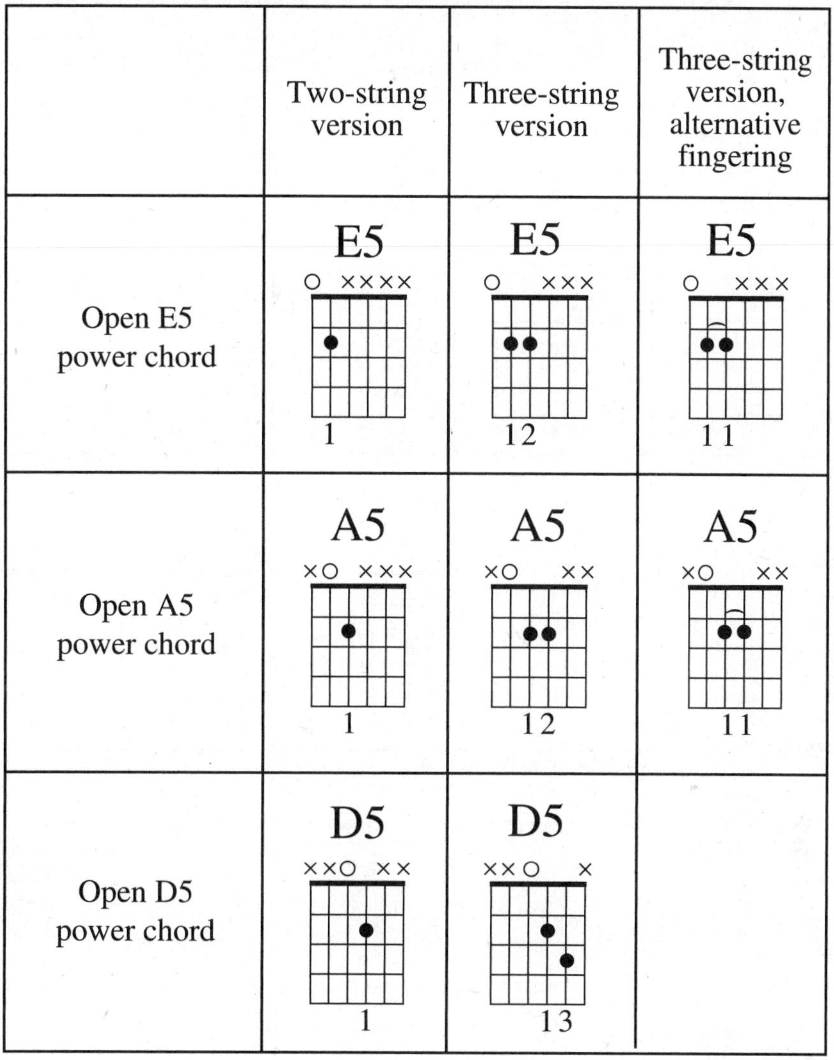
Two-string version
Three-string version
Three-string version, alternative fingering
Open E5 power chord
E5
1
E5
12
E5
11
Open A5 power chord
A5
1
A5
12
A5
11
Open D5 power chord
D5
1
D5
13

Figure 9-18: E5, A5, and D5 power chords.

© John Wiley & Sons, Inc.

to stand out more from the music. You can hear this kind of power chord sound in old songs such as "Johnny B. Goode" and "Peggy Sue." The progression shown in Figure 9-20 illustrates the power chords you use to produce this kind of sound. Play this progression by using either two- or three-string power chords. Watch Video Clip 42 to help capture the right feel for playing power chords.

	Two-string version	Three-string version	Three-string version, alternative fingering
E-based movable power chord	F5 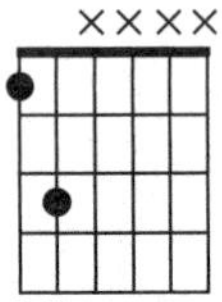 / 1 3	 F5 / 1 3 4	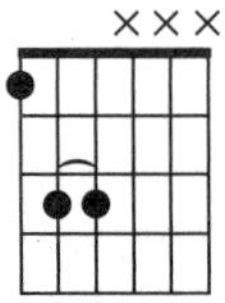 F5 / 1 3 3
A-based movable power chord	B♭5 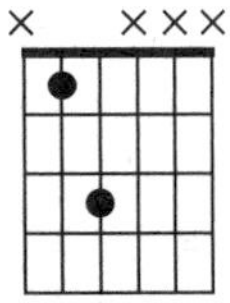 / 1 3	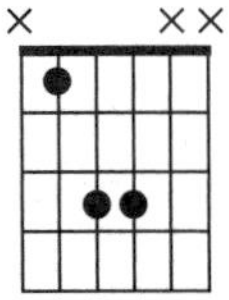 B♭5 / 1 3 4	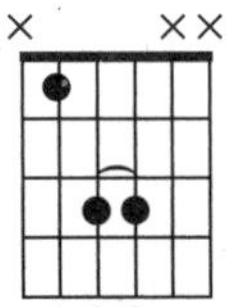 B♭5 / 1 3 3

Figure 9-19: F5 and B♭5 (movable) power chords.

© John Wiley & Sons, Inc.

Track 28, 0:00

Video Clip 42

Figure 9-20: A power chord progression in D.

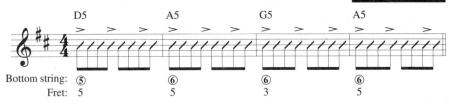

Bottom string ⑥ means chord is E-based; bottom string ⑤ means chord is A-based

© John Wiley & Sons, Inc.

The > symbol is called an *accent*. It tells you to play the accented notes a little louder than the other notes — to accentuate them. Sometimes accents form a rhythmic pattern that gives a song a certain flavor, such as a Latin flavor, a Bo Diddley flavor, a polka flavor, or even a tutti-frutti flavor.

In hard-rock and heavy-metal music, guitarists often like to use a heavy or ominous sound in their chords. They achieve this mood by playing low notes with *distortion* — a fuzzy-sounding signal that results if the signal is too powerful for the amp's circuitry and speakers to handle effectively.

Hard-rock and heavy-metal guitarists love to play power chords instead of full chords right off the bat, because power chords sound lower (mainly because they don't include the higher strings). In addition, the distorted tone really limits them to power chords, because full chords (chords with more than two different notes in them) can sound like mud with heavy distortion.

The progression shown in Figure 9-21 illustrates a typical heavy-metal riff, using both movable and open-position power chords. If you have an electric guitar and an amp or effect device that enables you to *overdrive* it (see Chapter 16), use distortion while practicing this progression, as you hear on Track 28. You can use either the two- or three-string version of the power chords, but the two-string version is what you hear on Track 28.

Track 28, 0:14

Figure 9-21: A heavy-metal power chord progression to bang your head to.

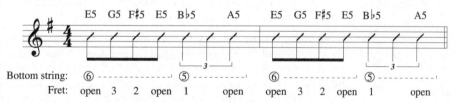

Bottom string ⑥ means chord is E-based; bottom string ⑤ means chord is A-based

© *John Wiley & Sons, Inc.*

To play a song with power chords right away, check out "Three Metal Kings" in the following section.

Songs with Barre Chords and Power Chords

Now the fun begins. You revisit a song that you may have already played at some point (refer to Figures 9-7 and 9-17), but in this section, we show you how playing a song is easier if you combine different chord forms.

Here is some useful information about the songs to help you along:

- ✔ **We Wish You a Merry Christmas:** To play "We Wish You a Merry Christmas," you need to know

  - How to play E-based barre chords (see the sections "Major Barre Chords Based on E" and "Minor, Dominant 7th, and Minor 7th Barre Chords Based on E," earlier in this chapter)

  - How to play A-based barre chords (see the sections "Major Barre Chords Based on A" and "Minor, Dominant 7th, Minor 7th, and Major 7th Barre Chords Based on A," earlier in this chapter)

  - How to play guitar dressed in a stuffy costume with a pillow strapped to your belly

  Chord progressions for this song appear twice in exercises in this chapter, first in the exercise in Figure 9-7, as practice for E-based barre chords, and then again in the exercise for Figure 9-17, as practice for A-based barre chords. In each of those exercises, your left hand must jump all over the fingerboard. By combining both kinds of barre chords (E-based and A-based), you can play this song with much less left-hand movement. Minimizing left-hand movement enables you to play both faster and more smoothly as well as to achieve better *voice leading,* or smoothness of motion between the individual notes of the changing chords. (Good voice leading produces a pleasing sound.)

- ✔ **Three Metal Kings:** To play "Three Metal Kings" (based on the classic Christmas carol "We Three Kings of Orient Are"), you need to know how to finger and play open-position and movable power chords up and down the neck (see the section "Fingering power chords," earlier in this chapter) and how to crank your amp up to 11 (à la Spinal Tap). Left-hand fingerings aren't indicated, so use any fingering that feels comfortable.

Note that we use tab, not rhythm slashes, to notate this song; that's because the music has a melodic, as well as a chordal, aspect and because some of the power chords exist in several different voicings.

Keep in mind that power chords are well suited to a heavier, distorted sound, and you can use them in place of full versions of chords because they usually contain the same bottom two or three notes. So if you're feeling a bit rebellious, a bit wicked, crank up your amp and play "We Wish You a Merry Christmas" with power chords, a distorted sound, and a *really* bad attitude.

We Wish You a Merry Christmas

Track 29

Video Clip 43

Three Metal Kings

Track 30

Video Clip 44

Chapter 10

Special Articulation: Making the Guitar Talk

In This Chapter

▶ Playing hammer-ons and pull-offs

▶ Practicing slides and bends

▶ Using vibratos and muting

▶ Playing in an integrated style

▶ Access the audio tracks and video clips at www.dummies.com/go/guitar

*A*rticulation refers to how you play and connect notes on the guitar. Look at it this way: If pitches and rhythms are *what* you play, articulation is *how* you play. Articulation gives your music expression and enables you to make your guitar talk, sing, and even cry. From a technical standpoint, such articulation techniques as *hammer-ons, pull-offs, slides,* and *bends* enable you to connect notes together smoothly, giving your playing a little "grease" (a good thing, especially in playing the blues). *Vibratos* add life to sustained (or held) notes that otherwise just sit there like a dead turtle, and *muting* shapes the sound of individual notes, giving them a tight, clipped sound.

As you start to incorporate articulation in your playing, you begin to exercise more control over your guitar. You're not merely playing "correctly" — you're playing with individual *style*.

This chapter shows you how to play all the articulation techniques you need to get your guitar talking. After we explain each technique, we present some *idiomatic licks* (musical phrases that naturally suit a particular technique or style) so you can play the technique in context.

Hitting Hammer-Ons

A *hammer-on* doesn't refer to playing the guitar while wearing a tool belt; a hammer-on is a left-hand technique that enables you to play two consecutive ascending notes by picking only the first note. The hammer-on derives its name from the action of your left-hand finger, which acts like a hammer striking the fretboard, causing the note of that fret to sound. This technique, which we describe in detail in the following sections, makes the connection between the notes sound smooth — far smoother than if you simply pick each note separately.

Note: In the tab (and standard) notation in this book, a *slur* (a curved line) connecting ascending notes indicates a hammer-on. The slur connects the first fret number, or note, of the hammer-on with the second. If more than two ascending notes are slurred, all the notes after the first are hammered.

Playing a hammer-on

An open-string hammer-on (or just *hammer,* for short) is the easiest kind to play. Following are the steps for the open-string hammer-on, as shown in Figure 10-1a:

1. **Pick the open G string (the 3rd string) as you normally do.**

2. **While the open string is still ringing, use a finger of your left hand (say, the 1st finger) to quickly and firmly strike (or slam or smack, as you prefer) the 2nd fret of the same string.**

   If you bring your finger down with enough force, you hear the new note (the 2nd fret A) ringing. Normally, your left hand doesn't *strike* a fret; it merely *presses* down on it. But to produce an audible sound without picking, you must hit the string pretty hard, as though your finger's a little hammer coming down on the fretboard.

Track 31, 0:00

Video Clip 45

Figure 10-1: Four kinds of hammer-ons.

© *John Wiley & Sons, Inc.*

Figure 10-1b shows a hammer-on from a fretted note on the 3rd string. Use your 1st finger to fret the first note at the 4th fret and strike the string; then, while that note's still ringing, use your 2nd finger to hammer down on the 5th fret. Check out Video Clip 45 to see all four hammer-ons in Figure 10-1.

After you master the open-string hammer-on, you're ready for several other types, which we cover in the following sections.

The double hammer-on

Figure 10-1c shows a *double hammer-on* on the 3rd string. Play the open string and hammer the 2nd fret with your 1st finger; then, while that note's still ringing, hammer the string again (at the 4th fret) with your 3rd finger, producing a super-smooth connection between all three notes.

Don't rush the notes together; rushing is a tendency as you first work with hammer-ons. Figure 10-1d shows a double hammer-on on the same string using three fretted notes. This type of hammer-on is the most difficult to play and requires some practice. Play the note at the 4th fret, fretting with your 1st finger; hammer the 5th-fret note with your 2nd finger; then hammer the 7th-fret-note with your 4th finger.

The double-stop hammer-on

You can also play hammer-ons as double-stops. The most common double-stop hammer-ons — and the easiest to play — are the ones where both double-stop notes lie on the same fret, enabling you to *barre* them (play them with one finger). (See Chapter 8 for details on double-stops.)

Figure 10-2a shows a *double-stop hammer-on* from open strings (the 2nd and 3rd). After striking the two open strings with the pick, and while the open strings are still ringing, slam down your 1st finger at the 2nd fret, across both strings at the same time.

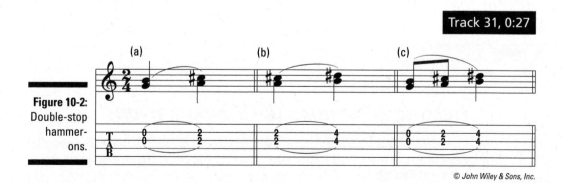

Track 31, 0:27

Figure 10-2: Double-stop hammer-ons.

© *John Wiley & Sons, Inc.*

Next, try a double-stop hammer-on from the 2nd fret to the 4th fret, also on the 2nd and 3rd strings, as shown in Figure 10-2b. Use your 1st finger to barre the 2nd fret and your 3rd finger to barre the 4th fret.

Now, to get really fancy, try a *double double-stop hammer-on,* on the same strings, as shown in Figure 10-2c. Start with the open strings; hammer the 2nd-fret barre with your 1st finger; then hammer the 4th-fret barre with your 3rd finger.

The hammer-on from nowhere

Figure 10-3 shows what we call a *hammer-on from nowhere.* It's not a typical hammer-on in that the hammered note doesn't follow an already-ringing lower note. In fact, the hammered note is on an entirely different string than the previous note. Using a left-hand finger, sound the hammered note in Figure 10-3 (the note with a short slur before it; it's on the 4th string) by fretting it very hard (hammering it) — hard enough that the note rings out without your striking it with the pick. You're hammering at the 7th fret.

Track 31, 0:47

Figure 10-3:
A hammer-on from nowhere.

© John Wiley & Sons, Inc.

Why would you even use this type of hammer-on, you ask? Sometimes, in fast passages, your right-hand picking pattern just doesn't give you time for that one extra pick attack when you need it. But you can sound the note anyway by fretting it hard enough with a finger of the left hand — hammering it from nowhere.

Getting idiomatic with hammer-ons

In Figures 10-4 through 10-7, you see some idiomatic licks using hammer-ons. (The little numbers next to the note heads in the standard notation indicate left-hand fingerings.)

✔ The lick in Figure 10-4 uses single-note hammer-ons from open strings. You may hear this kind of lick in a rock, blues, or country song. Try it out for a bit more practice with hammer-ons.

Track 32

Figure 10-4:
Single-note
hammer-on
from open
strings.

© John Wiley & Sons, Inc.

✔ Another cool trick is to strum a chord while hammering one of the notes. Figure 10-5 shows this technique — which James Taylor often employs — in the context of a musical phrase.

Track 33

Figure 10-5:
Strumming a
chord while
hammering
one of the
notes, in the
context of
a musical
phrase.

© John Wiley & Sons, Inc.

✔ Figure 10-6 shows single-note hammer-ons involving only fretted notes. You can hear this kind of lick in many rock and blues songs. Down-picks are indicated by the ⊓ symbol and up-picks are indicated by the V symbol. (The *sim.* means to keep playing in a similar manner — here referring to the picking pattern indicated.)

Keep your 1st finger barring the 5th fret for this lick as you play it. You get a smoother sound, and you find that it's easier to play, too.

✔ Figure 10-7 combines a double-stop hammer-on with a hammer-on from nowhere in 5th position. (See Chapter 7 for info on playing in position.) Try picking that last note, and you can easily see that the hammer-on from nowhere feels more comfortable than the picked version of the note.

Track 34, 0:00

Figure 10-6:
Single-note
hammer-ons
from fretted
notes.

© John Wiley & Sons, Inc.

Track 34, 0:08

Figure 10-7:
A double-
stop
hammer-
on plus a
hammer-on
from
nowhere.

© John Wiley & Sons, Inc.

Sounding Smooth with Pull-Offs

Like a hammer-on, a *pull-off* is a technique that enables you to connect notes more smoothly. It enables you to play two consecutive descending notes by picking only once with the right hand and, as the first note rings, pulling your finger off that fret. As you pull your finger off one fret, the next lower fretted (or open) note on the string then rings out instead of the first note.

You can think of a pull-off as sort of the opposite of a hammer-on, but that particular contrast doesn't really tell the whole story. A pull-off also requires that you exert a slight sideways pull on the string where you're fretting the picked note and then release the string from your finger in a snap as you pull your finger off the fret — something like what you do in launching a tiddly-wink.

Note: The tab (and standard) notation in this book indicates a pull-off by showing a slur connecting two (or more) descending tab numbers (or notes).

The following sections show you all you need to know about connecting notes with the pull-off technique, and when you're done reading the steps and licks we provide, you just may be able to pull it off.

Playing pull-offs

A pull-off (or *pull,* for short) to an open string is the easiest kind to play. Following are the steps for the open-string pull-off shown in Figure 10-8a:

1. **Press down the 3rd string at the 2nd fret with your 1st or 2nd finger (whichever is more comfortable) and pick the note normally with your right hand.**

2. **While the note is still ringing, pull your finger off the string in a sideways motion (toward the 2nd string) in a way that causes the open 3rd string to ring — almost as if you're making a left-hand finger pluck.**

   If you're playing up to speed, you can't truly pluck the string as you remove your finger — you're half lifting and half plucking . . . or somewhere in between. Experiment to find the left-hand finger motion that works best for you.

Track 35, 0:00

Video Clip 46

Figure 10-8:
Four kinds
of pull-offs.

© John Wiley & Sons, Inc.

Figure 10-8b shows a pull-off involving only fretted notes. The crucial factor in playing this kind of pull-off is that *you must finger both pull-off notes ahead of time.* We put that last part in italics because it's so important. This requirement is one of the big differences between a hammer-on and a pull-off. You must anticipate, or set up, a pull-off in advance. Following are the steps for playing the fretted pull-off shown in Figure 10-8b:

1. **Press down both the 2nd fret of the 3rd string with your 1st finger and the 4th fret of the 3rd string with your 3rd finger *at the same time.***

2. **Strike the 3rd string with the pick and, while the 4th-fret note is still ringing, pull your 3rd finger off the 4th fret (in a half pluck, half lift) to sound the note of the 2nd fret (which you're already fingering).**

Try to avoid accidentally striking the 2nd string as you pull off. Also, you can see that if you aren't already pressing down that 2nd-fret note, you end up pulling off to the open string instead of the 2nd fret!

After you get the hang of the preceding pull-offs, you can try your hand at the double pull-off and the double-stop pull-off in the following sections.

The double pull-off

Figure 10-8c shows a *double pull-off* to the open 3rd string. Start by simultaneously fretting the first two notes at the 2nd and 4th frets (with your 1st and 3rd fingers, respectively). Pick the string and then pull off with your 3rd finger to sound the note at the 2nd fret; then pull off with your 1st finger to sound the open string.

Figure 10-8d shows a double pull-off on the 3rd string, using only fretted notes. Start with all three notes fretted at the 4th, 5th, and 7th frets (using your 1st, 2nd, and 4th fingers, respectively). Pick the string and then pull off with your 4th finger to sound the 5th-fret note; then pull off with your 2nd finger to sound the 4th-fret note. Check out Video Clip 46 to see all four pull-offs in Figure 10-8.

The double-stop pull-off

You can also play pull-offs as double-stops. As is true with hammer-ons, the most common and easiest to play *double-stop pull-offs* are those where both double-stop notes lie on the same fret, enabling you to barre them. (See Chapter 8 for more info on double-stops.)

Figure 10-9a shows a double-stop pull-off to open strings on the 2nd and 3rd strings. After striking the notes at the 2nd fret, and while the strings are still ringing, pull off your 1st finger (in a half pluck, half lift) from both strings at the same time (in one motion) to sound the open strings.

Next, try a double-stop pull-off from the 4th fret to the 2nd fret, as shown in Figure 10-9b. Place your 1st finger at the 2nd fret, barring the 2nd and 3rd strings, and place your 3rd finger at the 4th fret (also barring the 2nd and 3rd strings) *at the same time.* Pick the strings and then pull your 3rd finger off the 4th fret to sound the notes at the 2nd fret of both strings.

Now try a *double double-stop pull-off,* on the same strings, as shown in Figure 10-9c. This type of pull-off is similar to what you play in the example shown in Figure 10-9b except that, after the notes on the 2nd fret sound, you pull your 1st finger off the 2nd fret to sound the open strings.

Track 35, 0:27

Figure 10-9:
Double-stop pull-offs.

© John Wiley & Sons, Inc.

Getting idiomatic with pull-offs

In Figures 10-10 and 10-11, you see two idiomatic licks using pull-offs.

- Figure 10-10 involves single-note pull-offs to open strings. You can hear this kind of lick in many rock and blues songs.

- Figure 10-5, in the section "Getting idiomatic with hammer-ons," earlier in this chapter, shows you how to strum a chord while hammering on a note of that chord. Figure 10-11 shows the opposite technique: strumming a chord while pulling off one note. The passage in Figure 10-11 leads off with two single-note pull-offs, just to get you warmed up.

Track 36, 0:00

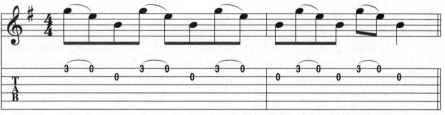

Figure 10-10:
Single-note pull-offs to open strings.

© John Wiley & Sons, Inc.

Track 36, 0:09

Figure 10-11: Strumming a chord while pulling off one of the notes.

© John Wiley & Sons, Inc.

Slipping Around with Slides

A *slide* is an articulation technique in which you play a note and then move your left-hand finger along the string to a different fret. This technique enables you to connect two or more notes smoothly and quickly. It also enables you to change positions on the fretboard seamlessly.

Many different types of slides are possible. The most basic includes those in the following list (we show you how to master these slides, except for maybe the last one, in the sections that follow):

- Slides between two notes where you pick only the first note.
- Slides between two notes where you pick both notes.
- Slides from an indefinite pitch a few frets above or below the target note. (The pitch is indefinite because you begin the slide with very little finger pressure, gradually increasing it until you land on the target fret.)
- Slides to an indefinite pitch a few frets above or below the starting note. (The pitch is indefinite because you gradually release finger pressure as you move away from the starting fret.)
- Slides into home plate.

Note: In the tab (and standard) notation, we indicate a slide with a slanted line (whether approaching a note, connecting two notes, or following a note).

Playing slides

The name of this technique, *slide,* gives you a pretty good clue about how to play it. You slide a left-hand finger up or down a string, maintaining contact with it, to arrive at a new note. Sometimes, you connect two notes (for example, you slide from the 7th fret to the 9th), and sometimes you connect a note (at a given fret) with an *indefinite* pitch (you produce indefinite pitches by picking a string while you gradually add or release finger pressure as you're sliding). We describe both techniques in the following sections.

Connecting two notes

Figure 10-12a shows a slur along with the slanted line. The slur indicates that this is a *legato slide,* which means that you *don't pick the second note.* Play the first note at the 9th fret normally, holding the note for one beat. At beat 2, while the string is still ringing, quickly slide your left-hand finger to the 12th fret, keeping full finger pressure the whole time. This action causes the note at the 12th fret to sound without being repicked.

Track 37, 0:00

Video Clip 47

Figure 10-12:
Two types
of slides:
one with the
second note
unpicked
and the
other with it
picked.

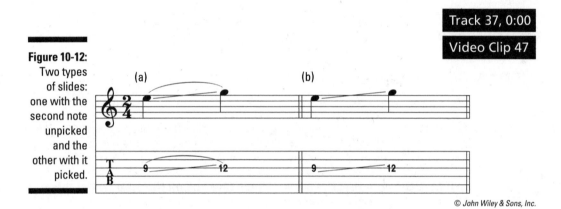

© John Wiley & Sons, Inc.

In Figure 10-12b, which notates a slide *without* a slur, you *do* pick the second note. Play and hold the 9th-fret note for a beat; then, at beat 2, slide up to the 12th fret — maintaining full finger pressure as you go — and strike the 3rd string with the pick just as you arrive at the 12th fret. Watch Video Clip 47 to see the differences between a slurred slide and a non-slurred slide.

If you play the slide in Figure 10-12b slowly enough, you produce what's known as a *glissando.* A glissando (or *gliss.* for short) is an effect that you hear on harps, pianos, and guitars, where all the notes between the two principal notes sound.

Working with indefinite pitch

What we call an *ascending immediate slide* is a quick slide, not in rhythm, that serves to decorate only one note and isn't something that you use to connect two different notes. In the example shown in Figure 10-13a, you slide into the 9th fret of the 3rd string from a few frets below. Follow these steps:

1. **Start the slide from about three frets below the target fret (the 6th fret if the 9th fret is your target), using minimal finger pressure.**

2. **As your finger slides up, gradually increase your finger pressure so, as you arrive at the target fret, you exert full pressure.**

3. **Strike the string with the pick while your left-hand finger is in motion, somewhere between the starting and target frets (the 6th and 9th frets, in this example).**

Track 37, 0:12

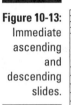
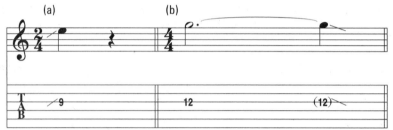

Figure 10-13: Immediate ascending and descending slides.

© John Wiley & Sons, Inc.

The slide shown in Figure 10-13b is what we call a *descending immediate slide.* This kind of slide usually occurs after you hold a note for a while. It gives a long note a fancy ending. Follow these steps:

1. **Pick the note that the tab indicates (the one on the 12th fret in this case) in the normal manner.**

2. **After letting the note ring for the indicated duration, slide your left-hand finger down the string, gradually releasing finger pressure as you go, to cause a fading-away effect.**

   After a few frets, lift your finger completely off the string — unless you want to play what's known as a *long slide.* In that case, you can slide your finger all the way down the neck, releasing finger pressure (and finally removing your finger from the string) toward the end of the neck, as near to the nut as you want to go.

Playing idiomatic licks using slides

Figures 10-14 and 10-15 show two idiomatic licks using slides.

- ✔ Figure 10-14 shows ascending immediate slides, including a barred double-stop slide. Use your 1st finger to play the barred double-stop at the 5th fret, sliding into it from only one or two frets below. This lick has a Chuck Berry sound to it.

✔ Figure 10-15 (which also contains a hammer-on and a pull-off) shows how you can use slides to smoothly change positions. (The small numbers in the standard notation indicate left-hand fingering.) Here, you move from 3rd position to 5th position and back to 3rd position. Notice that the tab indicates the slides with slurs — so don't pick the second note of each slide. And follow the downstroke and upstroke picking indications on the tab (⊓ and V) — you pick notes only five times, even though you actually play nine notes!

Track 38

Figure 10-14:
Some Chuck
Berry-ish
slides.

© *John Wiley & Sons, Inc.*

Track 39

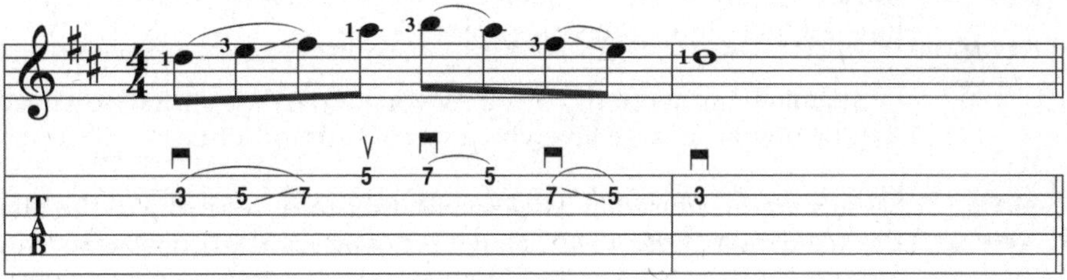

Figure 10-15:
Changing
positions by
using slides.

© *John Wiley & Sons, Inc.*

Stretching Out with Bends

More than any other type of articulation, the *string bend* is what makes your guitar talk (or sing or cry), giving the instrument almost voicelike expressive capabilities. *Bending* is nothing more than using a left-hand finger to push or pull a string out of its normal alignment, stretching it across the fingerboard toward the 6th or 1st string, thereby raising the pitch.

As you bend a string, the rise in pitch can be slight or great. Between the slightest and greatest bends possible are infinite degrees of in-between bends. It's those infinite degrees that make your guitar sing.

Note: The tab notation in this book indicates a bend by using a curved arrow and either a number or a fraction (or both) at the peak of the arrow. The fraction $\frac{1}{2}$, for example, means that you bend the string until the pitch is a half step (the equivalent of one fret) higher than normal. The numeral 1 above a bend arrow means that you bend the string until the pitch is a whole step (the equivalent of two frets) higher than normal. You may also see fractions such as $\frac{1}{4}$ and $\frac{3}{4}$ or bigger numbers such $1\frac{1}{2}$ or 2 above a bend arrow. These fractions or numbers all tell you how many (whole) steps to bend the note. But $\frac{1}{2}$ and 1 are the most common bends that you see in most tab notation.

Note: The standard notation in this book indicates a bend with a "pointed" slur connecting the unbent pitch with the sounding (bent) pitch (see Figure 10-17 for examples of pointed slurs).

You can check to see that you're bending in tune by fretting the target note normally and comparing that to the bent note. If the bend indicates a whole step (1) on the 7th fret of the 3rd string, for example, play the 9th fret normally and listen carefully to the pitch. Then try bending the 7th-fret note to match the 9th-fret pitch in your head.

You don't normally do a lot of string bending on acoustic guitars, because the strings are too thick. In electric guitar playing, where string bending is an integral technique, the strings are thinner.

In the following sections, we show you step by step what you need to know to play bends, and we give you a few licks to practice.

Strings are measured in *gauges,* with that term referring to the diameter of the string in inches. A light-gauge set of acoustic strings starts with the diameter for the 1st string at 0.012 inches, which is generally considered unbendable by all except the most dedicated masochists. (Guitarists refer to the entire set in shorthand as *twelves.*) For electric guitars, the most common gauges start with sets that use a 0.009 or 0.010 gauge for the top string (*nines* and *tens,* to use the vernacular). You can bend with 0.011s and 0.012s (*elevens* and *twelves*) on your guitar, but doing so isn't much fun unless you're seriously into pain.

Playing bends

Use the photo in Figure 10-16a as a starting point for playing a bend. You play this bend on the 3rd string with the 3rd finger, which represents a very common bending situation — probably the most common. Follow these steps:

1. **Place your 3rd finger at the 7th fret but *support* the 3rd finger by placing the 2nd finger at the 6th fret and the 1st finger at the 5th fret, all at the same time (see Figure 10-16a).**

   The 1st and 2nd fingers don't produce any sound, but they add strength to your bend. Supporting your bends with any other available fingers is always a good idea.

2. **Pick the 3rd string with your right hand.**

3. **After picking, use all three fingers together to push the string toward the 6th string, raising the pitch a whole step (to the pitch you normally get at the 9th fret — see Figure 10-16b).**

Figure 10-16:
Before
bending (a)
and after
bending (b).

a   b

Photographs courtesy of Jon Chappell

Pushing your hand into the neck as you execute the bend gives you added leverage. Also, using *light-gauge,* or thin, strings on your guitar makes bending easier.

Figure 10-17 shows what bends look like in standard notation and tab.

✔ Figure 10-17a shows what we call an *immediate bend.* Pick the note and then immediately bend it up.

✔ Figure 10-17b is called a *bend and release.* Pick the note and then bend it (without repicking) and unbend it (release it without repicking) to its normal position. Unlike the bend in Figure 10-17a, this bend isn't immediate; instead, you see it notated in a specific rhythm (that you can hear on Track 40). You can refer to this type of bend as a *bend in rhythm,* or a *measured bend.*

✔ Figure 10-17c shows a *prebend and release*. You prebend the note, or bend it *before* you strike it with the pick. Bend the note as you do in Figure 10-17a, but don't pick the string until after you bend it. After you pick the note, unbend (release without repicking) the string to its normal position. For music readers: Note that in standard notation, the pitch of the fret you finger — which is the pitch you release to (the unbent pitch) — is shown at the beginning of the figure as a small note head in parentheses.

Track 40

Video Clip 48

Figure 10-17: Three types of bends.

© John Wiley & Sons, Inc.

Check out Video Clip 48 to see how the left hand moves in the three types of bends in Figure 10-17.

Most often, as the examples in Figure 10-17 show, you push the string toward the 6th string (or toward the ceiling). But if you bend notes on the bottom two strings (the 5th and 6th strings), you *pull* the string toward the 1st string (or toward the floor) — otherwise, the string slides right off the fretboard.

Getting idiomatic with bends

In this section, you play a number of licks that feature a variety of bends, including the immediate bend, the bend in rhythm, the bend and release, the held bend, and the double-stop bend. We give you the details of each of these bends in the following sections.

Playing immediate bends in a rock solo

Figure 10-18 shows a very common bend figure that you can use in rock soloing. Notice the fingering that the standard notation staff indicates to use. Your left hand hardly moves — it's locked in 5th position (see Chapter 7 for more information on positions), with the 1st finger barring the 1st and 2nd strings at the 5th fret. The second note of the figure (5th fret, 2nd string) happens to be the same pitch (E) as your target bend, so you can use that second note to test the accuracy of your bend. Soon, you start to feel just how far you need to bend a string to achieve a whole-step or half-step rise in pitch. All the bends in this example are immediate bends.

After you play each 3rd-string bend, just before you pick the 2nd-string note, reduce your finger pressure from the bent note. This action causes the 3rd string to stop ringing as you pick the 2nd string.

Track 41

Figure 10-18: Bending the 3rd string in a classic rock 'n' roll lead lick.

© John Wiley & Sons, Inc.

Playing an immediate bend and a bend in rhythm in the same lick

In Figure 10-19, you bend the 2nd string, once as an immediate bend and once as a bend in rhythm. Listen to Track 42 to hear how this example sounds. Strictly speaking, because you're in 12th position, you should use your 4th finger to play the 15th fret. But we indicate (in the standard notation) for you to use the 3rd finger — because if you're up at the 12th fret, the frets are closer together, so your 3rd finger (which is stronger than your 4th) can easily make the reach. *Note:* The *8va* indication above the standard music notation in Figure 10-19 tells you to play the notes an octave higher than written.

Track 42

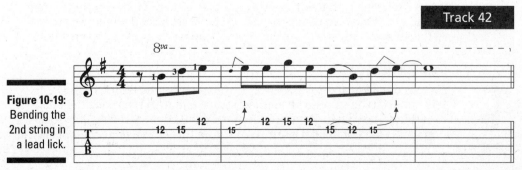

Figure 10-19: Bending the 2nd string in a lead lick.

© John Wiley & Sons, Inc.

Playing a bend and release

You play the examples shown in Figures 10-18 and 10-19 in what lead guitarists call a *box pattern* — a group of notes in one position that vaguely resembles the shape of a box. You can use this pattern for improvising lead solos. (For more info on box patterns and soloing, see Chapters 11 and 12.)

Figure 10-20 uses a small box pattern in the 8th position. This example features a bend and release, in which the bend is immediate and the release is in rhythm. Listen to Track 43 to hear this sound.

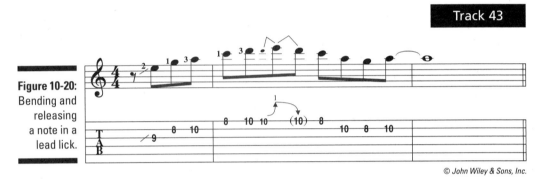

Figure 10-20: Bending and releasing a note in a lead lick.

Track 43

© John Wiley & Sons, Inc.

Bending one string in two directions

Although you bend most notes by pushing a string toward the 6th string, you may sometimes need to bend a string the other way, even on a middle or upper string (but *not* on the 1st string because it slides off the neck if you do). You need to use this type of opposite-direction bend if the note that follows a bend is on a string that's adjacent to the bent string. You need to bend *away* from the upcoming string; otherwise, your bending finger may accidentally touch it, inadvertently muting it.

Figure 10-21 shows two 1st-finger, half-step bends on the 3rd string. The first one bends toward the 6th string because the following note is on the 2nd string. (Remember that you're bending *away* from the following note.) The second one, however, bends toward the floor because the following note is on the adjacent 4th string. Again, you're bending away from the next note.

Trying a held bend

You can create an interesting effect by bending a note, letting it ring in its bent state, striking a note on another string, and then restriking the bent string and releasing it. Many Southern-rock and country-rock guitarists are fond of this kind of bend. Figure 10-22 shows this *held-bend* technique. In the tab, the dotted line after the upward-curved arrow indicates that you hold the bend not only as you strike the 2nd string but also as you restrike the 3rd string (the vertical arrow above that restruck 3rd string note indicates that the note is already bent); the downward-curved solid line shows the release of the bend. Make sure you bend the 3rd string toward the ceiling so your bending finger is out of the way of the 2nd string. Listen to Track 45 to hear how this lick sounds.

Figure 10-21:
Bending the same string in two different directions. The asterisks and footnotes tell you which direction to bend toward.

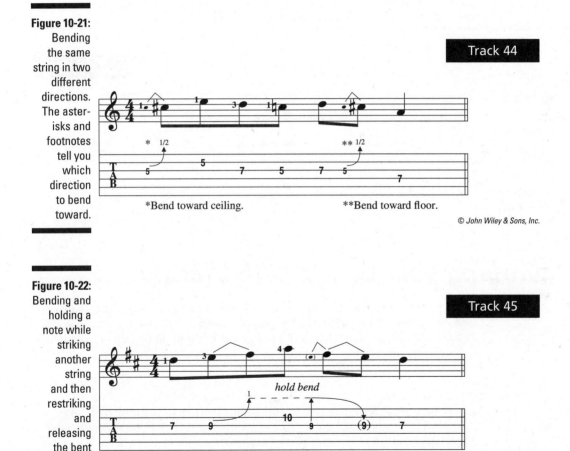

Track 44

*Bend toward ceiling.   **Bend toward floor.

© John Wiley & Sons, Inc.

Figure 10-22:
Bending and holding a note while striking another string and then restriking and releasing the bent note.

Track 45

© John Wiley & Sons, Inc.

Playing a double-stop bend

You can also play bends as double-stops (called *double-stop bends*) — you just bend two strings at the same time, usually by barring the two strings with one finger. (See Chapter 8 for more info on double-stops.) Figure 10-23 shows a double-stop bend of the 2nd and 3rd strings in the box pattern at the 5th fret. Use your 1st finger to play the 5th-fret double-stop; then use your 3rd finger to play the double-stop bend and release at the 7th fret. The double arrow in the tab tells you to bend both notes. By the way, the double-stop bend uses just a single arrow on the release only to avoid messiness in the notation — so go ahead and release both notes.

Track 46

Figure 10-23:
A double-stop bend and release.

© John Wiley & Sons, Inc.

Varying Your Sound with Vibrato

Think of the term *vibrato,* and you may imagine a singer's wavering voice or a violinist's twitching hand. On the guitar, however, *vibrato* is a steady, even (and usually slight) fluctuation of pitch, most often achieved by rapidly bending and releasing a note a slight degree. A vibrato can add warmth, emotion, and life to a held, or sustained, note.

The most obvious time to apply vibrato is whenever you hold a note for a long time. That's when you can add some emotion to the note by using vibrato. Vibrato not only gives the note more warmth, but it also increases the sustain period of the note. Some guitarists, such as blues great B.B. King, are renowned for their expressive vibrato technique. Both the tab and standard notation indicate a vibrato by placing a wavy line at the top of the staff over the note to which you apply the technique.

In the following sections, we describe different techniques for producing vibrato and give you some practice time with vibrato.

Looking at methods for producing vibrato

You can produce a vibrato in several ways:

- ✔ **You can slightly bend and release a note over and over again, creating a wah-wah-wah effect.** The average pitch of the vibrato is slightly higher than the unaltered note. The left-hand technique for this method is the same as the technique for bending — you move a finger back and forth, perpendicular to the string, creating a fluctuation of pitch.

- ✔ **You can very rapidly slide your finger back and forth along the length of a string, within one fret.** Although you're not actually moving your finger out of the fret, the pitch becomes slightly sharper as you move toward the bridge and slightly flatter as you move toward the nut. Consequently, the average pitch of the vibrato is the same as the unaltered note. This type of vibrato is reserved almost exclusively for playing classical guitar with nylon strings. (See Chapter 14 for more information on playing classical guitar.)

- ✔ **If your electric guitar has a whammy bar mounted on it, you can move the bar up and down with your right hand, creating a fluctuation in pitch.** In addition to giving you greater rhythmic flexibility and pitch range, the whammy bar enables you to add vibrato to an open string. (For more on the whammy bar, also called simply the *bar,* see Chapter 1.)

The first type of vibrato, the bend-and-release type, is the most common, by far, and is the one shown in the examples in this chapter. Support your vibrato finger with other available fingers by placing them all on the string at the same time. You can either move your whole hand by rotating it at the wrist and keeping the finger fixed, or you can move just your finger(s). Try both ways and see which feels more comfortable.

Practicing vibrato

You may find that playing a vibrato is easier if you anchor your left hand on the neck as you play. Squeeze the neck a little between the side of your thumb and the part of your palm that's about half an inch below your 1st finger. This action gives you better leverage and helps you control the evenness of the fluctuation.

Figure 10-24a shows a vibrato at the 9th fret of the 3rd string. Anchor your hand, as we describe in the preceding paragraph, and slightly bend and release the note over and over. Try the vibrato with each finger. Try it at different frets and on different strings. The notation for a vibrato never tells you how fast or slowly to bend and release — that's up to you. But whether you play a fast vibrato or a slow one, make sure you keep the fluctuations steady and even.

The notation *does* tell you, however, whether to make the vibrato *narrow* (that is, you bend the string only slightly — less than a half step — for each pulsation) or *wide* (you bend the string to a greater degree — about a half step or more). Figure 10-24a shows a regular (narrow) vibrato, and Figure 10-24b shows a wide vibrato, indicating the latter by using an exaggerated wavy line (with deeper peaks and valleys). Try playing a wide vibrato with each finger. Try it at different frets and on different strings.

Track 47

Video Clip 49

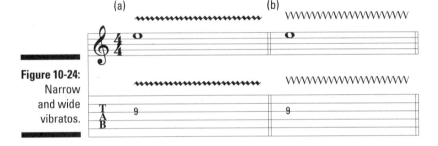

Figure 10-24: Narrow and wide vibratos.

© John Wiley & Sons, Inc.

If the note you're holding is a bent note (see the section "Stretching Out with Bends," earlier in this chapter), you create the vibrato by *releasing and bending* (instead of bending and releasing) — because the note's already bent as you start the vibrato. This action makes the average pitch lower than the held (bent) note, which itself produces the highest pitch in the vibrato.

After a long vibrato, guitarists often play a descending slide, gradually releasing finger pressure as they go, to give the vibrato a fancy little ending. Another trick is to play a long note without vibrato for a while and then add some vibrato toward the end of the note. This *delayed vibrato* is a favorite technique that singers often use.

To practice playing vibratos, play the examples shown in Figures 10-19, 10-20, and 10-23 again, but add vibrato to the final note of each figure. Be careful with the example in Figure 10-19 — the last note is bent, so you need to unbend (release) and bend the note to produce the vibrato. If you want, finish off each vibrato with a little slide-off. (See the section "Slipping Around with Slides," earlier in this chapter, for more information on this technique.)

Getting Mellow with Muting

To *mute* notes or chords on the guitar, you use your right or left hand to touch the strings so as to partially or completely deaden the sound. You apply muting for one of the following reasons:

- To create a thick, chunky sound as an effect
- To prevent unwanted noises from strings that you're not playing
- To silence annoying commercials on TV

The following sections show you how to use muting and provide a few passages for practice.

Creating a thick, chunky sound as an effect

To use muting to create percussive effects, lightly lay your left hand across all six strings to prevent the strings from ringing out as you strike them. Don't press them all the way down to the fretboard (which would cause the fretted notes to sound), but press them hard enough to prevent the strings from vibrating. Then strike the strings with the pick to hear the muted sound. The tab notation indicates this type of muting by placing Xs on the string lines (and in place of the actual notes on the standard staff), as shown in Figure 10-25a.

Figure 10-25:
Muting with the left hand produces a dead thud. Muting with the right hand gives the notes a thick, chunky sound.

Track 48

Video Clip 50

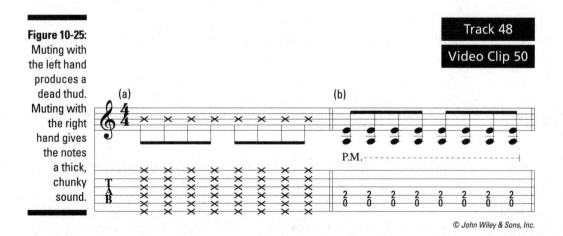

© *John Wiley & Sons, Inc.*

Although *left-hand muting* deadens the strings completely, *right-hand muting* deadens them only partially — to whatever degree you desire. With partial muting, you can still discern the strings' pitches. To accomplish this technique, place the heel (side) of your right hand against the bridge as you play. It may seem a little awkward at first, but don't worry. With a little practice, you can keep your hand on the bridge and still strike the strings with the pick. As you move your right hand toward the fretboard, you increase the amount of muting. That way, you can vary the degree of muting. The tab notation indicates this type of muting by placing the letters *P.M.* (for *palm mute*) above the tab staff, with a dotted line indicating how long to continue the muting, as shown in Figure 10-25b. Check out Video Clip 50 to see the left- and right-hand positions for muting.

Preventing unwanted string noise

As a beginner, you don't normally worry too much about preventing unwanted string noises — you're too involved in just getting your hands into a comfortable position on the instrument. But as an experienced guitarist, you prevent unwanted string noises all the time, sometimes without even being aware of it. Following are some examples of how you do so:

✔ If you finger, say, the 7th fret of the 3rd string with your 3rd finger, your 3rd finger leans slightly against the 2nd string, preventing it from ringing. And as you pick the string with your right hand, your pick also lands against the 2nd string, further preventing it from ringing.

✔ If you play an open-position D chord, and you don't want to strike the 6th string because it doesn't belong in the chord, you can bring your left thumb up around the neck ever so slightly to touch the 6th string, ensuring that it doesn't ring.

✔ If you play a chord that omits a middle string, you need to mute that string with a finger of the left hand. For example, a lot of people like to omit the 5th string if they play the open-position G chord (even though you normally fret that string for the chord), just because they think it sounds better. The finger that's playing the 6th string leans against the 5th, muting it completely.

Playing idiomatic licks using muting

If you strum the same chord over and over, especially a barre chord in a steady eighth-note pattern, you can create additional interest by sometimes lifting your left hand slightly to mute out the strings. The alternation of the normally fretted chord and the muted strings can create some interesting *syncopation* effects (effects where the normal, expected accentuation of notes is intentionally altered or disrupted). Figure 10-26 demonstrates this technique.

Track 49

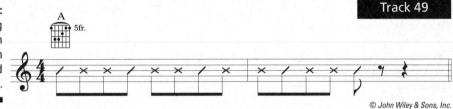

Figure 10-26: Achieving syncopation through left-hand muting.

© John Wiley & Sons, Inc.

Figure 10-27 demonstrates how to use right-hand muting in a typical hard-rock or heavy-metal rhythm-guitar figure. Keep the heel of your right hand against or near the bridge as you play the notes for which the tab indicates a palm mute *(P.M.)*. Don't deaden the notes so much, however, that you can't discern their pitches. Lift your right hand for the accented notes (indicated by the symbol >).

Track 50

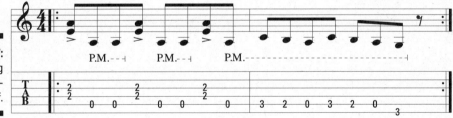

Figure 10-27: Palm muting in a hard-rock riff.

© John Wiley & Sons, Inc.

On Johnny Cash records and other classic country records, you can hear the sound of muted country guitars. Figure 10-28 is based on a simple C chord, but the palm muting gives the riff a country sound.

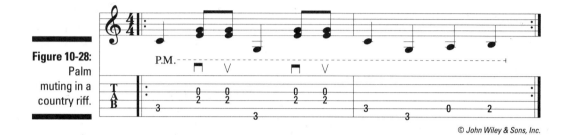

Figure 10-28:
Palm
muting in a
country riff.

© John Wiley & Sons, Inc.

Playing a Song with Varied Articulation

"The Articulate Blues" is a short solo piece, in the form of a 12-bar blues, that employs all the articulations we discuss in this chapter. (See Chapters 6, 11, and 12 for more on the 12-bar blues form.) It combines single notes, chords, and riffs. It's an integrated style of playing that real-life guitarists use. Looking at the song's notation, you see slides, pull-offs, bends, vibratos, and a hammer-on. The tab doesn't indicate any muting, but you can use that technique any time you want to avoid unwanted noises; in measure 5, for example, you can lean your left thumb lightly against the 6th string to prevent it from ringing while you play the A7 chord.

The Articulate Blues

Track 52

Video Clip 51

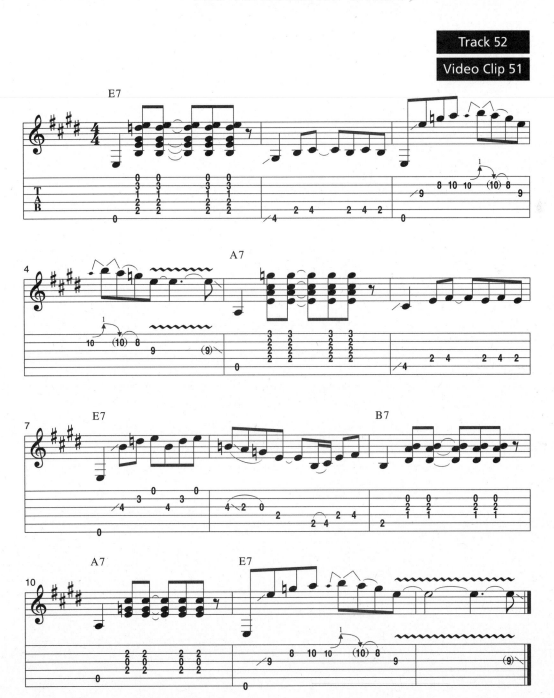

Part IV
A Pile of Styles

Top five concepts for playing rock and blues lead solos

- ✔ Play box patterns to produce authentic-sounding rock and blues lead lines.
- ✔ Add different articulations to the notes in the boxes, including hammer-ons, pull-offs, slides, and bends.
- ✔ Move from box to box among pentatonic scale patterns to give you the opportunity to play new notes that were unavailable in the box you came from.
- ✔ Vary your note choices by using pentatonic major as well as pentatonic minor scales.
- ✔ Add a little flavor to your solos through the judicious addition of little two-note chords, otherwise known as *double-stops*.

For a handy reference on the five pentatonic scale patterns, check out www.dummies.com/extras/guitar.

In this part . . .

- Emulate the playing of Chuck Berry and other rock guitar pioneers with classic rock 'n' roll techniques.

- Allow your guitar to complement the soulful substance of the blues with electric and acoustic blues techniques.

- Discover how to fingerpick folk songs to become the star of the campfire sing-along.

- Impress even scholarly musicians by mastering a few classical pieces.

- Discover jazz chords and melodies so that you can hang with the cool cats.

Chapter 11

Ready to Rock: Rock Guitar Basics

In This Chapter

▶ Getting a feel for classic rock 'n' roll

▶ Using modern-rock, country-rock, and Southern-rock techniques

▶ Playing rock songs

▶ Access the audio tracks and video clips at www.dummies.com/go/guitar

*P*laying rock 'n' roll guitar is arguably the most fun you can have with an inanimate object in your hands. With the volume turned up and your adrenaline flowing, nothing's quite like laying down a chunking rhythm or ripping through a searing lead to screaming, adoring fans — or even to your own approving smile coming back at you from the mirror. All you need to do is figure out how to play a couple of simple patterns and you can be gyrating like Elvis, duck-walking like Chuck Berry, and windmilling like Pete Townshend in no time.

Stripped of all bravado and showmanship, rock guitar is just like any other guitar style. You absorb it in simple, easy steps and then practice, practice, practice until it comes naturally. After you pick up some rhythm and lead passages and get the techniques down, the real work begins: standing in front of a mirror and perfecting your moves.

In this chapter, we hit all the high notes — classic rock, modern rock, country rock, and Southern rock sounds. Along the way, you can pick up some skills and techniques, such as playing from box positions and using alternative ways to tune your guitar.

Playing Classic Rock 'n' Roll

Classic rock 'n' roll is defined here as the straightforward style pioneered by Chuck Berry and heard in the music of the early Beatles, the Rolling Stones, the Who, the Beach Boys, and others who based their sound on a solid, chord-based rhythm guitar groove. It also includes the sound of the blues-based rockers, such as Jimi Hendrix, Led Zeppelin's Jimmy Page, and Cream's Eric Clapton.

In the following sections, we explain how to play both rhythm guitar and lead guitar in the classic rock 'n' roll style.

Rhythm guitar

Much of rock guitar playing involves what's known as rhythm guitar playing. To a guitarist, *playing rhythm* means supplying the accompaniment or backing part to a vocalist or other featured instrument. Mostly, this accompaniment involves strumming chords and, to a lesser extent, playing single-note or double-stop (two notes played at once; see Chapter 8) riffs in the lower register (the bottom two or three strings). Listen to the verses of Chuck Berry's "Johnny B. Goode" or the Beatles' "I Saw Her Standing There" for some good, unadulterated rhythm guitar, and check out the Beatles' "Day Tripper" for low-note riffing. Listen also to almost anything by the Who's Pete Townshend, who's (no pun intended) the quintessential rock rhythm guitarist and who immortalized the "windmill" technique — the sweeping circular motion of the right hand to play chords.

In the following sections, we discuss two elements of playing rhythm guitar: open-position accompaniment and the 12-bar blues progression.

Open-position accompaniment

The Chuck Berry style, which is a simple *rhythm figure* (accompaniment pattern) in *open position* (using open strings), gains its name from the fact that almost all of Berry's songs use this pattern. Figure 11-1 shows the pattern for this style.

The pattern in Figure 11-1 features a movement within the chord between two notes, the *fifth* and *sixth degrees* (steps) of the scale (that is, of the major scale that corresponds to whatever key you're playing in). (You know the *major scale;* it's what you get when you play all the white keys from C to C on a piano — the familiar *do-re-mi-fa-sol-la-ti-do.*) Knowing the degrees isn't important, except that musicians sometimes refer to this figure as the *5-to-6 pattern.*

To play this rhythm effectively, use the following techniques:

- ✔ Anchor the 1st finger (at the 2nd fret) and add the 3rd finger (at the 4th fret) as you need it.

- ✔ Don't lift the 1st finger while adding the 3rd finger.

- ✔ Pick the notes using all downstrokes.

Track 53

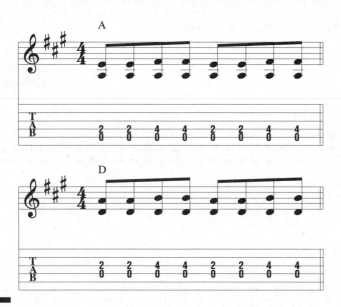

Figure 11-1:
The classic Chuck Berry rock 'n' roll accompaniment riff for A, D, and E chords.

© John Wiley & Sons, Inc.

Notice that all three chords (A, D, and E) in Figure 11-1 use the exact same fingering and that the open strings make the pattern easy to play.

The 12-bar blues progression

The 5-to-6 pattern in the preceding section sounds great, but to make it work for you, you need to put it into a progression. Figure 11-2 shows what's known as a *12-bar blues progression,* a common chord progression in tons of rock songs: "Johnny B. Goode," "Roll Over Beethoven," "Tutti Frutti," "At the Hop," and "Blue Suede Shoes," to name but a few.

Notice that the 12-bar blues progression in Figure 11-2 is in the key of A, uses the 5-to-6 pattern, and has major chord symbols above the notes. The 12-bar blues progression can occur in any key and often uses dominant-7th chords (as in Chapter 6) instead of major chords.

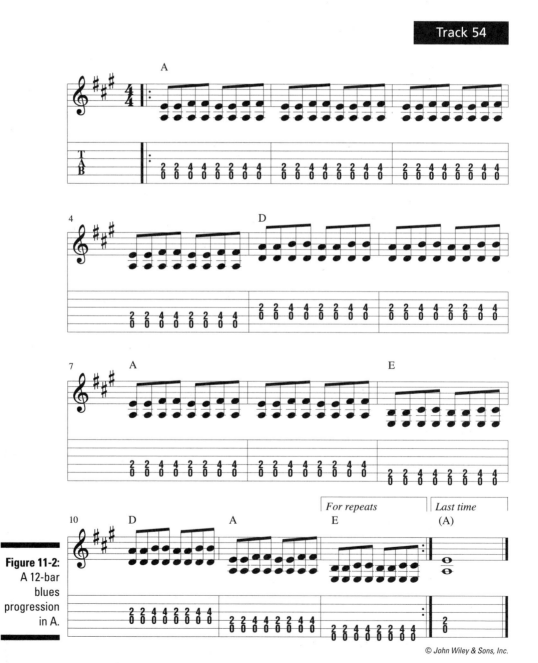

Track 54

Figure 11-2:
A 12-bar blues progression in A.

© John Wiley & Sons, Inc.

Lead guitar

After you gain a solid feel for a basic rock 'n' roll rhythm (see the preceding section), you may want to try some lead guitar, which simply involves playing single notes over an underlying accompaniment. You can play memorized *licks,* which are short, self-contained phrases, or you can improvise by making up melodies on the spot. In this section, we provide you with the building blocks for great classic rock solos, help you mix in some articulation, show you how to string it all together, and finish up with some tips on building your own solos.

What's behind Box 1? The pentatonic minor scale

You can play lead right away by memorizing a few simple patterns on the guitar neck, known as *boxes,* that produce instant results. Basically, guitarists memorize a finger pattern that vaguely resembles the shape of a box — hence the term *box position* — and use notes from that pattern (in various orders) over and over pretty much throughout a solo or a section of a solo. In soloing over a basic chord progression, you can keep using this one pattern even if the chords change. By learning the boxes in this chapter, your arsenal for soloing over the 12-bar blues will be almost complete. (For more on soloing, see Chapter 12.)

The first box we're going to show you is made up of notes of what's known as the *pentatonic minor scale,* and it's the most useful box for rock music (and is also the daddy of the blues boxes — see Chapter 12). You don't need to think about theory, scales, or chords — only the fingering, which you memorize. These patterns contain no "wrong notes," so by virtue of just moving your fingers around in time to a rhythm track, you can play instant rock 'n' roll lead guitar. You don't even need to add water (which is especially hazardous if you're playing an electric guitar).

The pentatonic minor scale is a five-note scale; its formula, in scale degrees (in comparison to a major scale that starts from the same note) is 1, ♭3, 4, 5, ♭7. If the notes of a C major scale, for example, are numbered 1 through 7 — C(1), D(2), E(3), F(4), G(5), A(6), B(7) — the notes of the C pentatonic minor scale are C(1), E♭(♭3), F(4), G(5), B♭(♭7). That's the theory anyway, but for now, you're just going to memorize a pattern and use your ear — not your brain — to guide your fingers.

Figure 11-3 shows a two-octave A pentatonic minor scale in 5th position. (See Chapter 7 for more about positions.) This example is your first box, here called *Box I.*

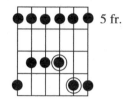

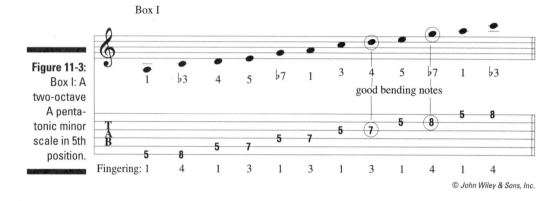

Figure 11-3: Box I: A two-octave A pentatonic minor scale in 5th position.

© John Wiley & Sons, Inc.

Before proceeding, make sure you understand how the neck diagrams and staff correspond. Note that the neck diagram doesn't show a chord, but a scale, where the notes are played one at a time, from lowest to highest (as shown in the standard notation and tab).

Notice that in Figure 11-3, we show you (beneath the notes in the standard notation) the scale degree (not so important) and (beneath the tab numbers) the fingering (very important) for each note; we also show you which notes are good for bending. Memorize the fingering until you can play it in your sleep. This pattern is *essential* to know if you want to play rock guitar. Memorize it. Really do it. Play it over and over, up and down. Really. (We mean it. Honest!)

We use the key of A for all the examples in this section because the backing chords (as shown earlier in Figure 11-2) are easy to play and the soloing notes fall around the middle of the neck, where they're comfortable to play. But if you want to play lead in other keys, move your box patterns up or down the neck the appropriate number of frets. For example, to play in the key of B, move your boxes up two frets.

Having a box to use in improvising lead guitar is what makes playing classic rock 'n' roll (or blues) so much fun; you don't need to think — you just gotta *feel*. Of course, you can't play just the five notes of the scale up and down, over and over — that would get boring very fast. Instead, you use your creativity to create licks by using the scale and adding *articulations,* such as bends, slides, and hammer-ons, until you have a complete solo. (See Chapter 10 for articulation techniques.) We show you how to add these articulations in the following section.

Adding articulations

The box pattern shows you *what* to play, but articulations show you *how* to play. Articulations include *hammer-ons, pull-offs, slides, bends,* and *vibrato.* These elements are what make a solo sound like a solo, give the solo expression, and personalize it. Chapter 10 explains each articulation step by step, but we tell you how to *use* articulations to make some righteous rock 'n' roll right here.

Figure 11-4 shows a four-bar lick, using notes of Box I (the pentatonic minor scale) in ascending and descending order that you connect by using hammer-ons and pull-offs. Notice how much smoother and more flowing the sound is, as opposed to what you hear if you pick every note separately.

Track 55

Figure 11-4:
Using
hammer-ons
and pull-offs
in Box I.

© John Wiley & Sons, Inc.

Bending notes is probably the coolest sound in lead soloing, but the trick is knowing which notes to bend and when to do so. When using Box I, guitarists really like to bend notes on the 2nd and 3rd strings because the tension feels right, and they get to bend toward the ceiling — their favorite direction. Start off by bending the 3rd-finger note on the 3rd string and the 4th-finger note on the 2nd string. (See Chapter 10 for info on how to bend a note.) Figure 11-5 shows a typical four-bar phrase featuring a 3rd- and 2nd-string bend in Box I.

Figure 11-6 shows a typical two-bar phrase featuring a double-stop bend in Box I. The note that's on the 7th fret of the 2nd string isn't part of the A pentatonic minor scale, but it sounds good anyway, and it's easy to play because the 3rd finger barres both notes of the double-stop.

Add some vibrato to the final note to give it some expression.

Track 56

Video Clip 52

Figure 11-5:
Bending the
3rd and 2nd
strings in
Box I.

© John Wiley & Sons, Inc.

Track 57

Figure 11-6:
A double-
stop bend in
Box I.

© John Wiley & Sons, Inc.

Building a solo using Box I

An improvised solo is something you create, and nobody can show you exactly what to play. But we can show you the tools for soloing so you can practice and get a feel for it. Beyond that, however, your personality does the talking.

For now, start by getting the feel of playing lead over the 12-bar blues accompaniment pattern we show you earlier in Figure 11-2, which is incorporated into the rhythm on Track 54.

Notice that each of the phrases (in Figures 11-4, 11-5, and 11-6) that we show you in the preceding section, "Adding articulations," alternates one *active* measure (containing lots of notes) with one *static* measure (containing just one note). This alternation between activity and rest prevents monotony. Play these phrases in the order we describe in the following instructions, and you have a ready-made 12-bar solo. (If you want, you can play the solo over and over.) To play such a solo, just follow these steps:

1. **For the first four bars of the solo, play the double-stop lick, shown in Figure 11-6, twice.**

2. **For the next four bars of the solo, play the hammer-on/pull-off lick, as shown in Figure 11-4.**

3. For the last four bars of the solo, play the "bending the 3rd and 2nd strings" lick (refer to Figure 11-5).

We notate the preceding steps in Figure 11-7. Playing this example gives you the feel of playing lead . . . your little solo sounds like a series of phrases — as it should. Video Clip 53 lets you see how the left hand smoothly blends the different phrases.

Track 58

Video Clip 53

Figure 11-7:
Putting together three Box-I licks to create one 12-bar solo.

© John Wiley & Sons, Inc.

Moving to Boxes II and III

The next two boxes, which we name here *Box II* and *Box III,* don't show notes on all six strings as Box I does, because guitarists generally play only the notes on the top two or three strings.

Box II consists of five notes, as shown in Figure 11-8. Notice that the two notes at the top of this box (at the 8th fret) are also part of Box I, but in Box I, you play them with the pinky or 3rd finger. This box shows notes from the A pentatonic minor scale in 8th position. Again, in Figure 11-8, we show you the scale degree and fingering for each note, and we show you which note is good for bending.

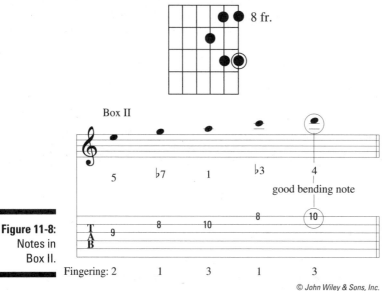

Figure 11-8:
Notes in
Box II.

© John Wiley & Sons, Inc.

Box II is popular because it features a good note for bending under the 3rd finger, and that note also happens to be the highest note in the box. In playing lead, *high* is good. You can play the highest note in the box and then make it even higher by bending it up a step. This technique produces quite a dramatic effect. Try it.

In Figure 11-9, you see a typical lick using Box II notes that features a bend on the highest note of the box.

Track 59

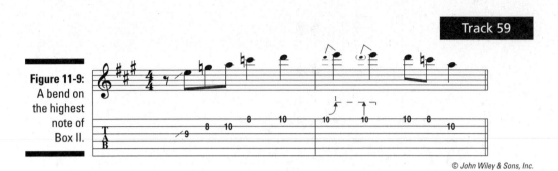

Figure 11-9:
A bend on
the highest
note of
Box II.

© John Wiley & Sons, Inc.

Box III is a funny one because some of its notes aren't in the A pentatonic minor scale — but guitarists use this box a lot anyway. The following list tells you all the stuff that Box III has going for it:

- Box III is easy to play and memorize — it's exactly like Box II but lies two frets higher on the neck.

- Box III has two notes — F♯ (the sixth degree) and B (the second degree) — that don't fall in the A pentatonic minor scale. And this is a good thing. These two notes are borrowed from the *parent major scale* (the major scale that starts on the same note — in this case, A), and sometimes guitarists like to add them to the pentatonic minor scale for variety and spice. The *predominance* of notes from the pentatonic minor scale is what gives classic rock 'n' roll (and blues) its flavor — not the total exclusion of all other notes.

- The good note for bending in Box III falls under the 3rd finger.

- The first degree of the scale, the note on which you often end a phrase, is under the 1st finger on the 2nd string in this box. You tend to apply vibrato to the ending note of a phrase (especially if you hold it), and this note provides an ideal finger and string on which to vibrato.

Figure 11-10 shows Box III (in 10th position for the key of A). Again, we show you the scale degree and fingering for each note, and we circle the note that's good for bending.

Often, guitarists concentrate on the 2nd and 3rd strings of Box III, as shown in Figure 11-11, which depicts a typical Box III phrase. Don't forget to vibrato that last note!

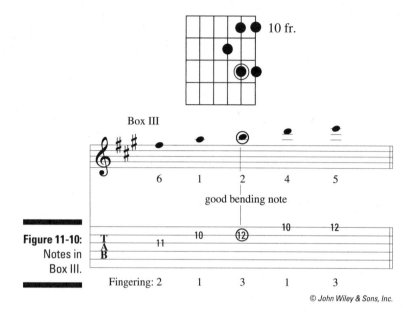

Figure 11-10:
Notes in
Box III.

© John Wiley & Sons, Inc.

Track 60

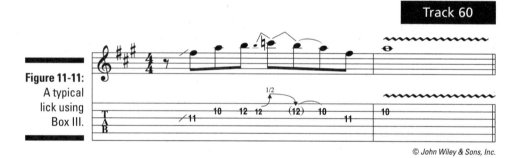

Figure 11-11:
A typical
lick using
Box III.

© John Wiley & Sons, Inc.

PLAY THIS!

If you want to play a song in classic rock 'n' roll style right now, skip to "Chuck's Duck" in the section "Playing Songs in the Rock Style," later in this chapter.

Building a solo by using Boxes I, II, and III

This section simply puts together licks from the three boxes that we describe in the preceding sections. You don't need any new information; you just need to piece together what you know if you read the information we provide in those sections. (If you haven't yet, we suggest you do so now, before you try the solo we describe here.) In other words, only *after* you make the bricks can you put them together to make a house.

Here, we show you how to build a ready-made 12-bar solo consisting of six two-bar phrases (using three boxes) that we show you in the preceding sections. Follow these steps:

1. **Play the Box I double-stop lick, as shown earlier in Figure 11-6.**

2. **Play the Box I "bending the 3rd string" lick, as shown in the first half of Figure 11-5 (shown earlier).**

3. **Play the Box III lick, as shown in Figure 11-11.**

4. **Play the Box I "bending the 2nd string" lick, as shown in the second half of Figure 11-5.**

5. **Play the Box II lick, as shown in Figure 11-9.**

6. **Play the Box I double-stop lick again, as shown in Figure 11-6.**

Figure 11-12 shows you the music to the preceding steps. Listen to Track 61 to hear how this solo sounds; watch Video Clip 54 to see and hear how it's done.

As you play this solo over and over, you get a feel for soloing with the three boxes over a 12-bar blues progression. The fun begins after you start making up your own solos. Following are some guidelines for creating your own leads:

✔ Think in terms of short phrases strung together. You can even play just one short phrase over and over, even though the backing chords change. A good way to make up a phrase is to make it a singable one. Sing a short phrase in your mind but use notes from the box.

✔ Add some articulation — especially bends, because they sound the coolest. Add vibrato to long notes that end a phrase, sometimes sliding down at the very end.

✔ Alternate between activity (lots of notes) and rest (a few notes or just one note or even silence for a few beats).

✔ Move from box to box to give your solo some variety.

Don't be inhibited or worry about making a mistake. In our opinions, you can't really make a mistake, because all the notes in the boxes sound good against all the chords in the backing progression. The only mistake you can make is to avoid soloing for fear of sounding lame. Soloing takes practice, but you gradually build confidence. If you're too shy to solo in front of people, start out by doing it along with the audio tracks, where no one can hear you. Pretty soon, no one can stop you.

Track 61

Video Clip 54

Figure 11-12:
Putting together six two-bar licks from all three boxes to build one 12-bar solo.

© John Wiley & Sons, Inc.

Listen to recordings to get new ideas as you become more confident in your playing. As you hear a recording, you may be able to figure out exactly what the guitarist is playing, because most guitarists use the same boxes, bends, vibratos, and so on that you do. Some good people to listen to for ideas are Chuck Berry, Jimi Hendrix, Eric Clapton, and Eddie Van Halen.

Mastering Modern Rock

Whereas classic rock 'n' roll rhythm guitar uses simple chords, *modern-rock* music makes use of chords other than basic major, minor, and 7th chords. *Sus chords, add chords, slash chords,* and unusual chords that result from retuning your guitar are all part of the modern-rock lexicon. These chords enable you to create entirely new rhythm guitar colors and textures that aren't possible in standard tuning. This sound was an especially important component of the '90s alternative movement. We explore the chords of modern rock in the following sections.

Sus chords and add chords

Chords are often built by taking every other note of a major scale. For example, if you build a three-note chord by taking every other note of the C major scale (C-D-E-F-G-A-B), you get C-E-G (a C major chord). The chord *members* (the individual notes that make up the chord) are labeled according to their scale degrees: C is "1" (or the *root* of the chord), E is "3" (or the *3rd* of the chord), and G is "5" (or the *5th* of the chord).

In *sus chords,* you replace the 3rd of a chord with the 4th, as in *sus4* (which you pronounce "suss-four") or sometimes with the second, as in *sus2.* The resulting sound is incomplete or unresolved but creates an interesting sound that's neither major nor minor.

An *add chord* is simply a basic chord (such as a major chord) to which you add an extra note. If you take a C chord and add a D note to it, for example, you have a *Cadd2* (which you pronounce "see-add-two") chord (with notes C-D-E-G). This chord is different from *Csus2,* which has no E. (The D took its place.)

The following sections cover open-position sus chords and add chords in more detail.

Open-position sus chords

Although you can play sus chords as movable barre chords (see Chapter 9), the open-position ones are the easiest to play and are the ones guitarists most commonly use. Figure 11-13 shows the fingerings for a progression that uses Asus4, Asus2, Dsus4, and Dsus2 chords.

Track 62, 0:00

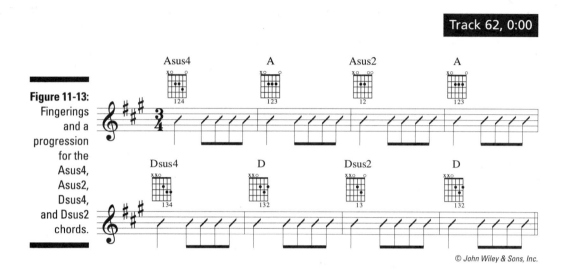

Figure 11-13:
Fingerings and a progression for the Asus4, Asus2, Dsus4, and Dsus2 chords.

© John Wiley & Sons, Inc.

Open-position add chords

You can play add chords as movable barre chords, but the open-position add chords are the most common and the easiest to play. Figure 11-14 shows the fingerings and a progression for the Cadd9 (which adds a D note, the ninth step of a two-octave C scale, to the three notes that make up the basic C major chord) and four-fingered G chords. The four-fingered G chord isn't an add chord, but you almost always use this G fingering before or after a Cadd9 chord.

Track 62, 0:15

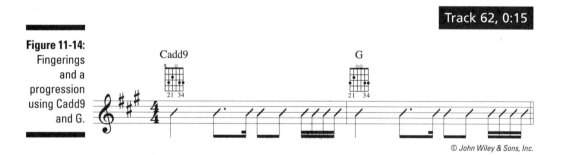

Figure 11-14:
Fingerings and a progression using Cadd9 and G.

© John Wiley & Sons, Inc.

Slash chords

Slash chords are colorful, interesting chords that add spice and flavor to modern rock music. A slash chord is, simply, a chord with a slash (/) in its name, as in Am/C (which you pronounce as "A minor over C"). To the left of the slash is the chord itself. To the right of the slash is the *bass* note for that chord. Often, the lowest-pitched note of a chord — the bass note — is the *root* of the chord (the note that gives the chord its name). So if you see a chord name such as Am, you assume that the bass note is A. But the root isn't always the lowest note of a chord. In fact, any note can serve as a bass note, be it a chord tone other than the root (such as the 3rd or 5th of the chord) or a note that isn't even a member of the chord at all. If you do have such a non-root bass note, you indicate that bass note by placing it to the right of the slash. So Am/C means that you're playing an A minor chord — but with a C as the lowest note.

Guitarists often use slash chords in progressions where the bass line forms an ascending or descending scale. This sort of bass pattern gives interest and unity to a progression. You can hear a progression such as this one in the song "Whiter Shade of Pale," by Procol Harum. Figure 11-15 shows another progression that uses slash chords in this manner. To bring out the bass line, in each measure, play only the bottom note of the chord on beat 1 and then strum the chord on beats 2 and 3 (what *Bass strum strum* means).

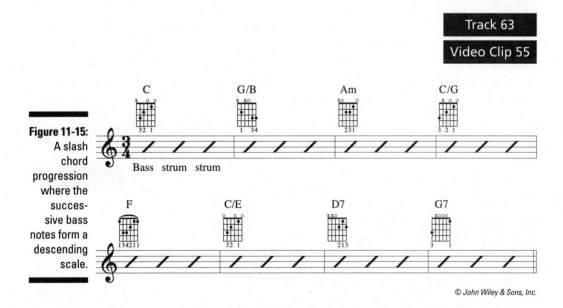

Figure 11-15: A slash chord progression where the succes-sive bass notes form a descending scale.

© John Wiley & Sons, Inc.

The chords in Figure 11-15 show Xs in the chord diagrams, which tell you which strings *not* to play. To keep a string from sounding, either avoid striking it with the right hand, or use the left-hand finger that's fretting the adjacent lower-pitched string to mute it by lightly touching it.

Alternate tunings

Modern-rock guitar music makes frequent use of *alternate tunings* — tunings other than the standard EADGBE tuning (refer to Chapter 2). By using alternate tunings, you can achieve new, exciting sounds that are impossible to attain in standard tuning. Alternate tunings may also enable you to play licks or chords that are difficult to finger in standard tuning but that are easy to finger in alternate tuning. But remember: After you retune your guitar, all your familiar fingerings are out the window. That's why picking up new licks and riffs in alternate tunings by reading tab can prove especially helpful. Artists as diverse as Joni Mitchell, the Rolling Stones, and Led Zeppelin make use of alternate tunings.

In the following sections, we describe two common types of alternate tunings: drop-D tuning and open-D tuning.

Drop-D tuning (DADGBE)

Drop-D tuning (so called because you detune, or *drop*, the low E string down to D) is the alternate tuning that's closest to standard tuning — you retune only the 6th string; so the open strings, from low to high, are D, A, D, G, B, E. To get into this tuning, lower (drop) your 6th string until it sounds an octave lower than your 4th string. This tuning enables you to play a D or Dm chord with a low D as a root on the 6th string, giving you a full, rich sound.

Figure 11-16 shows a typical passage in drop-D tuning. It has a bluesy sound. Bend the 3rd-fret note of the 6th string very slightly (only a quarter step, which is half as much as a half step). For music readers: Note that the standard notation indicates a quarter bend with a short slur after the note head in question.

Track 64, 0:00

Figure 11-16: A typical phrase in drop-D tuning.

© John Wiley & Sons, Inc.

An advantage of drop-D tuning is that you can play low power chords on the bottom two strings as two-string barres, which enables you to play power chord riffs more easily, as shown in Figure 11-17.

© John Wiley & Sons, Inc.

Figure 11-17: A low power chord riff in drop-D tuning.

Open-D tuning (DADF#AD)

In an *open tuning*, the open strings usually form a major chord. In *open-D tuning*, they form (big surprise) a D chord: from low to high, D, A, D, F#, A, D. In this tuning, most of the chords you play are nothing but open strings or one finger barring across all six strings. You can, for example, play a G chord simply by barring the entire 5th fret with your 1st finger. Joni Mitchell has made extensive use of this tuning in songs such as "Big Yellow Taxi."

To get into this tuning, follow these steps:

1. **Drop your 6th string until it sounds an octave lower than the open 4th string.**

2. **Drop your 3rd string so it matches the note at the 4th fret of the 4th string.**

3. **Drop your 2nd string so it matches the note at the 3rd fret of the 3rd string (and is one octave higher than the open 5th string).**

4. **Drop your 1st string so it matches the note at the 5th fret of the 2nd string (and is one octave higher than the open 4th string).**

If you raise all six strings by one whole step (the equivalent of two frets) from open-D tuning, you get open-E tuning (EBEG#BE), which you can consider as essentially the same tuning as open D, because the relationships between the strings remain the same, even though the actual notes differ. To hear a song in open-E tuning, check out the Allman Brothers' "Little Martha."

In Figure 11-18, you see a typical phrase using open-D tuning that sounds like something Joni Mitchell may have played on one of her early albums.

Another common alternate tuning that you may run across is open-G (DGDGBD, low-pitched to high), often used by Keith Richards of the Rolling Stones on such songs as "Brown Sugar" and "Start Me Up." (See Chapter 13 for an example that uses open-G tuning.)

Track 65

Open D tuning (low to high): D A D F♯ A D

Figure 11-18:
A typical
phrase in
open-D
tuning.

© John Wiley & Sons, Inc.

Getting a Feel for Country-Rock and Southern-Rock Lead Guitar

Since the days of the Eagles, the Grateful Dead, and the Allman Brothers Band, country rock and Southern rock have enjoyed mainstream success and appeal. The sound of these styles falls somewhere between that of straight country music and blues, although both are too rock-oriented for straight country yet not quite hard-edged enough to pass as blues-based rock. The slightly simpler, more major sound of these styles can be attributed to the chords the guitarists typically use and, to a greater extent, the scales that they use in the solo passages. To get a feel for this sound, listen to the music of the Byrds, the Allman Brothers Band, the Marshall Tucker Band, Pure Prairie League, Lynyrd Skynyrd, the Grateful Dead, and the Eagles.

In the following sections, we describe another approach to lead playing in which you use the *pentatonic major scale* — a scale that's different from the bluesier pentatonic minor scale that you play mainly in classic rock 'n' roll and blues. You can use the pentatonic major scale for Southern- and country-rock leads as well as for adding variety to blues-based leads.

The pentatonic major scale

You can define the notes of the pentatonic *minor* scale in any key as 1, ♭3, 4, 5, ♭7, as compared to the parent major scale. You practice the scale as a memorized box, which is just fine. The *pentatonic major scale,* on the other hand, uses the 1, 2, 3, 5, 6 notes of the parent major scale. It's a five-note scale that has no *chromatic alterations* (that is, notes that you alter by raising or lowering a half step), so it sounds just like a major scale with two notes left out. Again, the pentatonic major scale is a very useful scale because it practically makes music itself, and you can't play any "wrong" notes. (See the section "What's behind Box I? The pentatonic minor scale," earlier in this chapter, for more information on scale degrees and the pentatonic minor scale.)

After you master the pentatonic minor scale, the pentatonic major scale is a cinch. Just move the pentatonic minor scale down three frets and *voilà,* you have a pentatonic major scale. Play the same pattern, and the notes, theory, and all that nonsense take care of themselves.

Say, for example, that you know that you play the A pentatonic minor scale at the 5th fret against a chord progression in the key of A. Well, drop that lead pattern down to the 2nd position (where your left-hand index finger plays the notes on the 2nd fret), and you have an A pentatonic major scale, suitable for country-rock and Southern-rock progressions. (See Chapter 7 for info on positions.)

Figure 11-19 shows the A pentatonic major scale in 2nd position (Box I) and 5th position (Box II), along with the scale degree and fingering for each note and the good note for bending in each box (circled). Notice that the only real difference from the pentatonic *minor* scale is the starting fret.

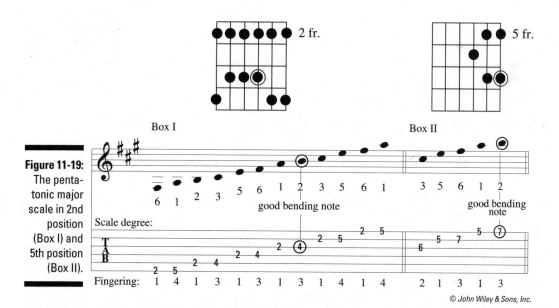

Figure 11-19: The pentatonic major scale in 2nd position (Box I) and 5th position (Box II).

© John Wiley & Sons, Inc.

Licks that you base on the pentatonic major scale

The good news is that, as is true of the pentatonic minor scale, the pentatonic major scale has all the right things going for it: Bending notes lie in good places; you use your index finger on each string of Box I for a solid feel; and the scale is especially suitable for the use of hammer-ons, pull-offs, and slides for more expressive possibilities.

The bad news is that, although you're still in A, the fingering is shifted, so you no longer can count on landing on the usual fingers to end your solo. But we don't think that this problem is an especially big one. With just a little reorientation (and your ear), you can find good alternative notes in no time.

Good notes for ending a pentatonic major solo in A are the 2nd fret of the 3rd string (Box I) and the 5th fret of the 1st string (Box I or II).

Figure 11-20 shows a four-bar lick to get you starting down that Southern country road. Notice that this lick features bends in both positions (Boxes I and II) and a slide from Box II back down to Box I to bring you home. Refer to Video Clip 56 to see how to execute the bends and the position shifts.

Track 66

Video Clip 56

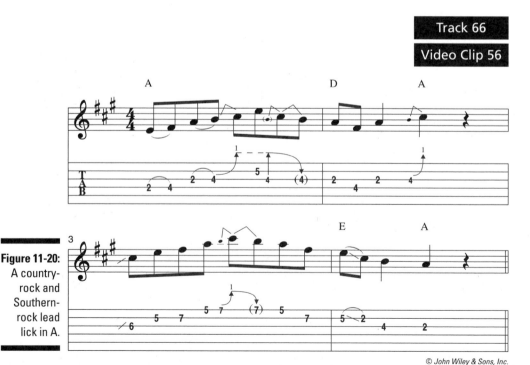

Figure 11-20: A country-rock and Southern-rock lead lick in A.

© John Wiley & Sons, Inc.

If you want to play a song in Southern rock style right now, check out "Southern Hospitality" in the section that follows.

Playing Songs in the Rock Style

Don your tour jackets and pile into your limousines, because you're going to be rockin' out in style in this section. The songs here cover two styles: the deliberate-sounding, classic rock 'n' roll of the late '50s and the easy-sounding twang of the country- and Southern-rock movements of the '70s.

Here is some special information about the songs to help you along:

✔ **Chuck's Duck:** To play "Chuck's Duck," you need to know how to play licks with the pentatonic minor scale (see the section "What's behind Box I? The pentatonic minor scale," earlier in this chapter); how to play double-stops and double-stop bends (see Chapters 8 and 10); and how to bend down on one knee and hop across a stage without requiring arthroscopic surgery afterward.

Double-stops, the pentatonic minor scale, and continuous eighth notes characterize the classic rock 'n' roll sound. Notice the quick, bursting bends on the 3rd string in bars 6 through 9.

✔ **Southern Hospitality:** To play "Southern Hospitality," you need to know how to play the pentatonic major scale (see the section "The pentatonic major scale," earlier in this chapter); how to play sus, add, and slash chords (see the section "Mastering Modern Rock," earlier in this chapter); and how to grow an overly long beard.

By taking the pentatonic minor scale and moving it down three frets, you have the pentatonic major scale, which you use to create a true country-rock and Southern-rock sound in the styles of the Eagles, the Allman Brothers Band, Lynyrd Skynyrd, and the Marshall Tucker Band. After playing the lead part, try the rhythm guitar part, which features sus, add, and slash chords. We've indicated the left-hand chord fingerings for you, but listen to Track 68 for the right-hand strumming pattern.

Chuck's Duck

Track 67

Video Clips 57

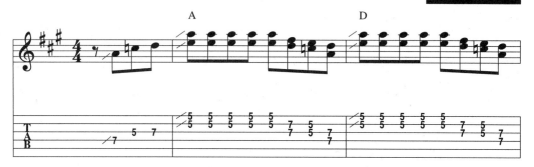

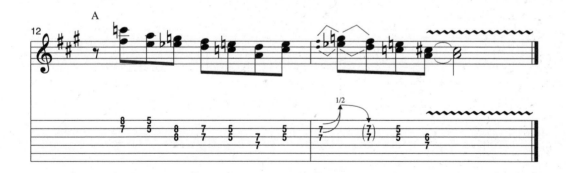

Southern Hospitality

Track 68

Video Clips 58

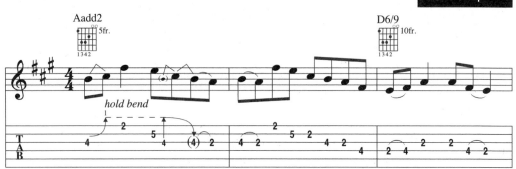

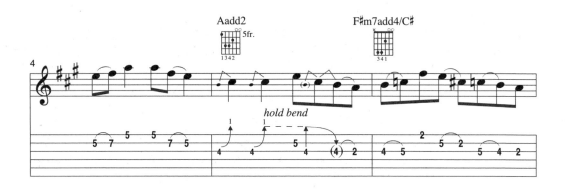

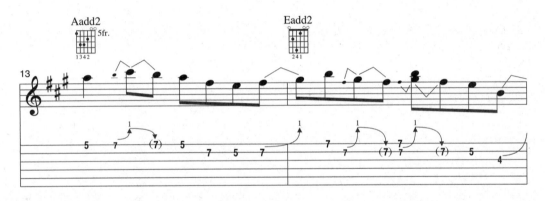

Chapter 12

Bluer Than Blue: Blues Guitar Basics

In This Chapter

▶ Tapping into electric blues

▶ Getting down with acoustic blues

▶ Practicing songs about heartbreak and sorrow and looking good doing it

▶ Access the audio tracks and video clips at `www.dummies.com/go/guitar`

*B*lues is one of the most popular forms of guitar music, both for the listener and the player. And why not? Who could resist the easy rhythms, the expressive melodies, and the soulful lyrics of the blues? Not every form of music can warm your heart as the singer is lamenting his death-row plight for a murder he didn't commit while his baby runs off with his best friend. Ah, the sweet sorrow.

But before we get too sentimental, we want to tell you why playing the blues just seems born for the guitar. One reason is that it's a relatively easy style to play (especially if you compare it to jazz or classical music): Blues accompaniment patterns are accessible and comfortable to the hands, and blues melodies fall particularly well on the guitar's neck because of the scales the style uses. Plus, blues isn't technically demanding, and you play it best by ear with the heart guiding the way.

Playing great blues — following in the musical footsteps of such legends as B.B. King or Stevie Ray Vaughan — may be difficult, but playing pretty good blues right away is still fairly easy if you know the form, a couple of scales, and some simple blues moves.

In this chapter, we cover electric and acoustic blues. Along the way, we introduce you to more boxes (first introduced in Chapter 11), the *blues scale,* Roman-numeral naming, and *turnarounds,* among other topics.

Plugging into the Electric Blues

Electric blues is the kind of blues that all the giants of the genre play: Buddy Guy, B.B. King, Albert King, Albert Collins, Johnny Winter, and Duane Allman, among others. Electric-blues guitar playing breaks down fairly neatly into two categories: rhythm and lead. We explore both categories in the following sections.

Blues rhythm guitar

Rhythm playing is what you do whenever you're not playing lead — such as accompanying a singer or another featured instrument by playing chords, background figures, and repeated low-note riffs. Rhythm generally requires less technical proficiency than playing lead does and relies more on the guitarist's "feel" than on his technique. To put chord playing into some kind of context, you want to begin with the most popular form, or progression, in the style, the *12-bar blues,* and you want to get a handle on a rhythm known as the *shuffle* feel (also called the *swing* feel or *triplet* feel).

Starting with the 12-bar blues form

Blues and rock guitar are similar in that each leans heavily on the 12-bar blues form for song structure (see Chapter 11). Taking the key of A as an example, the 12-bar blues progression consists of four bars of A, two bars of D, two bars of A, one bar of E, one bar of D, and two bars of A. In music notation, the 12-bar blues progression looks like the example shown in Figure 12-1.

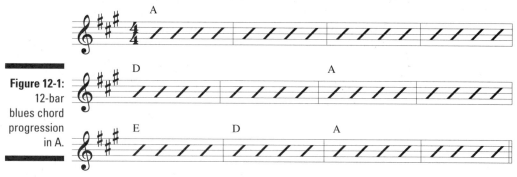

Figure 12-1: 12-bar blues chord progression in A.

© John Wiley & Sons, Inc.

Chords in any common progression, including the blues progression in Figure 12-1, are often referred to by Roman numerals. These numerals identify the chords generically rather than by key. You always assign Roman numeral I to the chord that names the key you're in. Then, you count up alphabetically, letter by letter, assigning other numbers to chords.

For example, in the key of A (as in Figure 12-1), the A chord is I (Roman numeral one), the D is IV (four), and the E is V (five). (You can count letter names on your fingers, starting from A, to confirm that A is I, D is IV, and E is V.) In the key of G, on the other hand, G is I, C is IV, and D is V. By using such a system, if you decide to switch keys, you can always just say, "Start playing at the IV (four) chord in bar 5." If you know which chords are I, IV, and V in that key, you're ready to play. See Table 12-1 for a handy reference that shows the I, IV, and V chords in common keys.

Table 12-1	I, IV, and V Chords in Common Keys		
Key	**I**	**IV**	**V**
A	A	D	E
C	C	F	G
D	D	G	A
E	E	A	B
F	F	B♭	C
G	G	C	D

If you're playing your blues accompaniment by using barre chords (see Chapter 9), you can remember which chords are which merely by their position on the neck. Say, for example, that you're playing a blues progression in A. If you make an E-based barre chord at the 5th fret (A), you're playing the I chord in A. If you switch to the A-based barre chord form at that same fret, you're now playing the IV chord, or D. Move that same A-based barre two frets higher on the neck — to the 7th fret — and you're playing the V chord, E. See how easy playing the blues can be! Use those same positions anywhere on the neck — an E-based barre chord at any fret, following it with an A-based barre chord at the same fret, and moving that barre up two frets — and you know the I-IV-V progression for whatever key goes with the starting fret.

The following are two important variations of the 12-bar blues form:

- **Quick IV:** Still using the key of A as an example, you substitute a D (IV) chord for A (I) in bar 2. Ordinarily, you must wait until bar 5 to play the IV chord, so switching to it in bar 2 feels pretty quick, hence the name.

- **Turnaround:** In a turnaround, you play a V chord instead of a I chord on the last bar (bar 12). This change helps draw the music back to the I chord of the first bar, turning the progression around to the beginning. A turnaround allows you to repeat the progression over and over, as desired. Blues guitarists base many licks just on the turnaround at the progression's end. (For more information on turnaround licks, see the section "Turnarounds" later in this chapter.)

Try substituting 7th or 9th chords (A7, D9, or E9, for example) for the basic I-IV-V chords to make the music sound even bluesier (see the following section for more on 9th chords).

Shuffling the beat with a triplet feel

Blues relies heavily on a rhythmic feel known as a *triplet feel* (sometimes called a *shuffle feel* or a *swing feel*). In a triplet feel, you divide each beat into three parts (instead of the normal two). You can hear this feel on Track 69 (the recording of Figure 12-2), but here's a good way to get an understanding of the difference between straight feel and triplet feel. Recite each of the following phrases out loud, snapping your fingers on each capitalized syllable. (Make sure you snap your fingers — it's important!)

1. TWIN-kle TWIN-kle LIT-tle STAR.

   That's a straight feel — each finger snap is a beat, and each beat you divide into two parts.

2. FOL-low the YEL-low brick ROAD.

That's a triplet feel — each finger snap is a beat, and each beat you divide into three parts. Because a lot of blues uses a triplet feel, you need to know how to play a 12-bar blues accompaniment with that feel.

Figure 12-2 shows you an accompaniment — here with the quick IV (bar 2) and turnaround (bar 12) variation — consisting of nothing more than strummed chords in a triplet rhythm. Typically, the last bar of a blues song uses a progression in which you approach the final chord from one fret above or below it (see measure 13). See the chord diagrams on the figure for the fingerings of the 9th chords in the song.

If you know how to play a rock boogie-woogie accompaniment (in Chuck Berry style — see Chapter 11), you should have no trouble at all playing Figure 12-3, which is actually the same boogie accompaniment (but with the quick IV variation), except that you play it in a triplet feel. Again, you approach the last chord from a fret above. Play along with Video Clip 37, if you find it helps to stay on track.

Note: In the music in Figures 12-2 and 12-3, the equivalency (♪♪=♪ ♪) that appears next to the words *Triplet feel* indicates that you should substitute triplet (or shuffle) eighth notes for straight eighth notes. In triplet eighths, you hold the first note of each beat a little longer than the second.

Track 69

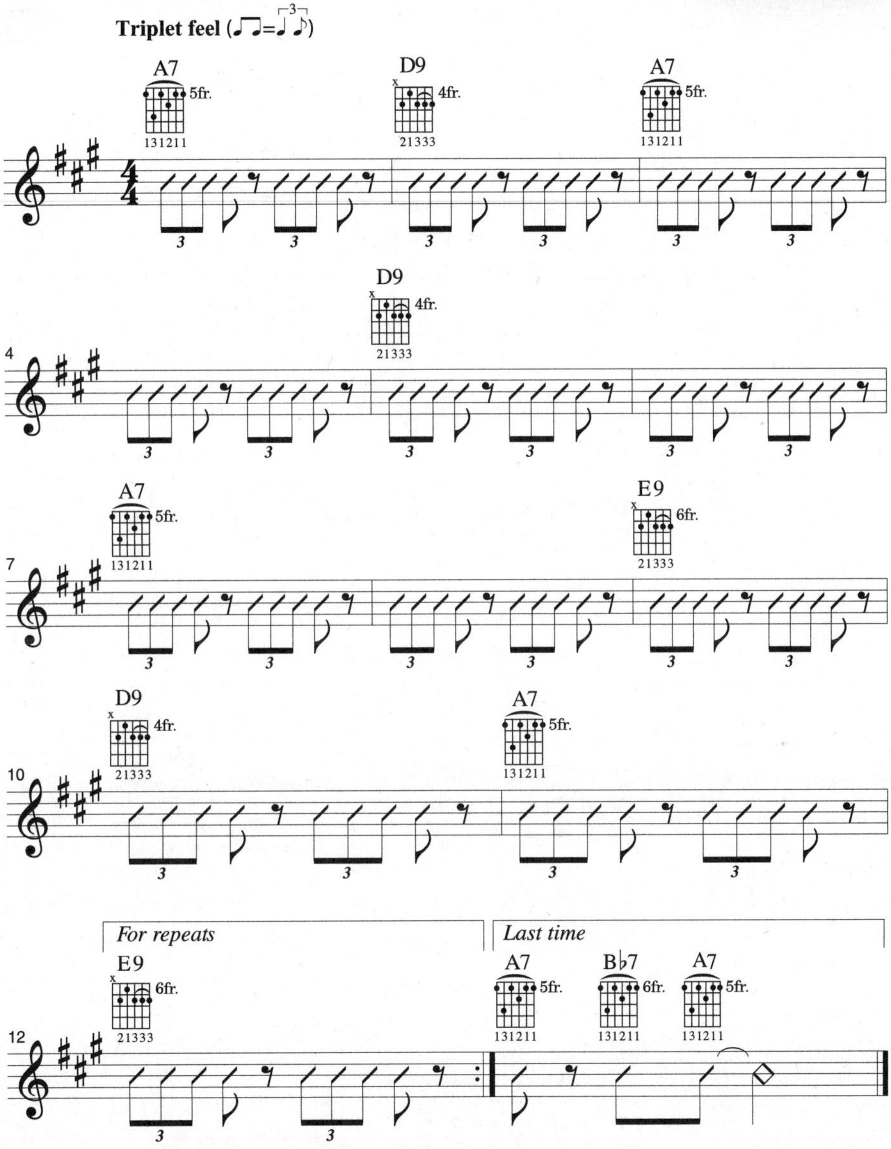

Figure 12-2: A 12-bar blues accompaniment with strumming in a triplet feel.

© John Wiley & Sons, Inc.

Track 70

Video Clip 59

Triplet feel (♪♪ = ♪ ♪)

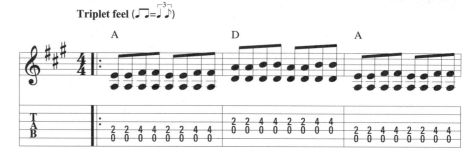

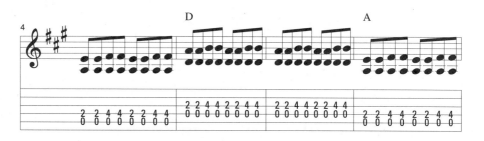

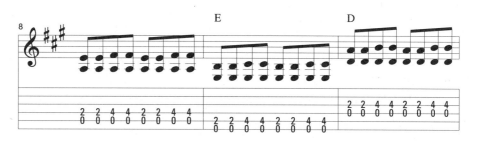

For repeats

Last time

Figure 12-3:
A 12-bar blues accompaniment with a boogie riff in triplet feel.

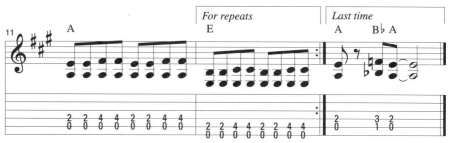

© John Wiley & Sons, Inc.

Breaking down blues lyrics and structure

In dealing with the blues, one good way to keep the song's structure straight is to think of the 12-bar progression as three four-bar phrases. You can do so because the lyrics of a typical blues song usually fall in an AAB form (which means that the first two sections of the song are the same and the third one is different), with each of the three sections taking up four bars. A typical blues song, for example, may go something like the following:

- **First phrase:** "I woke up this morning; I was feeling mighty bad." This phrase you sing over the first four bars of the 12-bar progression (I, I, I, I or I, IV, I, I for the quick IV variation).

- **Second phrase:** "I woke up this morning; I was feeling mighty bad." This phrase repeats the same lyrics that you sing in the first phrase, and you sing it over the second four bars of the progression (IV, IV, I, I).

- **Third phrase:** "I can't stop thinking I lost the best gal I ever had." This phrase is different from the first two phrases, and you sing it over the last four bars of the progression (V, IV, I, I — or V, IV, I, V if you're going to repeat the progression).

Usually, you sing each vocal phrase within the first two measures of the four-bar phrase, giving the instrumentalist (maybe even you!) a chance to play some cool blues licks during measures 3 and 4 of each phrase, which gives the song a kind of question-answer feeling. But even if you're not using a vocalist on a particular song, the instrumentalists can still play the tune with this two-bar plus two-bar, question-answer mentality in each four-bar phrase.

Blues lead guitar

Blues lead is the single-note melodic line, consisting of a mixture of composed lines and improvised phrases. A great lead solo includes both these elements in one seamless, inspired whole. The following sections provide you with the tools and techniques you need to create your own bluesy-sounding licks and solos.

Beginning with boxes

Blues guitarists improvise mostly by using *boxes* — just as rock guitarists do. A box is a fingerboard pattern — usually outlining a pentatonic minor scale — that vaguely resembles the shape of a box. (See Chapter 11 for info on pentatonic minor scales and boxes.) By using notes in a box, you can improvise lead lines that automatically sound good as you play them over a 12-bar blues accompaniment.

You may already know how to use boxes to play rock 'n' roll lead guitar, which employs the same scales and chords as blues. (And we describe these in Chapter 11.) If so, you should have no trouble understanding the example in Figure 12-4, which shows the three boxes you can use for soloing in the key of A that we introduce in Chapter 11; we circle the notes that are good for bending. (For information on bending, see Chapter 10.)

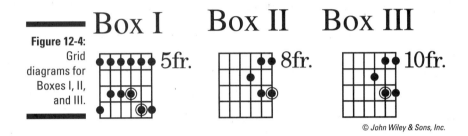

Figure 12-4: Grid diagrams for Boxes I, II, and III.

© John Wiley & Sons, Inc.

Figure 12-5 shows two new boxes that you can also use for blues soloing:

- The one we're calling *Box IV* (because no standard names or numberings exist for the boxes) is similar to Box III, except that we move it up three frets to the 13th position (for the key of A) and we eliminate the two notes on the 1st string (see Chapter 7 for info on playing in position). Again, we circle the good note for bending. Play the notes in this box by using your 2nd finger on the 3rd string and your 1st and 3rd fingers on the 2nd string.

- *Box V* is sometimes thought of as a lower extension of Box I — because it contains Box I's 5th-fret notes on the bottom two strings and because you often move back and forth between those two boxes. Use your 1st and 3rd fingers to play the notes on both strings.

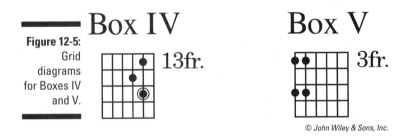

Figure 12-5: Grid diagrams for Boxes IV and V.

© John Wiley & Sons, Inc.

You may notice that Box I covers all six strings while the other boxes cover only two or three strings. Actually, what we're showing you in Boxes II through V are *partial boxes*. Full-box versions (using all six strings) exist for these, but in the full versions, you end up with some "bad" or uncomfortable fingerings, such as playing the important notes with fingers 2 and 4 instead of the stronger 1 and 3 or having the good notes for bending end up under a bad finger for bending. That's why most guitarists use just the partial boxes, as shown in these figures.

If you know how to play typical licks by using Boxes I, II, and III, the lick in Figure 12-6 that uses Box IV should give you no trouble. Play with a triplet feel, and make sure you apply vibrato to the last note for a real blues effect. (See Chapter 10 for details about playing vibrato.) Notice how the bend falls under the 3rd finger — the best finger for bending.

Track 71, 0:00

Video Clip 60

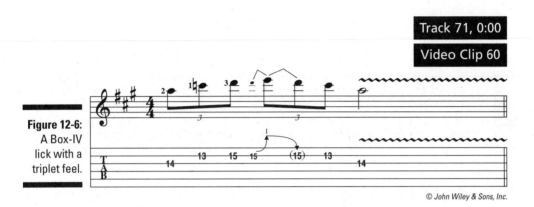

Figure 12-6: A Box-IV lick with a triplet feel.

© John Wiley & Sons, Inc.

Figure 12-7 shows a typical lick that uses Box V. A common blues technique is to *slide* on the 5th string (3rd finger) back and forth between Box V and Box I. (See Chapter 10 for info about slides.) See how nicely all the notes fall under the 1st and 3rd fingers, even as you move between the boxes.

Track 71, 0:10

Figure 12-7: A Box-V lick with a slide up to Box I.

© John Wiley & Sons, Inc.

Adding depth with additional notes

The pentatonic minor scale produces good blues notes, but adding two more notes gives you an even richer sonic palette of note choices. The flatted 5th and the major 3rd help give more definition to a line by introducing a *dissonant,* or tension-filled, note (the flatted 5th) and another note (the major 3rd) that reinforces the major quality of the I chord.

A *flatted 5th* is a note that's a half step (or one fret) lower than the regular 5th of a scale. In the A pentatonic minor scale, for example, the E note is the *5th*. (Count letter names from A to E on your fingers to confirm that E is five notes above A.) The E♭ note is, therefore, the *flatted 5th*. A *major 3rd* is a note that's a half step (or one fret) higher than the regular (minor) 3rd of a pentatonic minor scale. In the A pentatonic minor scale, for example, the C note is the *minor 3rd*. The C♯ note is the *major 3rd*. (See Appendix A for more info on sharps and flats.)

Creating the blues scale with the flatted 5th

The five-note pentatonic scale works great for basic blues, but for a *really* funky, crying sound, toss in the *flat-5* note (E♭ in the key of A) now and then (the flat 5 is just another name for the flatted 5th). Adding the flat-5 note to the pentatonic scale creates the six-note *blues scale*. The flat 5 is particularly dissonant but adds some spice to the more "vanilla-sounding" quality of the straight pentatonic minor scale. But as with any spice, whether salt, fennel, or a flat 5, add it sparingly and judiciously.

Boxes I, II, and IV, as shown in Figure 12-8, consist of notes from the pentatonic minor scale. The notes in circles indicate the added E♭ — the ♭5 (flat 5) — this time and not the bending notes. Box I shows the complete (two-octave) A blues scale in 5th position, while Boxes II and IV show partial blues scales that are good to use for improvising.

Figure 12-8:
Grid showing the addition of the flat 5 (♭5) to Boxes I, II, and IV.

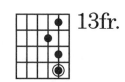

© John Wiley & Sons, Inc.

Figure 12-9 shows a typical Box-I blues lick, using the blues scale. Notice that you can produce the E♭ in two ways: by playing it at the 8th fret of the 3rd string or by bending the *7th-fret* note (the typical good note for bending in Box I) up a half step.

Figures 12-10 and 12-11 show a typical blues-scale lick, first using Box II (in 8th position) and then (the same lick) using Box IV (in 13th position). Again, you play the ♭5 both straight and as a bent note (with the 3rd finger) in each position.

Track 72, 0:00

Figure 12-9:
A blues-scale lick using Box I.

© John Wiley & Sons, Inc.

Track 72, 0:13

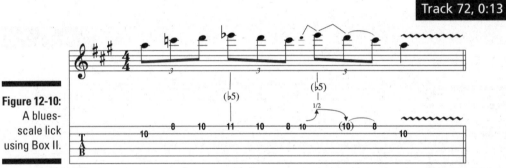

Figure 12-10:
A blues-scale lick using Box II.

© John Wiley & Sons, Inc.

Track 72, 0:23

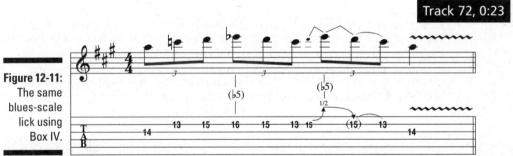

Figure 12-11:
The same blues-scale lick using Box IV.

© John Wiley & Sons, Inc.

Borrowing the major 3rd

Another note that blues players commonly add to the pentatonic minor or blues scale is the major 3rd. You can think of this note as one that you "borrow" from the pentatonic major scale or from the full major scale. In the key of A, the added major 3rd is C♯, and Figure 12-12 shows where it falls in Box I (the note in the circle). It's the only note you play with your 2nd finger if you're using Box I (unless you're also using the flat 5 we describe in the preceding section).

Figure 12-12:
Grid
showing the
addition of
the major
3rd to Box I.

© John Wiley & Sons, Inc.

Very often, you hammer on the major 3rd from the minor 3rd a fret below it, as shown in Figure 12-13. (Refer to Chapter 10 for how to play hammer-ons.)

Track 73, 0:00

Figure 12-13:
A lick using
the major
3rd with
Box I.

© John Wiley & Sons, Inc.

Even though you use the pentatonic *minor* scale for soloing, the *key* of a typical blues song is *major* (as in A major) because the rhythm guitarist plays *major* background chords (which contain major 3rds). In double-stop licks, often heard in the music of Chuck Berry and the Beach Boys, the end of a descending lead lick usually contains a major 3rd to help establish the key as major rather than minor, as shown in Figure 12-14.

Track 73, 0:10

Figure 12-14:
A double-
stop riff
using the
major 3rd
with Box I.

© John Wiley & Sons, Inc.

Using short phrasing

Although blues soloing uses many of the same techniques, scales, chords, and boxes as rock soloing does, the two styles are different in the area of *phrasing.* Lots of steady-flowing eighth notes often characterize rock soloing (think of the solo to "Johnny B. Goode"). But blues soloing (think B.B. King) more often employs phrases that are shorter and sparser (more separated) than those of rock. (See Appendix A for more info on eighth notes.)

In a typical blues melody, you may hear a very short phrase, some empty space, and then a repetition of the same phrase. Usually, these short phrases have a vocal quality to them in that they're expressive, often conveying pain or sorrow. Sometimes, if the guitarist is also the singer, the vocal phrases and the guitar phrases are practically one and the same. Figure 12-15 shows you a short passage that demonstrates the short-phrase concept. Notice how the same figure (the pull-off from the 8th fret to the 5th) sounds good but different if you play it against a different chord (first against A7 and then D7). Repeating a figure after the chord changes is a typical blues technique.

Track 74

Figure 12-15: A riff showing typical blues phrasing.

© John Wiley & Sons, Inc.

Making blues moves

Figure 12-16 shows four typical blues moves. A *blues move* is nothing more than a short, cool-sounding *lick* (a self-contained musical phrase). Track 75 demonstrates how these moves sound if you play them in the context of a progression.

Blues moves are easy to create because they're so short. Make up your own and see how they sound as you play them over the 12-bar blues progressions shown earlier in Figures 12-2 and 12-3.

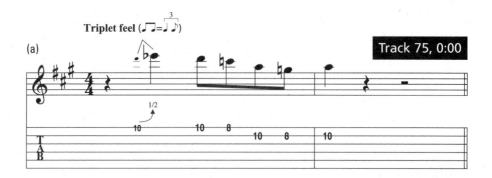

Triplet feel

(a) Track 75, 0:00

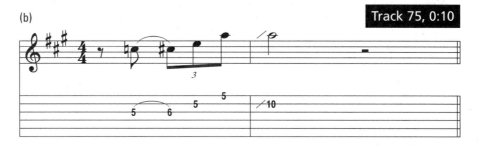

(b) Track 75, 0:10

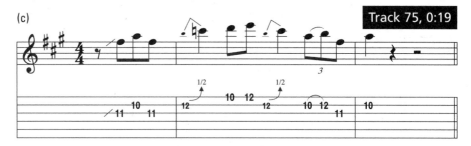

(c) Track 75, 0:19

Figure 12-16: Riffs showing four typical blues moves.

(d) Track 75, 0:29

© John Wiley & Sons, Inc.

If you want to play an electric blues song right now by using the blues moves of Figure 12-16, skip ahead to "Chicago Shuffle" in the section "Playing Blues Songs," later in this chapter.

Getting to the Root of Acoustic Blues

Blues guitar today is most often heard on electric guitar. B.B. King, Buddy Guy, Muddy Waters, Johnny Winter, Stevie Ray Vaughan, Albert King, Albert Collins, and Eric Clapton, for example, are all known for their electric guitar playing. But blues started out as an acoustic form, played fingerstyle (see Chapter 13), and still evokes images of the rural Mississippi Delta, where it originated and flourished.

In the following sections, we talk about the general concepts behind acoustic blues and show you some specific techniques that will have you playing in no time.

Looking at general concepts

Although you play electric blues in various keys by using movable boxes (see the section "Blues lead guitar," earlier in this chapter), you play acoustic blues (sometimes called *Delta Blues*) in open position (usually playing low on the neck and using a combination of open strings and fretted notes), almost always in the key of E. The following sections describe the basics you need to play acoustic blues.

Playing the melody and the accompaniment simultaneously

The basic idea behind acoustic blues is that you're playing a solo that incorporates both the melody (which you often improvise) and the accompaniment at the same time. This method is opposite that of electric blues, where one guitarist plays the melody (the lead) while another guitarist plays the accompaniment (the rhythm).

The essence of the style is as follows: Your right-hand thumb plays the *root* of each chord (the note the chord is named after) in steady quarter notes on the bass strings. (See Appendix A for more info on quarter notes.) Meanwhile, your right-hand fingers play melody notes that you take from the E pentatonic minor scale or the E blues scale, in open position. (For more information on the pentatonic minor scale and the blues scale, see Chapter 11 and the section "Blues lead guitar," earlier in this chapter.) You can use either scale or mix them up. Figure 12-17 represents a grid showing the E pentatonic minor/E blues scales in open position. Without the circled notes, you have the E pentatonic minor scale; with the circled notes — the flat-5 (♭5) notes, or B♭ in this key — you have the E blues scale.

Notice that the scale in Figure 12-17 is actually Box I in open position! For the left-hand fingering, play in 1st position — that is, use the same finger number as the fret number. Because your right-hand thumb is usually steadily plucking away at the low strings, you usually take your melody notes from the high strings.

Figure 12-17:
Grid
showing
the open-
position E
pentatonic
minor and
E blues
scales.

© John Wiley & Sons, Inc.

Figure 12-18 shows a simple exercise that demonstrates the basic acoustic blues style by using the E blues scale, first descending and then ascending. Make sure you play in a triplet feel, as on Track 76. You can see how you can play both the melody and accompaniment at the same time — and doing so isn't even difficult. That's because the bass part is so easy to play! Watch Video Clip 39 to see how the right-hand thumb and fingers interact.

Track 76

Video Clip 61

Figure 12-18:
Combining
steady bass
notes with
treble notes
from the E
blues scale.

© John Wiley & Sons, Inc.

Employing repetition

An important aspect of acoustic blues (and electric, too) is *repetition*. This idea involves a *motive* (a short musical phrase) that you repeat, sometimes once, sometimes over and over. In acoustic blues, you can achieve this effect in one of the following two ways:

✔ **Repeat a phrase *at the same pitch* as the background chord changes.** In Figure 12-19, the chord changes from E to A. (The different bass notes that the thumb plays imply the chord change.) The motive, however, repeats at the same pitch. Notice how the same notes sound different if you play them against a different chord (even an implied one). This technique is a blues staple.

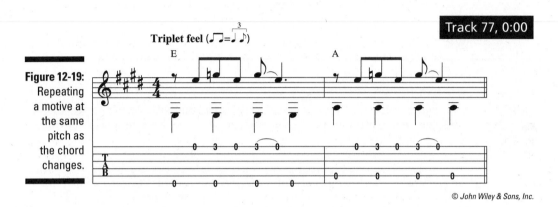

Track 77, 0:00

Figure 12-19: Repeating a motive at the same pitch as the chord changes.

© John Wiley & Sons, Inc.

✔ **Repeat a phrase *at a different pitch* as the background chord changes.** If you use this technique, the relationship between the melody and background chord stays the same. This type of repetition is shown in Figure 12-20. Barre the 5th fret to play the A chord in the second measure. (We cover barre chords in Chapter 9.)

Notice in Figure 12-20 that, for each chord, you use a hammer-on to move from the minor 3rd to the major 3rd. This technique is common in the acoustic-blues style. (See Chapter 10 to get the full scoop on hammer-ons.)

Track 77, 0:11

Figure 12-20: Moving a motive to a new pitch as the chord changes.

© John Wiley & Sons, Inc.

Eyeing specific techniques

You can use these two simple techniques, which we discuss in detail in the following sections, to give your acoustic blues playing more variety:

- ✔ Alternating the *texture* (that is, combining different musical patterns, such as playing one bar of rhythm and then a bar of lead) creates an unexpected, less homogeneous sound.

- ✔ Combining open strings with fretted ones creates some unusual results by enabling some notes to ring while others move melodically.

Alternating the texture

Alternation refers to the practice of playing the melody and bass parts one at a time, in an alternating fashion, instead of at the same time. Rather than having the thumb constantly play bass notes while the fingers simultaneously play melody notes, you can sometimes play just melody notes or just bass notes. This technique not only adds variety to the music's texture, but it also enables you (because *all* your fingers are available) to play some coolersounding, more-difficult, trickier licks that may otherwise be impossible.

Figure 12-21 shows a phrase that begins with only the melody (which you play in double-stops, a common acoustic blues technique) and ends with only bass (playing a boogie groove). You can see how the bass part — instead of playing merely quarter notes on the low roots — becomes more elaborate if you don't need to worry about melody notes. (See Chapter 8 for info about double-stops.)

Track 78, 0:00

Video Clip 62

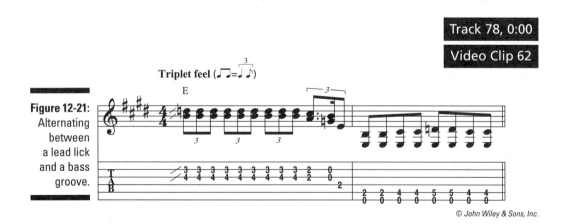

Figure 12-21: Alternating between a lead lick and a bass groove.

© John Wiley & Sons, Inc.

An effective and fancy little trick is to play an actual bass lick (that is, a bass *melody* instead of just a boogie figure) in an *alternation* scheme. The example in Figure 12-22 begins like that of Figure 12-21. That's the melody's turn in the

Track 78, 0:13

Figure 12-22: Alternating between a lead lick and a bass lick.

© John Wiley & Sons, Inc.

alternation scheme. Then, in bar 2, the bass part takes its turn, so you can go to town with an exciting bass lick. Typically, these bass licks use notes of the E pentatonic minor (or E blues) scale with some major 3rds (on the 4th fret of the 6th string) and major 6ths (on the 4th fret of the 5th string) thrown in.

Combining open strings with fretted strings

Another important acoustic-blues technique is alternating between an open string and a fretted note (on an adjacent string) that's the same pitch or a nearby pitch. You usually play this technique on the treble strings, but you can play it in the bass part as well.

In the example shown in Figure 12-23, you play the first high E on the 2nd string (a fretted note); next, you play the E on the 1st string (an open note), and then you play it back on the 2nd string again. The open E then recurs after you play some nearby notes on the 2nd string. Then, the same idea occurs with the Bs on the fretted 3rd and open 2nd strings. Measure 2 (with the bass part playing alone) illustrates the same idea in a bass-part setting. On beats 3 and 4, the open D on the 4th string alternates with the 5th-string D and nearby notes.

Track 78, 0:26

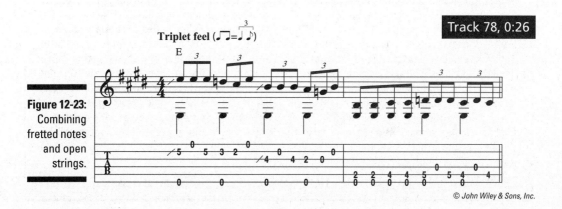

Figure 12-23: Combining fretted notes and open strings.

© John Wiley & Sons, Inc.

Turnarounds

In a typical acoustic blues solo, you play the 12-bar blues progression over and over; otherwise, your entire solo ends up very, very short. Ordinarily, as you get to the end (bars 11 and 12) each time through, you play a fancy little lick known as a *turnaround lick* that's designed to both punctuate the ending and set you up to go back (or turn around) to bar 1 again.

In a broad sense, if you're in the key of E, the turnaround puts you on some kind of B or B7 chord (because that chord best leads back to the E chord — the chord in bar 1 of the next time through). But if you simply play an E7 chord in bar 11 and a B7 in bar 12, you miss out on a world of musical delights, as the following examples demonstrate.

The power of slide guitar

Slide guitar is an important addition to blues-guitar technique. In playing slide, you don't use your left hand to fret the guitar by pressing the strings to the fretboard, as you normally do. Instead, you hold a metal or glass bar (the *slide*) over the neck and *stop* (shorten the vibrating length) the strings by pressing the slide lightly against the strings at a given fret. To play in tune, you must position the slide directly over the fret wire itself, not behind it as you do in normal fretting.

For the slides themselves, you can use anything from the neck of a wine bottle to a medicine bottle (the cough medicine Corrocidin made the ideal vessel and was a favorite of Duane Allman's) to a small length of brass pipe. The back edge of a knife works in a pinch, too. Today, specially made glass and brass slides, available in music stores, come in various diameters to accommodate different finger sizes. Most people usually wear the slide on the ring finger or pinkie, which leaves the other fingers free for fretting. The slide material itself determines the weight and tone, and whether you choose a heavier or lighter slide is a subjective matter.

Because the slide lays across the strings in a straight line, playing chords where the notes are on different frets becomes rather difficult. Many guitarists solve this problem by tuning the guitar to an open tuning, such as G or D. (See Chapter 11 for info on open tunings.) Many slide-blues greats used (or still use) open tunings. Robert Johnson played in open G; Duane Allman played in open D or E; Bonnie Raitt plays in open A; and Derek Trucks plays in open E.

The quality of lead guitar becomes sustained, expressive, and vocal-like if you play with a slide. Because the slide rides on top of the strings and doesn't use the frets for its pitches, the response is more like that of a violin or a voice, where the pitch change is smooth and continuous as opposed to the more "detached" sound that results from normal fretting. As you listen to the great slide artists, listen especially to their *phrasing.* That's the best way to appreciate slide guitar's emotional power — in the expressive execution of the melodic line.

Figure 12-24 shows four commonly played acoustic blues turnarounds. Notice that most turnarounds employ some kind of *chromatically moving* line (that is, one that's moving by half steps).

Figure 12-24: Four typical turnarounds in E.

© *John Wiley & Sons, Inc.*

If you feel pretty good about playing the figures in the "Getting to the Root of Acoustic Blues" section, you're ready to play the song "Mississippi Mud" in the following section. And don't be afraid to get your hands dirty!

Playing Blues Songs

B.B. King once said, "I have a right to sing the blues," and if you're ready to try playing a couple of authentic blues songs, you have that right, too! The two songs in this section employ many of the techniques we present throughout this chapter.

As you first attempt to play these pieces, don't try to rush the process. In blues, feel comes before technique, and the best way to develop a feel is to keep the tempo slow and manageable while you work your way up. Focus on your feel and let the technique catch up on its own. It always does — we promise.

Here is some special information about the songs to help you along:

- **Chicago Shuffle:** To play this song, you need to know how to play single-note blues lines (see the section "Blues lead guitar," earlier in this chapter); how to piece together separate blues moves into a cohesive whole (see the section "Making blues moves," earlier in this chapter); and how to boogie like your back ain't got no bone.

  The lead guitar in this piece uses several devices common to blues lead playing: short phrases with wide spaces between them, repetition, the blues scale, double-stops, and a turnaround at the end. (For more info on these techniques, see the earlier sections of this chapter.) The rhythm part (not notated here, except by chord names) is the same pattern that you use in the preceding Figure 12-3 (also not notated there, but you can hear it on the audio tracks). Notice that this particular progression includes a quick IV.

- **Mississippi Mud:** To play this song, you need to know how to play an independent bass line with the thumb working against a melody that you play with the fingers (see the section "Playing the melody and the accompaniment simultaneously," earlier in this chapter); how to alternate textures smoothly (see the section "Alternating the texture," also earlier in this chapter); how to play a turnaround; and how to get your mojo workin'.

  This song features many of the acoustics blues concepts covered throughout this chapter: E pentatonic minor scale in open position, steady bass notes, alternation (the bass plays alone in measure 2, for example), repetition of a lick at the same pitch even though the background chord changes (measure 5), fretted note/open string combination (measure 9), and a turnaround lick (measures 11 to 12).

Chicago Shuffle

Track 80

Video Clip 64

Mississippi Mud

Track 81

Video Clip 65

Chapter 13

Around the Campfire: Folk Guitar Basics

In This Chapter

▶ Practicing fingerstyle

▶ Introducing the capo

▶ Playing arpeggio, thumb-brush, Carter, and Travis styles

▶ Trying your hand at folk songs

▶ Access the audio tracks and video clips at www.dummies.com/go/guitar

*I*n terms of a guitar style, *folk* means a lot more today than just playing "Jimmy Crack Corn" around a campfire with a bunch of doleful cowboys and a cook named Stumpy wheezing on an out-of-tune harmonica. Although folk guitar did enjoy a humble beginning as a plaintive strumming style to accompany simple songs, it has since evolved as a popular music category all its own.

Folk guitar has progressed from cowboy ditties of the 19th century through Appalachian songs and ballads in the '30s and '40s, to the hits of early country artists such as Jimmie Rodgers, Hank Williams, and Johnny Cash, to the rockabilly of the late '50s. In the '60s, folk music enjoyed a popular revival, beginning with the Kingston Trio and continuing all the way through the heyday of Bob Dylan, Joan Baez, and Peter, Paul, and Mary. From there, folk guitar crossed over into the mainstream, via the sophisticated pop-folk stylings of John Denver, James Taylor, Joni Mitchell, and Crosby, Stills & Nash. In the 21st century, folk music and folk guitar continue to thrive in the music of such artists as Sam Beam (better known by his stage and recording name, Iron & Wine), California's Brett Dennen, and England's Kate Rusby.

In this chapter, we cover a wide range of approaches to playing folk guitar, including arpeggio, thumb-brush, and Carter and Travis styles. As well, we show you how to use the capo to change keys, create new sounds with open tunings, and play harmonics.

Playing Fingerstyle

Folk music favors *fingerstyle* playing (a style in which you pluck the strings with your right-hand fingers instead of a pick). Think of Peter, Paul, and Mary's "Puff the Magic Dragon," Bob Dylan's "Don't Think Twice, It's All Right," Arlo Guthrie's "Alice's Restaurant," and Fleetwood Mac's "Landslide," and you can hear the easy, rolling patterns that the fingers produce in the accompaniment.

You also hear fingerstyle in rock (the Beatles' "Blackbird," Kansas's "Dust in the Wind," the intro to Led Zeppelin's "Stairway to Heaven," and the intros to Metallica's "One" and "Nothing Else Matters"), country, and blues. And, of course, you play all classical guitar music fingerstyle (we cover classical guitar in Chapter 14).

Fingerstyle playing opens a world of musical possibilities that the pick simply can't deliver. For example, you can play two or more lines simultaneously while fingerpicking: Your right-hand thumb plays the bass line while the fingers play the melody and *inner voices* (filler or background notes on the middle strings, between the melody and bass) for an even fuller and more complex sound.

In the following sections, we describe the technique and right-hand position you use to play fingerstyle.

Fingerstyle technique

In fingerstyle guitar, you pluck the strings with the individual right-hand fingers instead of striking them with the pick. In most cases, you play the strings one at a time, in some form of repeated pattern, while your left hand holds down a chord. Typically, the thumb, plucking downward, plays the low (bass) strings, and the fingers, plucking upward, play the high strings (one finger per string).

After you strike each note, move your finger away so as not to rest against the adjacent string. This technique enables all the strings to ring out and produce chords instead of merely a succession of individual notes. In this way, you play the guitar much as you would a harp, except that playing this way on a guitar looks so much cooler than it does on a harp.

Right-hand position

As you play with the fingers, you want to rotate your right hand slightly so the fingers are more or less perpendicular to the strings. Figure 13-1 shows a before-and-after picture of the right hand in the normal, pick-holding position and then in a rotated, perpendicular placement better suited to fingerstyle playing. By keeping your right hand perpendicular to the strings, you meet them dead-on — as opposed to at an angle if you keep your hand unrotated and in line with the arm. (Incidentally, this position represents the same perpendicular approach that you use for playing classical guitar. See Chapter 14 for more info about right-hand position.)

a

Figure 13-1:
The right hand in pick position (a); the right hand in fingerstyle position (b).

b

Photographs courtesy of Cherry Lane Music

You can do what many guitarists do and grow your right-hand fingernails a little long so, as you pluck, you produce a brighter or louder sound. If you want a super-bright sound, use fingerpicks — plastic or metal devices that you actually wear on your thumb and fingers — or adhere acrylic nails to your own natural nails (a common procedure at any nail salon and an emergency measure that many classical guitarists use if they break a nail just before a concert).

Note: The music notation in this book indicates the right-hand fingers by the letters *p* (thumb), *i* (index), *m* (middle), and *a* (ring). This scheme comes from classical guitar notation. The letters *p, i, m,* and *a* are the first letters of the Spanish words for the fingers (classical guitar being very big in Spain): *pulgar* (thumb), *indice* (index), *medio* (middle), and *anular* (ring). Sometimes you see the English equivalents of *t, i, m,* and *r.* You don't ordinarily use the little finger of the right hand in fingerstyle playing.

Using a Capo

A *capo* is a device that clamps down across the fingerboard at a particular fret. Capos can operate by means of elastic, springs, or even threaded bolts, but they all serve the same purpose — they shorten the length of all the strings at the same time, creating, in effect, a new nut. All the "open" strings now play in higher pitches than they do without the capo.

How much higher? A half step for each fret. If you place the capo at the 3rd fret, for example, the open E strings become Gs (three half steps higher in pitch than E). All the strings become correspondingly higher in pitch as well — B becomes D; G becomes B♭; D becomes F; and A becomes C. (By the way, you can't play anything below the capo — only above it on the neck.)

To correctly set the capo, place it just *before* the 3rd fret (toward the tuning pegs), *not* directly over the 3rd metal fret wire. Figure 13-2 shows a capo set correctly on the guitar at the 3rd fret. See Chapter 17 for information on different kinds of capos.

Why should you use a capo?

> ✔ **A capo enables you to instantly change the key of a song.** Say you know how to play "Farmer in the Dell" in the key of C and only in the key of C. But you want to accompany a singer (maybe yourself) whose vocal range is better suited for singing "Farmer in the Dell" in the key of D.
>
> No problem. Put your capo at the 2nd fret and simply play the song in C as you normally do. The capo causes all the strings to sound two halfsteps higher than normal, and the music sounds in D! In fact, you can move the capo to any fret, sliding it up and down the neck, until you find the fret (key) that's perfect for your vocal range.

Figure 13-2:
A capo on
the guitar
neck. Notice
that the
capo sits
just before
the fret —
not directly
on top of it.

Photograph courtesy of Jon Chappell

Of course, if the notes and chords in the song you're playing have no open strings, you can simply change positions on the neck (using movable chords) to find the best key for singing. Use a capo only if the song requires the use of open strings.

✔ **A capo gives the guitar a brighter sound.** Just place a capo on the neck (especially high on the neck). The guitar will sound more like a mandolin (you know, that teardrop-shaped little stringed instrument that you hear gondoliers play in films set in Italy).

Capos can prove especially useful if you have two guitarists playing a song together. One can play the chords without a capo — in the key of C, for example. The other guitarist can play the chords in, say, the key of G with a capo at the 5th fret, sounding in C. The difference in *timbre* (that is, the tone color or the quality of the sound) between the two instruments creates a striking effect.

✔ **A capo allows you to move, to any key, certain open-string/fretted-string combinations that exist in only one key.** Some people refer to capos as "cheaters." They think that if you're a beginner who can play only in easy keys (A and D, for example), you need to "cheat" by using a capo to play in more difficult keys. After all, if you're worth your salt as a guitarist, you could play in, say, B♭ without a capo by using barre chords.

But in folk-guitar playing, the combination of open strings and fretted ones is the essence of the style. Sometimes these open-string/fretted-note combinations can become quite intricate.

Think, for example, of the introduction to "Fire and Rain," by James Taylor, which he fingers in the key of A. James plays it, however, by using a capo at the 3rd fret, causing the music to sound three half-steps higher, in C, because that key best fits his vocal range. So why not just play the song in C without a capo? Because the fingering makes that option impossible; the necessary open strings that James plays don't exist in C — only in A!

✔ **A capo "moves" the frets closer together as you go up the neck.** Playing with a capo requires less stretching in the left hand, making some songs a little easier to play.

Throughout this chapter, as you play the various exercises and songs, experiment with the capo. See how you can use a capo to find the best key for your vocal range. And even on the instrumental selections, experiment by placing the capo at various frets to see how that placement affects the timbre. You're sure to like what you hear.

Sometimes, engaging or disengaging a capo causes the strings to go out of tune. Be sure to check your tuning and make any necessary adjustments whenever you attach or remove the capo.

Aiming for Arpeggio Style

To play in *arpeggio* style (also known as *broken chord* style), hold down a chord with your left hand and play the notes one at a time, in succession, with your right, allowing the notes to ring out or sustain. This technique produces a lighter flowing sound to the music than you get by playing all the notes at once, as you do in strumming. In the following sections, we explain how to play the basic arpeggio style as well as the related "lullaby" pattern.

Playing arpeggio style

To play in arpeggio style, put your right-hand fingers on the strings in the basic fingerstyle position — thumb (*p*) against the 6th string, index finger (*i*) against the 3rd string, middle finger (*m*) against the 2nd string, and ring finger (*a*) against the 1st string. All the fingers are now ready to pluck. (See the earlier section "Right-hand position" for details.)

Even without actually fingering a left-hand chord (because all the strings you're plucking are open strings in an Em chord), you can still play an Em arpeggio by plucking first *p*, then *i*, then *m*, and finally *a*. You should hear a pretty Em chord ringing out.

Just so you know how this pattern looks in notation, see Figure 13-3, which shows you exactly how to play the open strings of an Em chord in arpeggio style.

Track 82, 0:00

Video Clip 66

Figure 13-3:
An open-
string Em
arpeggio.

© John Wiley & Sons, Inc.

Now try arpeggiating up (from low-pitched to high-pitched strings) and back down on the open Em chord. Again, use only the 6th, 3rd, 2nd, and 1st strings. Instead of playing just *p-i-m-a,* as before, play *p-i-m-a-m-i.* See the notation in Figure 13-4 to check that you're playing the correct notes.

Track 82, 0:07

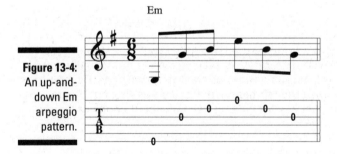

Figure 13-4:
An up-and-
down Em
arpeggio
pattern.

© John Wiley & Sons, Inc.

Next, try fingering the various chords in Chapters 4 and 6, and playing *p-i-m-a* or *p-i-m-a-m-i.* But for each new chord, make sure your thumb hits the correct bass string — the *root* of the chord (the 6th string for all the E and G chords, the 5th string for all the A and C chords, and the 4th string for all the D chords). (The *root* of a chord is simply the note from which the chord takes its name; for example, the root of a C chord is a C note.)

Many arpeggio patterns are possible because you can pluck the strings in lots of different orders. The *p-i-m-a* and the *p-i-m-a-m-i* patterns are two of the most common.

To play a song right now using the *p-i-m-a-m-i* arpeggio pattern, skip to the section "Playing Folk Songs," later in this chapter, and check out "House of the Rising Sun."

Picking out the "lullaby" pattern

Some guitarists refer to the accompaniment pattern shown in Figure 13-5 as the *lullaby* pattern because it's a pretty-sounding pattern suitable for playing accompaniments to lullabies.

Track 83, 0:00

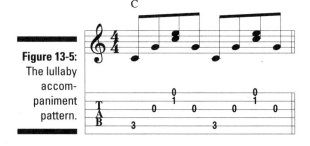

Figure 13-5: The lullaby accompaniment pattern.

© John Wiley & Sons, Inc.

This pattern incorporates a double-stop (two notes sounded at once; see Chapter 8) into an arpeggio pattern. After playing *p* and *i* individually, you play *m* and *a* together (at the same time) on the top two strings. Be sure to hold down each chord with the left hand while the notes ring out. Again, use a capo to find your best key for singing (we talk about capos earlier in this chapter).

To play a song right now using the lullaby pattern, skip to the section "Playing Folk Songs," later in this chapter, and check out "The Cruel War Is Raging."

Tackling the Thumb-Brush Technique

The *thumb-brush* technique is an accompaniment pattern that has a "boom-chick" sound. Here, the thumb plays normally (plucking a bass string down-ward), but the fingers strike (brush) the top three or four strings with the backs of the nails in a downward motion (toward the floor). The fingers actually strum the strings as a pick does, but you don't move your arm or your whole hand. Basically, you curl your fingers into your palm and then quickly extend them, changing from a closed-hand position to an open-hand position, striking the strings with the nails in the process.

Figure 13-6 shows two measures of the thumb-brush pattern on a C chord. Don't worry about hitting *exactly* three strings with the finger brush. Getting a smooth, flowing motion in the right hand is more important. Watch Video Clip 67 to see how the right-hand fingers brush the strings.

Track 83, 0:10

Video Clip 67

Figure 13-6:
A simple thumb-brush pattern on a C chord.

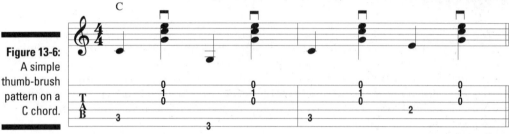

© John Wiley & Sons, Inc.

A variation of the simple thumb-brush is the *thumb-brush-up* (which yields a "boom-chick-y" sound). After strumming with the backs of the nails of the middle and ring fingers, you use the flesh of your index finger to pluck the 1st string (upward). You invariably perform this technique in an eighth-note rhythm on beats 2 and 4 (one, two-and, three, four-and). (See Appendix A for more info on eighth notes.)

Figure 13-7 shows a two-measure pattern, using the thumb-brush-up technique. Keep the downstrokes and upstrokes steady, with no break in the rhythm. (Make sure you listen to Track 84 for this one, and don't be discouraged if this pattern takes a little getting used to.)

Don't think of the upstroke with the finger as a fingerpicking move but as an upward brush with the whole hand. In other words, keep the right hand loose and flowing as you pull it upward to strike the 1st string with your 1st finger.

You can use the thumb-brush or thumb-brush-up pattern for any song that has a "boom-chick" or "boom-chick-y" sound, such as "Jingle Bells" or "I've Been Working on the Railroad."

Track 84, 0:00

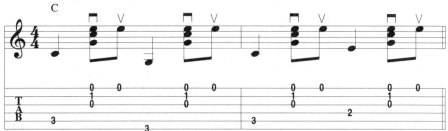

Figure 13-7:
The thumb-
brush-up
pattern on a
C chord.

© John Wiley & Sons, Inc.

Considering Carter Style

In *Carter style* (named after the famous Carter family, whose members included June Carter, "Mother" Maybelle, and "Uncle" A. P.), you play the melody on the low strings with the thumb while the fingers provide an accompaniment in the form of brushes. This style works well for songs with melody notes that fall mostly on beats 1 and 3. (The brushes occur on beats 2 and 4.) But if a melody note falls on beat 2 or 4, you can simply omit the brush on that beat.

You can play this style just as easily with a pick as you can with the fingers, so try it both ways and see which is more comfortable for you.

Figure 13-8 shows a passage that you can play by using Carter style, where the melody falls entirely on the lower strings. The melody comes from a traditional melody, called "Wildwood Flower," that the Carter family made famous. Woody Guthrie wrote his own lyrics and called it "The Sinking of the Ruben James."

Track 84, 0:09

Video Clip 68

Figure 13-8:
Carter style
puts the
melody in
the bass
and the
accompani-
ment in the
treble.

© John Wiley & Sons, Inc.

To play a song right now in Carter style, skip to the section "Playing Folk Songs," later in this chapter, and check out the tune "Gospel Ship."

Trying Travis Picking

Travis picking, named after country guitarist Merle Travis, is probably the most popular fingerstyle folk technique. Here, the thumb alternates between two (and sometimes three) bass strings in steady quarter notes while the fingers pluck the treble (higher) strings, usually between the quarter notes (on the off-beats). The result is a driving, rhythmic feel that you can use for a variety of settings from ragtime to blues, to the rolling 4/4 accompaniment pattern that you hear in Simon and Garfunkel's "The Boxer," Kansas's "Dust in the Wind," Garth Brooks's "Much Too Young (To Feel This Damn Old)," and Phish's "Dog Faced Boy."

This technique is more complex than the ones we discuss in the preceding sections, so we show you how to play it step by step in the following sections.

The basic pattern

You can create different Travis patterns by varying the timing you use to hit the treble strings. What remains the same is the steady rhythm that you play with the thumb. One pattern of treble strings is so popular that we're calling it the "basic Travis pattern." You can play it by following these steps:

1. **Start out by fingering a D chord with your left hand and holding the chord down throughout the measure.**

2. **Using only your thumb, alternate between plucking the 4th and 3rd strings in steady quarter notes, as shown in Figure 13-9a.**

   The thumb part is the foundation of the pattern. The standard notation marks the thumb part by using downstems (descending vertical lines attached to the note heads). Play this thumb part several times so it's rock steady.

3. **Now add the 2nd string to the pattern by plucking it with your index finger after beat 2 (between the thumb notes), as shown in Figure 13-9b.**

   Make sure the 2nd string continues to ring as your thumb hits the 4th string on beat 3. Play this partial pattern several times until it feels natural. Listen to Track 85 for the rhythm.

4. **Now add the 1st string to the pattern by plucking it with your middle finger after beat 3 (between the thumb notes), as shown in Figure 13-9c.**

   Play this partial pattern several times until it feels comfortable.

5. **Finally, add the 1st string (which you play by using the middle finger) to beat 1, playing the 4th string simultaneously with your thumb, as shown in Figure 13-9d.**

   In Travis picking, playing a treble string and bass string together is known as a *pinch*.

A variation of the basic pattern is sometimes called *the roll*. This pattern uses no pinches, and you pluck every off-beat, as shown in Figure 13-9e. Typically, you play the last off-beat only if you don't change chords as you go to the next measure. If you do change chords, leave out the last off-beat.

Track 85

Video Clip 69

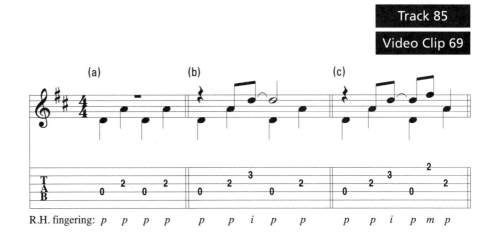

Figure 13-9:
Travis
picking, step
by step.

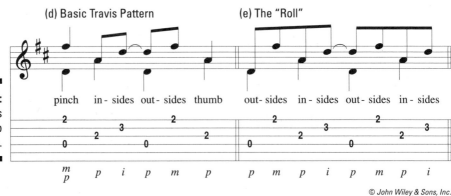

© John Wiley & Sons, Inc.

You can create other variations of the basic pattern by adding or omitting pinches and off-beats — but *never* omit the thumb notes. You can create these variations as you go, using them to break the monotony of one pattern that you otherwise repeat over and over.

For the basic Travis pattern, an easy way to remember which strings to hit and the order in which to hit them is to think of the four-note group of strings you pluck as a set of *outside strings* and a set of *inside strings.* On the D chord, for example, the 1st and 4th strings are "outside" and the 2nd and 3rd strings are "inside." Look at Figure 13-9d again. Say the following phrase as you play: "Pinch, insides, outsides, thumb." The following steps relate this phrase to the corresponding actions you take:

1. **Pinch:** On beat 1, play the outside strings (4th and 1st) as a pinch — the thumb striking the 4th string and the middle finger striking the 1st simultaneously.

2. **Insides:** On beat 2, play the inside strings (3rd and 2nd) one at a time — the thumb striking first and then the index finger.

3. **Outsides:** On beat 3, play the outside strings (4th and 1st) one at a time — the thumb striking first and then the middle finger.

4. **Thumb:** On beat 4, play just the thumb on the bass string of the inside set (the 3rd string).

Note that you don't normally use your ring finger when playing Travis patterns.

Accompaniment style

After you know the basic Travis pattern, you can create an entire accompaniment to a song by simply stringing together a series of chords and applying the appropriate pattern for each chord. You can play the pattern for any chord by memorizing the following information:

✔ Which group of four strings to play for each chord. (See the chart shown in Figure 13-10.)

✔ Which right-hand fingers to use on those strings. (The thumb and middle finger play the outside strings, and the thumb and index finger play the inside strings.)

✔ The phrase *pinch, insides, outsides, thumb.* By using this phrase (see the preceding section), you can play any pattern for any chord.

Figure 13-10 shows which four strings you can use for various chords and identifies the "inside" and "outside" strings for each group. Try the groups indicated for each chord, playing both the basic Travis pattern and the roll.

To play a song right now using Travis-style accompaniment, skip to the section "Playing Folk Songs," later in this chapter, and check out "All My Trials."

Solo style

You can use Travis picking to create exciting instrumental solos by placing the song's melody in the treble (as pinches or off-beats) while the bass — along with other, strategically placed off-beats — provides an accompaniment. In this solo style, you don't necessarily play strict four-string groupings (as you would in accompaniment style) — the melody pretty much dictates the groupings, which sometimes expand to five strings.

	Higher group	Lower group
4th-string root D, Dm, D7, 4-string F	insides ⎡①②③④⎤ outsides	
5th-string root C, C7, A, Am, A7, B7	insides ⎡①②③④⑤⎤ outsides	insides ⎡②③④⑤⎤ outsides
6th-string root E, Em, E7, G, G7	insides ⎡①②③④⑥⎤ outsides	insides ⎡②③④⑥⎤ outsides (not good for G7)

Figure 13-10: Inside and outside string pairs for various chords in Travis picking.

© John Wiley & Sons, Inc.

Figure 13-11 shows how a melody — in this case, "Oh, Susanna" — plays in a solo Travis-picking style. Notice that beats 1 and 2 in each full bar are pinches (the thumb and finger play the strings together), because both the melody and bass fall on these beats. Other melody notes fall on the off-beats, coming in between bass notes.

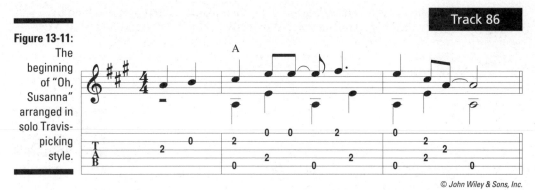

Figure 13-11:
The beginning of "Oh, Susanna" arranged in solo Travis-picking style.

© John Wiley & Sons, Inc.

To play a song using Travis solo style right now, skip to the section "Playing Folk Songs," later in this chapter, and check out "Freight Train."

Open tuning

You can create some interesting effects if you Travis pick in open tunings. Figure 13-12 is a passage in open-G tuning (D-G-D-G-B-D, low pitched to high) that sounds like something Joni Mitchell may have played on one of her early albums. The only unusual thing here is that you tune the guitar differently. Nothing in the right hand changes from a normal Travis pick. Video Clip 70 helps you orient your left hand on the neck as it descends through the different positions.

To get into open-G tuning, follow these steps:

1. **Drop your 6th string until it sounds an octave lower than the open 4th string.**

2. **Drop your 5th string until it sounds an octave lower than the open 3rd string.**

3. **Drop your 1st string until it sounds an octave higher than the open 4th string.**

Notice that in Figure 13-12, you use only one four-note grouping (5th, 4th, 3rd, and 2nd). The 5th and 3rd strings are open until the very end, when you play the barred twelfth-fret harmonics. Think "pinch, insides, outsides, thumb" throughout this example (see the earlier section "The basic pattern" for more about this phrase).

A *harmonic* is a pretty, high-pitched, bell-like tone that you produce by lightly touching a string (with the fleshy part of a left-hand finger) at a certain fret (usually the 12th, 7th, or 5th) directly over the metal fret wire rather than in front of it, as you would when fretting normally, and then striking the string.

Track 87

Video Clip 70

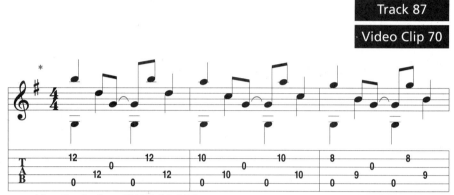

*Open G tuning (low to high): D G D G B D

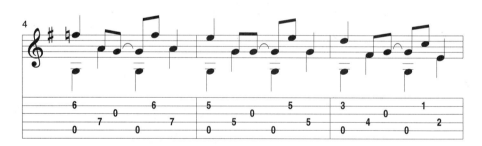

Figure 13-12: Travis picking in open-G tuning.

© John Wiley & Sons, Inc.

Playing Folk Songs

The range of songs that we present in this section runs the gamut from a simple accompaniment pattern that you repeat over and over to a solo-style treatment of a tune, with independent bass, superimposed melody on top, and a couple of tricks thrown in. In these five songs, you find just about every fingerpicking approach possible that's appropriate for songs in the folk vein. Don't let the simple nature of the songs themselves deceive you, however; the guitar parts here make them sound full and complete. After you get these arrangements down, all you need is the requisite flannel shirt and hiking boots, and you're on your way to a career in hoboing, labor organizing, and political protest.

Here is some information about the songs to help you along. Some of the songs employ a technique known as a *bass run*. This technique is a single-note line — played by the thumb — that leads to the next chord and serves to break up the monotony of a repeated pattern.

✔ **House of the Rising Sun:** To play "House of the Rising Sun," you need to know how to play an up-and-down arpeggio pattern (see the section "Playing arpeggio style," earlier in this chapter); how to finger basic major and minor chords (see Chapter 4); and how to make a song about a wasted life in a house of ill repute sound light and frothy.

The up-and-down arpeggio pattern *(p-i-m-a-m-i)* makes a nice accompaniment for "House of the Rising Sun" and other songs like it. Your left hand should hold down each chord for the entire measure. Think *broken chords* (where the notes ring out) and not *individual notes* (where the notes stop short). Notice that the fingers play only the top three strings for every chord in the song, even though the thumb changes strings from chord to chord.

✔ **The Cruel War Is Raging:** To play "The Cruel War Is Raging," you need to know how to play the lullaby pattern (which we describe earlier in the "Picking out the 'lullaby' pattern" section); how to finger basic major and minor chords (see Chapter 4); and how to coo a baby to sleep with a song about annihilation and destruction.

Be sure to hold down each chord with the left hand while the notes ring out. Use a capo to find your best key for singing (see the section "Using a capo" earlier in this chapter).

✔ **Gospel Ship:** To play "Gospel Ship," you need to know how to play a Carter-style solo (see the section "Considering Carter Style," earlier in this chapter); how to play hammer-ons and pull-offs (see Chapter 10); and whether any person on the planet actually knows the lyrics to this song.

Hammer-ons, pull-offs, and bass runs are an important part of Carter style, as you see in this arrangement, loosely based on the traditional song "Gospel Ship." The standard notation helps you determine which notes you play with the thumb (the ones with the stems going down) and which you play with the fingers (the ones with the stems going up). This song works equally well, however, if you use a pick. Try it both ways.

- **All My Trials:** To play "All My Trials," you need to know how to play a Travis-style accompaniment (see the section "Accompaniment style," earlier in this chapter); how to play hammer-ons (see Chapter 10); and how to convincingly sing a song about toil and hardship without sounding pretentious because you've led a life of relative ease and privilege.

  Measure 1 uses the lower string group for the G chord, because if you use the higher set, you end up with an incomplete chord. Because measure 2 has only two beats, you play only half the pattern in that measure. Measure 5 begins as if you're using the higher string set (to smoothly resolve the high note of the previous bar), but then on beat 2, it switches to the lower string set, again to avoid an incomplete chord. Measure 9 incorporates a little bass line into the pattern on the way from G to Em. In measure 12, a pinched hammer-on adds an extra-folky flavor.

- **Freight Train:** To play "Freight Train," you need to know how to play a Travis-style solo (see the section "Solo style," earlier in this chapter); how to play hammer-ons (see Chapter 10); and how to sound like a simple hobo while playing a sophisticated fingerpicking arrangement with four new techniques.

  A bass run breaks up the monotony in measures 4 and 8. In measure 9, you're fingering an E chord, and you can use your 1st finger, flattened into a barre, to play the 1st string, 1st fret. Use your left thumb, wrapped around the neck, to finger the 6th string in bars 11 and 12. Measure 14 features a fancy little trick — you hammer a treble note at the same time that you strike a bass note. In measure 15, the bass alternates among three notes, not two.

House of the Rising Sun

Track 88

Video Clip 71

The Cruel War Is Raging

Track 89

Video Clip 72

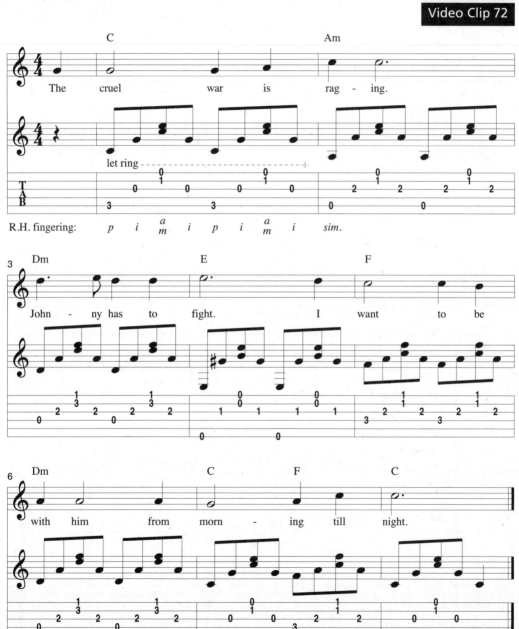

Gospel Ship

Track 90

Video Clip 73

All My Trials

Track 91

Video Clip 74

Freight Train

Track 92

Video Clip 75

Chapter 14

Maestro, If You Please: Classical Guitar Basics

In This Chapter

▶ Prepping to play classical guitar

▶ Getting the hang of free strokes and rest strokes

▶ Playing arpeggios and counterpoint

▶ Practicing classical pieces

▶ Access the audio tracks and video clips at www.dummies.com/go/guitar

Classical guitar not only suggests a certain musical style but also implies an approach to the instrument that's quite different from that of any other style, whether folk, jazz, rock, or blues. Classical guitar encompasses a long tradition of techniques and practices that composers and performers have observed through the ages and to which they still adhere, even with the advent of more modern and avant-garde musical compositions.

To play the great music of Bach, Mozart, and Beethoven — and to have it sound authentic — you *must* play it in the classical style. Even if you have no intention of becoming a serious classical guitarist, you can improve your tone, technique, and phrasing by practicing classical techniques.

Don't get the impression that, because it adheres to certain disciplines, classical music is all rigid rules and regulations. Many guitarists with careers in both the pop and classical fields feel that some aspects of classical guitar playing are liberating, and these rugged individualists have actually tried to infuse classical techniques into pop and rock playing. Steve Howe of Yes, Michael Hedges, and Chet Atkins have each appropriated classical techniques into their own inimitable styles. Still, we can't quite picture Metallica having the same headbanging effect if they were to perch on straight-backed chairs with left legs raised and wrists folded at right angles.

In this chapter, we get serious about classical guitar and present the correct sitting position and the proper right- and left-hand positions. In addition, we show you how to use rest strokes and free strokes to bring out a melody from within an arpeggio pattern and how to combine melodies to create counterpoint.

Getting Ready to Play Classical Guitar

You always play classical guitar on a nylon-string guitar (as opposed to the steel-string models used for many other styles), in a sitting position. Beyond that, you must employ certain right-hand *strokes* (methods of plucking the strings) to get the expected sound. In addition, you must adopt a new approach to left-hand positioning. We show you how to do all these things in the following sections.

Knowing how to sit

Real classical guitarists (that is, most real classical guitarists) sit differently from other guitarists in that they hold the guitar on the *left* leg instead of on the right one. They also elevate the left leg about six inches by using a footstool. If you perform this balancing act, you accomplish the following goals:

- ✔ You rest the guitar's treble side (the side closer to the higher-pitched strings) on the left leg, with the back of the instrument resting against your abdomen. The weight of your right arm on the bass side holds the instrument in place (balanced, so to speak). Your hands are thus completely free to play — and only play. You don't need to use your hands to keep the guitar from falling to the floor (unless you jump up suddenly to answer the phone).

- ✔ You position the guitar so the left hand can play any fret at the correct (perpendicular) angle — see the "Using the correct left-hand position" section later in this chapter. This angle allows you to play the higher positions (7th and up) more easily than you can in the steel-string acoustic sitting position (see Chapter 3).

The truth is, however, that a lot of people who attempt classical guitar simply don't even bother with all this stuff about how to hold the instrument. Why? Because it's too much trouble. Where would you even get a footstool? (Okay, you can get one at your local music store — maybe.) If you just want to try out a few classical-guitar pieces for the fun of it, hold the guitar as you normally do. The music police aren't likely to arrest you, and you can still hear the beautiful arrangement of the notes, even if you're not playing strictly "by the rules."

However, if you're really serious about playing classical guitar, buy a footstool and refer to Figure 14-1, which shows the correct sitting position. You can also use a special gizmo that pushes the guitar up from your leg, enabling you to keep both feet flat on the floor. These devices are gaining popularity because they don't create the uneven pull on your leg and back muscles that often results from elevating one leg and keeping the other flat. Oh, and if you want to pursue classical guitar, learn to read music (if you can't already), because lots of printed classical guitar music comes without tab. (To get started in music reading, see Appendix A. Also check out *Classical Guitar For Dummies,* written by yours truly and published by John Wiley & Sons, Inc.)

Figure 14-1: Sitting position for classical guitar.

Photograph courtesy of Jon Chappell

What's important is to make sure you sit upright and at the edge of the chair, elevating your left leg (or the guitar) and holding the instrument at the center of your body. Keep the head of the guitar (where the tuning pegs connect) at about the same height as your shoulder, as shown in Figure 14-1.

Figuring out what to do with the right hand

After posture, your right-hand approach is the most critical consideration for achieving a true classical guitar sound. You must play with your right hand in the correct position and execute the correct finger strokes.

Using the proper right-hand position

The most important concept about right-hand position is that you hold your fingers — index, middle, and ring — perpendicular to the strings as they strike. (You normally don't use the little finger in classical guitar.)

This positioning is no easy feat. Why? Because your hand, which is an extension of your arm, naturally falls at about a 60-degree angle to the strings. Try it. See? But if you hold your fingers at an angle, you can't get maximum volume from the strings. To get the strongest sound (which you need to do to bring out melodies from the bass and inner voices), you must strike the strings at a 90-degree angle — perpendicular.

Rotate your right hand at the wrist so the fingers fall perpendicular to the strings and your thumb stays about 1½ inches to the left (from your vantage point) of your index finger, as shown in Figure 14-2. Rest your right-hand thumb and fingers (index, middle, and ring) on the 6th, 3rd, 2nd, and 1st strings, respectively, as shown in the figure. This setup is the basic classical-guitar position for the right hand. Are your fingers perpendicular to the strings?

Figure 14-2:
Correct
right-hand
position.

Photograph courtesy of Jon Chappell

If you're serious about perfecting classical right-hand technique, here's a tip to force your fingers into the correct position: Place all four fingers (thumb, index, middle, and ring) on the *same string* (say, the 3rd), lining them up in a row. By positioning your fingers this way, your thumb can't rest to the right of your index finger. Then, without turning your hand, move each finger to its normal place: thumb to the 6th string, index staying on the 3rd, middle to the 2nd, and ring to the 1st. Refer to Figure 14-2 to make sure your thumb is in the correct position with respect to the fingers (to the side and not behind them).

Taking care of your fingernails

Your right-hand fingernails affect the tone of your playing. If your nails are very short, only the flesh of your finger hits the string, and the resulting tone is rather mellow and soft. Conversely, if your nails are very long, only the nail hits the string, and the tone is sharper and more metallic. Most classical guitarists grow their nails somewhat long so both the flesh and the nail hit the string at the same time, producing a pleasing, well-rounded tone.

Some guitarists own a special fingernail-care kit that contains scissors or clippers, nail files, emery boards, and fine abrasive cloths to enable them to keep their nails at a desired length, shape, and smoothness.

If you're serious about playing classical guitar, grow your nails a bit long and cut them so they're rounded, following the same contour as your fingertips. Then file or buff them with a nail file or emery board. Grow only the right-hand nails. You must keep the left-hand nails short so they don't hit the fretboard as you press down the strings, preventing the notes from sounding out correctly. But if you're playing classical guitar casually, for fun or just to try it out, don't worry about the length of your right-hand nails. Lots of people play classical guitar with short nails (and with the guitar set on their right leg, too!).

Changing tone color

You can alter the tone color of the strings by placing your right hand at different points along the string — closer to the bridge or closer to the fretboard or directly over the sound hole. If you play directly over the sound hole, the tone is full and rich. As you move toward the bridge, the tone becomes brighter and more metallic; and as you move toward the fretboard, the tone becomes more rounded and mellow.

Why do you need to change *timbre* (tone color)? Mostly for the sake of variety. If you're playing a piece with a section that repeats, you may play over the sound hole for the first pass and then on the repeat play closer to the bridge. Or maybe you're approaching the climax in a piece and you want to heighten the effect by playing with a brighter, more metallic sound. You can then play closer to the bridge.

Using the correct left-hand position

As you're fingering frets in the classical style, try to think of your left hand as a piece of machinery that you lock into one position — a position that you can characterize by right angles and perpendicularity (to achieve ease of playing and optimal sound). As you move up and down the neck or across the strings, the little machine never changes its appearance. You simply move it along the two directions of a grid — as you would an Etch-a-Sketch. Here's how the machine works:

- ✔ Keep your fingers rounded and arched so the tips come down to the fingerboard at a 90-degree angle and place them perpendicular to the strings.

- ✔ Straighten your thumb and keep it pretty much opposite the index finger as you lightly press it against the back of the guitar neck. As you move to higher frets, bring your thumb along, always keeping it opposite the index finger. You can move it across the neck as your fingers do, but don't ever allow it to creep above the fingerboard.

✔ Move your arm with your hand so your hand stays perpendicular to the strings. As you play the lower frets, keep your elbow out, away from your body. At the higher frets, bring your elbow in, closer to your body.

Theoretically, no matter what string or fret you play, your left hand position looks the same — as shown in Figure 14-3. Of course, special requirements of the music *could* force you to abandon the basic left-hand position from time to time. So think of the preceding guidelines as just that: guidelines.

Figure 14-3:
Correct
left-hand
position.

Photograph courtesy of Jon Chappell

If you've been playing other guitar styles (such as rock or blues) for a while, you probably often see your left thumb tip coming all the way around the neck, sticking out above the 6th string. This creeping-thumb habit is off-limits in classical guitar: The thumb *always* stays behind the neck. Fortunately, we have a good way to cure you of this habit (although you must be willing to suffer a little pain). Have a friend hold a sharp object (such as a pencil) while watching you play. Every time your thumb peeks out from behind the neck, have your friend lightly poke your thumb with the sharp object! This training method may hurt a bit, but after a few pokes, your thumb stays tucked away behind the neck, where it belongs. This method is how children in Charles Dickens' time learned correct left-hand technique.

Focusing on Free Strokes and Rest Strokes

If you had a golf or bowling coach, he'd probably lecture you on the importance of a good follow-through. Well, believe it or not, the same thing goes for plucking a guitar string. Your finger can follow through after plucking a string in one of two ways, giving you two kinds of strokes. One is the *free stroke,* which you use for arpeggios and fast scale passages. The other, the *rest stroke,* you use for accentuating melody notes. The thumb, however, virtually always plays free strokes, even when playing melodies. (Free strokes are used in both classical and folk playing; rest strokes are unique to classical guitar.) The following sections describe both strokes.

Playing free strokes

If you pluck a string at a slightly upward angle, your finger comes to rest in the air, above the next adjacent string. (Of course, it doesn't stay there for long, because you must return it to its normal starting position to pluck again.) This type of stroke, where your finger dangles *freely* in the air, is called a *free stroke.* Figure 14-4 shows you how to play a free stroke.

Figure 14-4: The free stroke. Notice that, after striking a string, the right-hand finger dangles in the air.

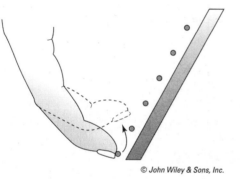

© *John Wiley & Sons, Inc.*

In classical guitar, you use free strokes for playing nonmelodic material, such as *arpeggios* (chords played one note at a time instead of all at once). Try arpeggiating the open strings (thumb on the 6th string, index finger on the 3rd, middle on the 2nd, and ring on the 1st), using all free strokes.

Figure 14-5 is an excerpt from a Spanish piece, "Malagueña," that just about every guitar player picks up at some time or other. You play the melody with the thumb while the middle finger plays free strokes on the open high-E string. Classical guitar notation indicates the right-hand fingers by the letters *p, i, m,* and *a,* which stand for the first letters of the Spanish names for the fingers: The thumb is *p (pulgar),* the index is *i (indice),* the middle is *m (media),* and the ring is *a (anular).* You also see these notations used in fingerstyle folk guitar (see Chapter 13 for details). View Video Clip 76 to see how the right-hand thumb brings out the melody.

Track 93, 0:00

Video Clip 76

Figure 14-5: A free-stroke exercise (from the classical piece "Malagueña").

© John Wiley & Sons, Inc.

Playing rest strokes

REMEMBER

The *rest stroke* uses a different kind of follow-through from the free stroke. Instead of striking the string at a slightly upward angle, pluck straight across (not upward) so your finger lands, or *rests,* against the adjacent lower-pitched string. By coming straight across the string (instead of coming across at an upward angle), you get the maximum sound out of the string. That's why rest strokes are good for melody notes; the melody notes are the prominent ones — the ones that you want to accentuate. Figure 14-6 shows how to play a rest stroke.

Use rest strokes to accentuate melody notes in a classical piece that includes inner voices — filler or background notes on the middle strings (played with free strokes) — and bass notes.

PLAY THIS!

Play the two-octave C major scale shown in Figure 14-7 *slowly,* using all rest strokes. Change from 2nd to 5th position at the end of measure 1 by smoothly gliding your 1st finger along the 3rd string, up to the 5th fret. (See Chapter 7 for info on playing in position.) On the way down, shift back to 2nd position by smoothly gliding your 3rd finger along the 3rd string, down to the 4th fret. Alternate between *i* (index finger) and *m* (middle finger) as you go. Video Clip 77 shows how your alternating index and middle fingers should look.

For the sake of speed and accuracy, alternating between two right-hand fingers (usually *i* and *m*) is customary for playing classical-guitar melodies.

Figure 14-6:
The rest stroke. Notice that, after striking a string, the right-hand finger rests against the next string.

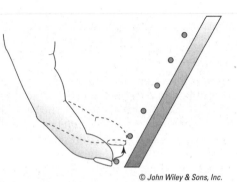

© John Wiley & Sons, Inc.

Video Clip 77

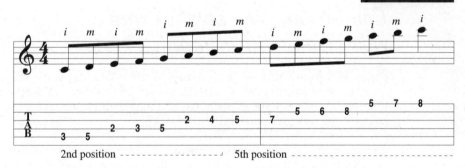

Figure 14-7:
The C-major scale with rest strokes, using alternating fingers.

© John Wiley & Sons, Inc.

Surveying Arpeggio Style and Contrapuntal Style

You play most classical guitar pieces in either an arpeggio style or a contrapuntal style, which we discuss in detail in the following sections.

- ✔ In *arpeggio* style, you hold chords with the left hand while plucking the strings in succession with your right hand (so each string rings out and sustains). Usually, you simultaneously play a melody on the top strings (using rest strokes) over the arpeggios.

- ✔ *Contrapuntal* classical guitar music usually has two parts — a bass part that you play with the thumb, and a treble part (the melody) that you play (usually by using free strokes) with alternating fingers (for example, *i* and *m*). The word *contrapuntal* refers to the *counterpoint* style, where you play two or more melodies (usually with different or contrasting rhythms) simultaneously — sort of like what you get if two people with opposing ideas talk at the same time. In music, however, the separate lines support rather than negate each other. Imagine if political debates had that effect!

Combining free strokes and rest strokes in arpeggios

Figure 14-8 shows an exercise in arpeggio style. You play the first note of each measure and the notes with stems that point down in the standard notation with the thumb; the other notes you play with the fingers (*i* on the 3rd string, *m* on the 2nd, and *a* on the 1st).

The notes you play on the 1st string have an *accent mark* (>) over them in standard notation. Accent marks tell you to *accentuate* (or stress) certain notes by playing them louder to bring them to the fore. In other words, use the more powerful rest stroke for accented notes and free strokes for all other notes. The *sim.* means to keep playing the same fingering pattern throughout the exercise.

Be sure to hold down all the notes of each measure simultaneously with the left hand, for the duration of the measure.

Before combining rest strokes and free strokes, play Figure 14-8, using all free strokes to get the feel of the piece. After you're comfortable with it, add the rest strokes to the notes on the 1st string.

© John Wiley & Sons, Inc.

Figure 14-8: An arpeggio exercise combining free strokes and rest strokes.

Trying a contrapuntal exercise

Figure 14-9 is an excerpt from a composition by an unknown composer of the Baroque era — an era during which contrapuntal music was very popular. Play the downstem notes (in the standard notation) by using the thumb. Use alternating fingers (free strokes) to play the melody. Check out Video Clip 78 to get the hang of playing two independent lines simultaneously.

The piece doesn't indicate any particular right-hand fingering. As long as you apply the concept of alternating fingers (even loosely) to attain speed and

Track 93, 0:48

Video Clip 78

Figure 14-9:
A contra-
puntal
exercise.

© John Wiley & Sons, Inc.

accuracy, you can use whatever fingering feels most comfortable to you. No single way is really right or wrong.

We do indicate the left-hand fingering, however, because this particular fingering is the only one that's feasible for this piece. The slanted line in front of the 2 on the second beat of measure 3 and the third beat of measure 5 indicates that you're using the same finger you used to play the previous note.

Practice by playing only the top part with the (alternating) fingers a few times. Then play the bass line alone with the thumb a few times. Then play both parts simultaneously. Listen to Track 93 to help you with the rhythm.

Playing Classical Pieces

Playing classical guitar pieces is never a hassle because you don't need to sing and you don't need an amplifier. You can do it any time, any place (as long as you have a nylon-string guitar).

Standard classical guitar notation uses some special symbols for indicating barre chords (see Chapter 9 for the scoop on barre chords). The symbol *C* with a Roman numeral after it indicates a barre across all six strings. (The Roman numeral tells you which fret to barre.) A *C* with a line (|) through it indicates a partial barre (fewer than six strings). And a dotted horizontal line to the right of the *C* tells you how long to hold down the barre.

The songs you play in this chapter are ones that all classical players meet at one time or another. They're great if you want a life full of Romanza that's always exciting and never Bourrée.

- **Romanza:** To play "Romanza," you need to know how to play free strokes and rest strokes (see the section "Focusing on Free Strokes and Rest Strokes," earlier in this chapter); how to barre chords (check out Chapter 9); and how to roll your *r*'s while saying "Romanza" (to sound truly continental).

  "Romanza" is a simple arpeggiated piece that gives you an opportunity to accentuate the melody notes with rest strokes (all of which you play on the 1st string with the *a* finger). For practice, you can play the piece by using all free stokes, adding the rest strokes later. Use the thumb to play all the bass notes (downstems in the standard notation). Use the right-hand fingering that we give you in the first measure throughout the piece. In measures 9 through 10, make sure you keep your 1st finger barred at the 7th fret with your 2nd finger pressing down at the 8th fret (3rd string) *the whole time*. Stretch your little finger up to the 11th fret for the first beat of measure 10. Note that this is reflected in the left-hand fingering indications.

- **Bourrée in E minor:** To play "Bourrée in E minor," you need to know how to play a melody by using alternating fingers while playing a bass line with the thumb (see the section "Trying a contrapuntal exercise," earlier in this chapter); how to barre chords (see Chapter 9); and how to pronounce and spell *bourrée*.

  A bourrée is a dance people did a couple hundred years ago (just slightly before the advent of the "funky chicken"). This contrapuntual piece is an excerpt that's loads of fun to play because it sounds beautiful and intricate, but it's actually rather simple to play. Leo Kottke plays a fingerstyle version of it, and Jethro Tull did a jazz arrangement of it. Play all the bass notes (downstems in the standard notation) by using the thumb. Alternate fingers (for example, *m-i-m-i* and so on) with the right hand. The alternation doesn't need to be strict. Use what feels the most comfortable to you. We indicate some left-hand fingerings at the very beginning to get you going. After that, use whatever fingering feels natural.

For inspiration, listen to recordings of this piece by classical guitarist John Williams, as well as the folk version by Kottke and the swing-jazz version by Jethro Tull. Heavy metal guitarist Yngwie (pronounce *ing-vay*) Malmsteen even does a version with ear-splitting stun-gun distortion. Although J. S. Bach never imagined all these wacky settings for his unprepossessing little dance suite segment, they all sound great.

Romanza

Track 94

Video Clip 79

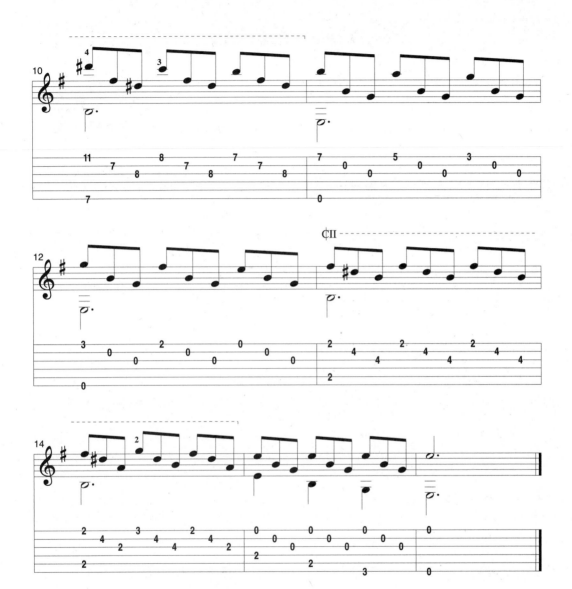

Bourrée in E minor

Track 95

Video Clip 80

Moderately

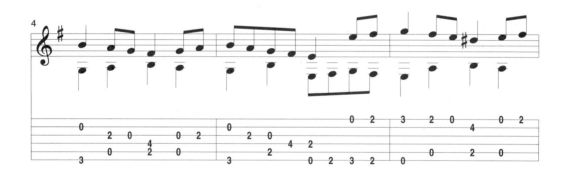

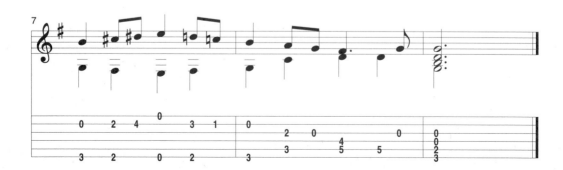

Chapter 15

Sunglasses and Berets: Jazz Guitar Basics

. . . .

. . . .

*J*azz is a form of music that instrumentalists created when they began taking liberties with existing song forms, improvising off composed melodies, and varying harmonic structures. Guitarists followed the early efforts of other instrumentalists like the great trumpeter Louis Armstrong, who was one of the first early masters of melodic improvisation.

Jazz guitar can be difficult to master because *improvisation* (making up music on the spot) is such an important part of the style. Normally, making up the music is the job of the composer. But in jazz, the performers are (usually) expected to improvise — and to do that well, you need to know far more than what you can learn in one chapter of a *For Dummies* book! But fret not. We show you some simple things to make you *sound* like a jazz guitarist, which will help get you on your way.

In this chapter, we put on our shades and help you get hip to jazz chords, jazz progressions, chord-melody style, chord substitutions, and single-note lead playing. We also show you the difference between inside and outside chords, and how to jazz up a melody.

Introducing a Whole New Harmony

Jazz guitar differs from rock and blues guitar most significantly in the following ways:

- ✔ Jazz guitar doesn't use distortion, favoring a softer, mellower tone.

- ✔ Jazz melodies are more harmonically sophisticated, observing more closely the chord constructions — which are themselves more complex.

- ✔ Jazz lines often employ more *skips* (musical distances of more than a step — for example, A to C) than rock or blues lines do.

A jazz guitarist's approach to chords is deeper than a rock or blues player's. In rock and blues, guitarists typically use one scale to play over all the chords, but in jazz, they may use many scales. They also must be aware of the notes that make up each chord, as arpeggiating, or playing chord tones in succession, is a hallmark of the jazz sound.

Most of the music you hear — pop, rock, blues, folk, and classical (especially classical music from the 17th and 18th centuries, like that of Bach and Mozart) — relies on traditional harmony (basic chords and progressions, like those found in Chapters 4 through 14). But jazz harmony uses what most people call (big surprise) jazz chords. *Jazz chords* often contain more notes than basic chords, or sometimes they can have the same number of notes as basic chords, but one or more of their notes is chromatically altered (raised or lowered a half step). We discuss both extended chords and altered chords in the following sections.

Extended chords

Simple major and minor chords are made up of only three notes — the 1st, 3rd, and 5th degrees of the major or minor scale whose starting note is the same as the chord's root. (For more on scale degrees and building chords, see Chapter 11.) These chords are called triads (three notes). Seventh chords are made up of four notes — the 1st, 3rd, 5th, and 7th degrees of the chord's namesake scale.

In jazz, you find chords made up of five or more notes. By continuing to take every other scale degree, you can go beyond the 7th to create 9th chords (using the 1st, 3rd, 5th, 7th, and 9th degrees), 11th chords (1st, 3rd, 5th, 7th, 9th, and 11th), and 13th chords (1st, 3rd, 5th, 7th, 9th, 11th, and 13th). These chords that include notes beyond the 7th are called *extended chords*.

Usually, not all the members of an extended chord are actually played. For example, in a 13th chord, you may play only four or five of the seven notes, so it's possible to play a 13th chord by using only four strings.

Altered chords

Jazz chords often contain notes that are altered (raised or lowered a half step). These alterations produce all sorts of funny-sounding chord names, like C7♭9, B♭13♯11, and G7♯5. And each of these jazz chords — and dozens of them exist — has a unique sound.

In playing jazz versions of popular songs, altered chords are usually substituted for more traditional chords — but knowing which chord to substitute, and when, is no easy feat and requires the skill of an accomplished jazz musician. (For more details, see the section "Making substitutions," later in this chapter.) Also, turn to the "Playing Jazz Songs" section later in this chapter to see some typical chord substitutions.

Supporting the Melody: Rhythm Comping

Comping is the term jazz players use when referring to playing the background or accompaniment. For the guitarist, comping translates into rhythm guitar — playing the chords. Jazz guitarists generally employ inside chords, outside chords, and full chords, which we explain in the following sections.

Inside chords

Inside chords are chords that don't use the 1st (high E) string. They're usually four-note chords played on the 2nd, 3rd, 4th, and either 5th or 6th strings. Jazz guitarists love to play inside chords — and they have a lot to choose from.

Inside voicings

Figure 15-1 shows 15 typical inside jazz-chord voicings. *Voicing* is the particular arrangement of notes in a chord chosen over another arrangement to suit a musical purpose or situation. Each chord in Figure 15-1 is movable and is shown at the lowest possible position on the neck. To produce other chords of the same type, just move the chord one fret for each half step. For example, the first chord shown is B7♯9. To play C7♯9, move the chord up one fret.

Some of the chord names may look strange. Here's how to pronounce the first three, left to right along the top row (after that you should have the hang of it): "B seven sharp nine," "B seven flat nine," and "F sharp six nine." A little circle in a chord name (°) stands for diminished (which usually tells you to lower the 5th a half step). The next-to-last chord (in the bottom line) is pronounced "F sharp diminished seven."

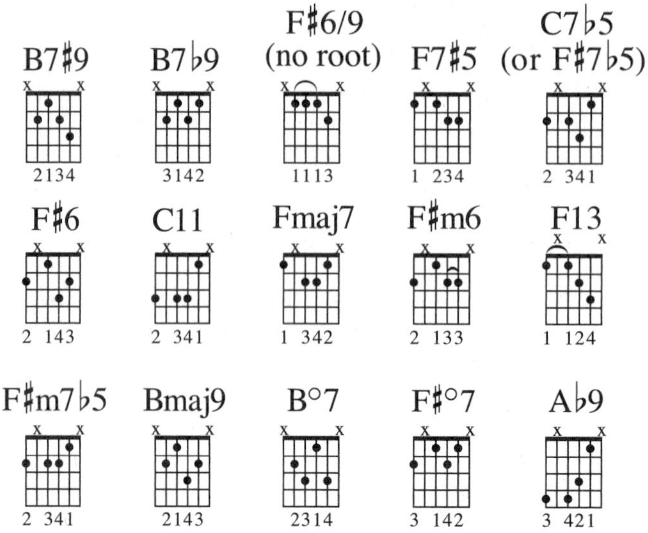

B7#9   B7b9   F#6/9 (no root)   F7#5   C7b5 (or F#7b5)

2134   3142   1113   1 234   2 341

F#6   C11   Fmaj7   F#m6   F13

2 143   2 341   1 342   2 133   1 124

Figure 15-1:
Various inside jazz chord voicings.

F#m7b5   Bmaj9   B°7   F#°7   Ab9

2 341   2143   2314   3 142   3 421

© John Wiley & Sons, Inc.

If you do nothing more than strum some of these chords, you sound jazzy right away. Actually, jazz players especially like to finger these chords around the middle of the neck, or slightly above it (usually between, say, the 4th and 11th frets). Try strumming them there.

Inside moves

Jazz guitarists like to exercise good voice leading; that is, they like their chord changes to sound smooth and economical. Often in jazz progressions, the only difference between one chord and the next is that one of the notes has moved a fret or two (see Figures 15-2 and 15-4). This economy of movement makes the music easier to play and, at the same time, makes the music sound pleasing.

Figure 15-2 shows three typical moves (progressions) consisting of inside chords that jazz players use. Play each chord once, and then play the next chord — you sound just like a jazz player. Try the progressions at different frets — these moves are movable!

Outside chords

Outside chord is a term used for a chord, especially a jazz chord, that uses only the top four strings — the low E and A strings get the night off. With outside chords, you often don't have the *root* (the note the chord is named after) on the bottom, or you don't include a root at all.

Track 96, 0:00

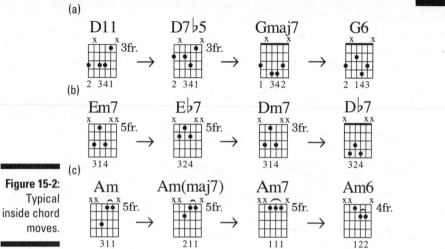

Figure 15-2:
Typical inside chord moves.

© John Wiley & Sons, Inc.

Outside voicings

Figure 15-3 shows 11 typical outside jazz chord voicings. Again, each is shown at the lowest possible position on the neck, and each is movable. Try playing them somewhere between the 4th and 11th frets, where jazz guitarists most like to play these chords.

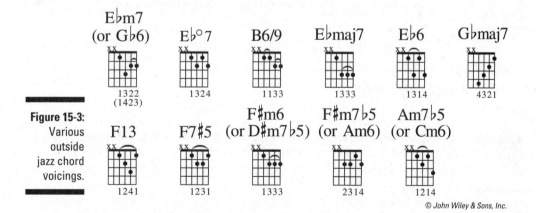

Figure 15-3:
Various outside jazz chord voicings.

© John Wiley & Sons, Inc.

Outside moves

As with the inside moves that we describe earlier in this chapter, the outside moves in Figure 15-4 display the principle of good voice leading, which is so important in jazz guitar. The last move, Figure 15-4c, looks like a bit of an exception because you must jump around the neck, but this move is actually pretty common. You can take the diminished-7th chord shape and move it up or down three frets without changing the chord (you're changing the *voicing*, or order of the notes, but you're still playing the same four notes). When jazz guitarists play a diminished 7th chord, they often move it up the neck in this fashion for the sake of variety or to provide a sense of movement.

Track 96, 0:17

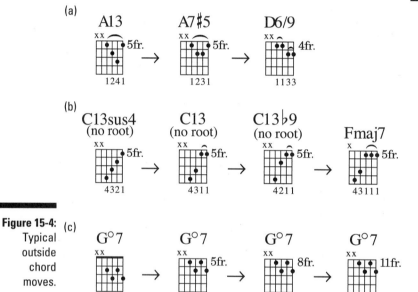

Figure 15-4: Typical outside chord moves.

© John Wiley & Sons, Inc.

Full chords

Not all jazz chords are limited to four-note inside or outside chords. Figure 15-5 shows five different full jazz chords (chords that use five or six strings) that can be played at any fret (but shown here at the lowest possible position).

Figure 15-5: Various full-chord jazz guitar voicings.

B9 B13 B9♭5 F♯m6 D♭maj7
21333 21334 21341 2 1333 43111

© John Wiley & Sons, Inc.

Playing Solo: Chord-Melody Style

Chord-melody style, as its name implies, is a jazz solo style that incorporates both the melody and chords of a song. You can hear this style of playing in the music of such jazz greats as Johnny Smith, Jim Hall, and Joe Pass. Chord-melody style often involves jazzing up an existing non-jazz song. Although the melody of the song is usually played straight (as composed), the performer changes the chords from traditional ones to jazz versions. These jazz chords, when they take the place of straight chords, are called substitutions.

Although playing a written-out chord-melody solo isn't especially difficult, creating one yourself (which is what jazz guitarists do) is no easy task. For starters, you need to know how to harmonize (put chords underneath) a melody; then you need to know how to apply chord substitutions. These skills go beyond merely playing the guitar — they enter the realm of composing and arranging. That's why we're not going to show you how to do it.

In the following sections, we give you an idea of what's involved and then show you an easy way to cheat, so you *sound* like you're creating a chord-melody solo. Then in the "Playing Jazz Songs" section of this chapter, you can play "Greensleeves" as a chord-melody arrangement by reading the tab.

Making substitutions

Substitutions are jazzy chords that you use in place of straight chords. These chords come in one of two general forms:

- ✔ **Same root:** Sometimes you substitute a chord with the same root but use an extended version or chromatic alteration (see the "Introducing a Whole New Harmony" section, earlier in this chapter). For example, if the chord progression of the song starts with C and goes to A7, you may substitute Cmaj7 and A7♭9, just to make it sound jazzy.

- ✔ **Different root:** Other times, you can substitute chords that don't even have the same root. Instead, the substitute chord may have other notes in common with the original. Taking the same example, instead of playing C and A7, you may play something like C6/9 and E♭7, because A7 and E♭7 have two notes in common (C♯/D♭ and G).

Anyway, you can make countless possible chord substitutions, and it can take years of playing jazz to develop an intuitive feel for knowing which chords can substitute where.

Faking it with three chords

Instead of learning hundreds of substitutions, try faking a chord-melody solo by using three simple chords. Look again at the first three movable chord shapes in Figure 15-3: the outside voicings for m7, °7, and 6/9. Because these chords have a somewhat ambiguous sound, they usually won't sound wrong no matter where you play them or what order you put them in; they just sound jazzy.

You can stick with one chord for a while, moving it to different frets — sliding up or down one fret at a time sounds cool. Or you can switch freely among the chords, playing them at various frets. Make up the rhythm as you go. If you like, you can use Figure 15-6 to get started and to see an example of what we're talking about. Check out Video Clip 81 to get a feel for the appropriately loose and easygoing approach. Have fun with it!

Track 96, 0:40

Video Clip 81

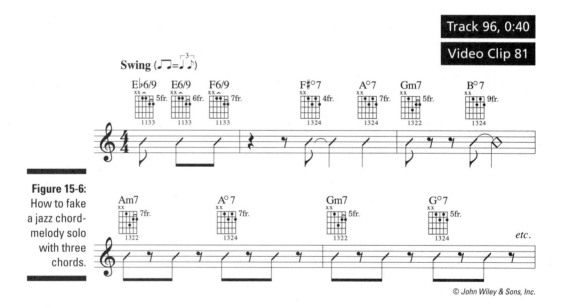

Figure 15-6:
How to fake a jazz chord-melody solo with three chords.

© John Wiley & Sons, Inc.

Taking the Lead: Jazz Melody

Playing lead in jazz is very similar in approach to playing lead in blues or rock. You play mostly single-note melodies — either composed or improvised — and licks (short passages idiomatic to the style). You don't have to vary your technique much either; play the notes with a pick, in alternate-picking fashion (see Chapter 5). What does change is the feel and the approach to the melodies. Vocabulary, phrasing, and tone separate jazz lead playing from other guitar styles.

You can create a jazz melody or make your lead playing sound jazzier by applying a few simple principles. The following three techniques can have you sounding like a jazz icon in no time.

Introducing altered tones

One thing jazz does is introduce chromatically altered tones, or tones not within the key. In blues, the notes are added sparingly; in jazz, any tone can be altered and included in the improvised melody. As long as an altered note is resolved (brought to a logical conclusion via an "in the key" melody note or a *chord tone*), any note is fair game.

Figure 15-7 shows a melody played two ways: first in the straight, composed way and then with chromatically altered tones added. Notice that this figure is in a triplet feel, also called swing feel. Many jazz pieces are played with a swing feel. (For more information on the triplet feel, see Chapter 12.) View Video Clip 82 to see how your left hand must shift down to 4th position to play the slide in bar 2 of the altered-tone version.

Track 96, 0:52

Video Clip 82

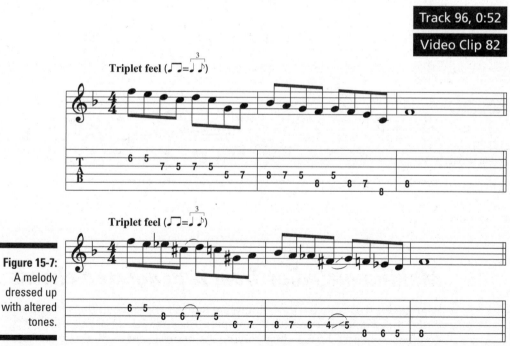

Figure 15-7:
A melody dressed up with altered tones.

© John Wiley & Sons, Inc.

Approaching target notes

Part of jazz's loose and liquid quality results from the way you sometimes approach a principal (or target) melody note from one fret above or below. In doing so, you add spice and variety to your playing.

Figure 15-8 shows a melody played two ways: in its straight context and then with principal melody notes approached from a fret above or below (arrows indicate principal notes). Video Clip 83 shows how the left hand goes to 4th position in the first two bars of the altered version to incorporate the altered and target notes effectively.

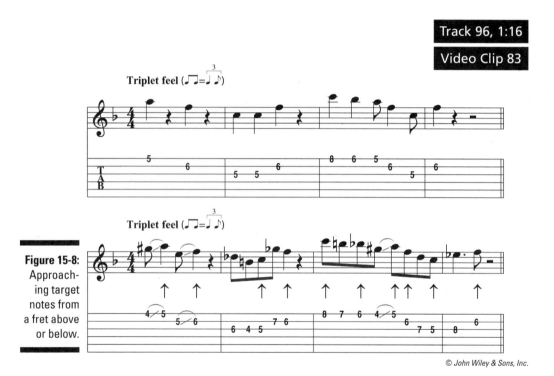

Track 96, 1:16

Video Clip 83

Figure 15-8: Approaching target notes from a fret above or below.

© John Wiley & Sons, Inc.

Making melodies from arpeggiated chords

Sometimes, to produce a jazzy-sounding line, all you have to do is play the chord tones contained in the rhythm part. Because jazz chords are often complex — like a C7♭9♯5 — just playing the chord tones as an arpeggio (one at a time, in succession) creates instant jazz (see Figure 15-9). In general, though, good jazz playing incorporates a healthy mix of arpeggios and linear (stepwise) playing. Check out both the right-hand and left-hand movements in Video Clip 84 to see how to play arpeggios smoothly.

Track 96, 1:43

Video Clip 84

Figure 15-9: Playing a melody as arpeggiated chord tones.

© John Wiley & Sons, Inc.

Playing Jazz Songs

In the songs that follow, you find a wide range of jazz techniques: extended chords, altered chords, inside and outside chords, chord substitutions, altered tones, and melodies formed from arpeggiated chord tones.

You can play "Greensleeves" either with a pick or fingerstyle. Play "Swing Thing" with a pick (both the chords and the melody). Here are some hints that will help you understand and play the songs:

- ✔ **Greensleeves:** We treat this old English folksong to a chord-melody solo arrangement. The straight chords for this song are Em, D, C, B, and so on, but here, as is typical in a jazz chord-melody arrangement, we've used jazzy chord substitutions. To play this song, you need to know how to play jazz chord forms, how to combine single-note melody with chords (see the earlier section "Playing Solo: Chord-Melody Style"), and how to look cool while playing a 16th-century folksong.

  Work on smoothly blending the single melody notes with the chord-supported melody notes. When playing the chords, be sure to bring out the top note by plucking it slightly harder or rolling the chord (arpeggiating it) slightly so the melody voice stands out.

- ✔ **Swing Thing:** This song employs some typical jazz moves in both the rhythm and lead. To play this piece, you need to know how to play inside chord forms (see the "Inside chords" section, earlier in this chapter), how to play single-line eighth notes up the neck (see Chapter 7), and how to bop till you drop.

  The progression begins with a typical comping figure in F. The lead part follows a II-V-I-VI progression (Gm7-C7-F-D7), over which a series of variations are written. Note the arpeggio pattern in the first half of bar 6, which is followed by a triplet of chromatically altered tones. These are two examples of typical jazz techniques discussed in this chapter. See how many more you can find.

Greensleeves

Track 97

Video Clip 85

Swing Thing

Track 98

Video Clip 86

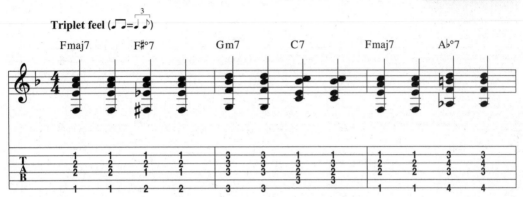

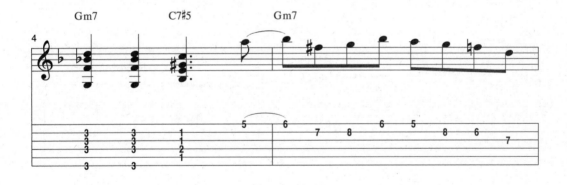

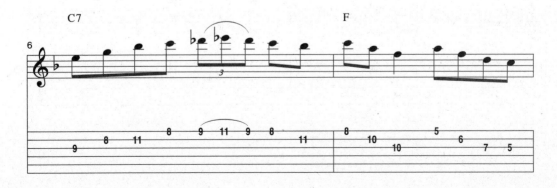

Swing Thing (continued)

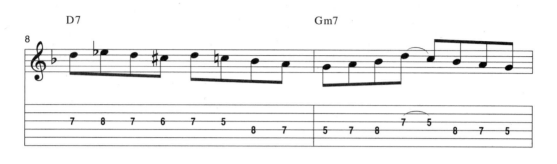

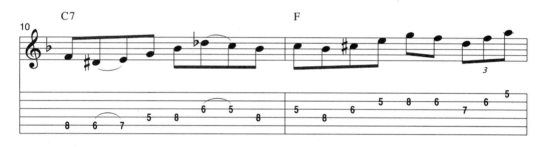

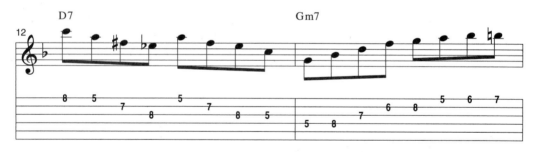

Part V
A Guitar of Your Own

Top five ways to maintain your guitar

- ✔ Cleaning your guitar's hardware and surfaces is the best hedge against wear and tear and corrosion and is essential for keeping your guitar in good shape.

- ✔ Tightening loose parts ensures your guitar plays buzz- and rattle-free.

- ✔ Adjusting the neck keeps playability manageable and the intonation true.

- ✔ Adjusting the bridge is sometimes necessary after adjusting the neck or changing string gauges.

- ✔ Replacing worn parts involves everything from swapping out cracked tuning machine buttons to stripped strap button screws so that your guitar remains happy, healthy, and safe.

For an in-depth discussion of four essential guitar effects, go to www.dummies.com/extras/guitar.

In this part . . .

✔ Avoid rookie mistakes and keep the hassle to a minimum when buying your first guitar.

✔ Match music styles to guitar models to best decide on the guitar for your particular taste.

✔ Complete your setup and enhance your sound with amps, effects, cases, and accessories.

✔ Know how to change your strings so that you always play in tune and with good tone.

✔ Protect and preserve your instrument so that it remains in tip-top playing condition.

Chapter 16

Shopping for a Guitar

*B*uying a new guitar is an exciting proposition. You go to the music store and immediately face a world of possibilities, a supermarket of tantalizing choices. Every guitar on the wall seems to scream, "Pick me! Pick me!" Should you resist, exercise restraint, and avoid the models you know you can't afford?

Heck no. Be bold and just try any model that strikes your fancy. After all, you're not asking to test drive the Ferrari appearing in the showroom window; you're simply asking the salesperson to see how different guitars feel and sound. And you're not being frivolous, either. Playing a range of guitars helps you understand the differences between high-quality, expensive guitars and acceptable but affordable guitars.

So indulge yourself. Even if you think you may not have enough experience to recognize the subtle distinctions between a good guitar and a great guitar, at least expose yourself to them. And don't wait until the day you decide to buy an instrument to pick one up for the first time. Make several visits to the music store before you're ready to buy and then take the time to absorb your experiences. Try to visit a few different music stores if you can. Some stores may be the exclusive dealer of a specific brand in your region; other retailers may not be able to sell that brand of guitar. Also, you pick up far more knowledge about what makes a good, playable guitar than you may think just by handling several different instruments. So get out there and get some hands-on experience.

Buying a guitar can be a similar experience to thinking you have the basics of a foreign language down pat and then visiting the country where it's spoken: You practice for weeks, but the first time a native starts speaking to you, you're completely flustered. But don't rush it; hang in there. You're just buying a guitar; you're not in a strange land trying to find the closest restroom facilities. You're eventually going to sort it all out, with the help of this chapter.

First Things First: Developing a Purchasing Plan

Before you walk into your local music store ready to plop down your hard-earned dough on a new guitar, you need to take stock of what you're doing. You need to ask yourself some tough questions about your pending purchase — and you need to do so *now*. Don't simply wait until you get to the store to develop a buying strategy (which, by that time, usually translates into no strategy at all). Keep in mind that the two most important factors in making any purchasing decision — especially concerning a guitar, where passions tend to run high — are to develop a plan and to gather all the information you need to make the best choice.

Start developing your purchasing plan by answering some specific questions about exactly what you want in a guitar — and how much you can spend to attain it. Narrowing your scope doesn't mean that you can't change your mind after you get to the store and see all the nifty instruments available or that you can't let on-the-spot inspiration and whim play a significant part in your final decision. ("I just *can't* decide between these two guitars . . . oh, what the heck! Just give me *both* of them!") But you *do* need a point from which to depart.

In focusing on the instrument of your (practical) dreams, ask yourself the following questions:

> ✔ **What's my level of commitment?** Regardless of your current ability, do you realistically envision yourself practicing every day for the next five years, pursuing a dedicated program of guitar excellence? Or do you first want to see whether this whole "guitar thing" is going to stick? Just because you can *afford* a $1,000 guitar doesn't mean that you should necessarily buy one. You can buy a quality instrument for much less than a grand. Before plunking down any cash, honestly determine the importance of the guitar in your life and then act responsibly according to that priority. (Or completely ignore this advice and go crazy, you guitar-playing rebel, you!)

✔ **What's my spending limit?** The answer to this question is critical because, often, the more expensive the guitar, the greater its appeal. So you need to balance your level of commitment and your available resources. You don't want to have to give up food for six months and live in a cardboard box just because you got carried away in a moment of buying fever at the music store. You can very easily overextend yourself. If you don't set a limit on how much you can spend, you can't know whether you exceed that limit . . . or by how much.

✔ **Am I a new-guitar person or a used-guitar person?** You're going to have a much easier time comparing attributes among new guitars. And prices of new instruments are pretty much standardized, though variation does exist among different types of retailers — large, urban stores versus mom-and-pop establishments, online retailers versus brick-and-mortar sellers, and so on.

Both retail and online operations offer a warranty against any manufacturer defects on new instruments. You don't find any comparable protection if you're buying a guitar from a newspaper ad (although music stores also sell used instruments, usually with their own, store-issued warranties) or from Craigslist, eBay, or other online classified service. But on the other hand, you *can* sometimes get a really good deal on a used instrument . . . *if you know what to look for.* And, of course, if you want a vintage instrument, you're looking at a used guitar by definition.

Grasping How a New Guitar Is Priced

In the not too distant past, a new guitar's cost was based on its *list*, or retail, price (set by the manufacturer), which the retailer then discounted to the selling price, or the actual amount you, the buyer, paid. Needless to say, the list price was much higher than the discounted price, from several hundred to even a couple thousand dollars more, especially if you were dealing with a high-end instrument. And the discount varied according to the customer and the policy or the whim of the individual retailer.

But the old pricing method, where the retailer advertises the list price along with his discount selling price, is almost entirely obsolete. Much more common now is to see just the vendor's advertised selling price. This practice encourages the retailers to offer the lowest price they can right at the outset (without forcing the customer to negotiate for it), in order to stay competitive. You may still find some variation in price for the same instrument among large retailers and between large and small retailers (who often can't offer a large discount because they don't deal in high-volume inventories). But pricing for new guitars tends to be fairly consistent. If you're at all unsure whether you're getting the lowest price, you can always ask the salesperson, "Is this the best you can do?" or "Is this the absolute lowest price? I saw this same make and model online from Uncle Bubba's Fly-by-Night Guitar

Emporium for 75 dollars less." Many retailers have a price-matching policy and honor any legitimate competitive offer, rather than lose a sale to a competitor. But if the retailer can't move any further on the price, you can accept the terms or try to do better.

If you're thinking about buying a used guitar, from a private owner in a newspaper ad or an online service like Craigslist or eBay, be very cautious when assessing the quality and condition of the guitar, especially if photos are the only things you have to go on (which is almost always the case). Also, be aware that most posted prices (also known as *asking prices*) from private owners are too high. Be prepared to dicker to get a better price for such a guitar — even if it's exactly what you're looking for.

After you feel that you have satisfactory answers to the preceding questions, proceed to the second prong of your guitar-purchasing attack plan: *gathering information on the specific guitar for you.* The following section helps you become more knowledgeable about guitar construction, materials, and workmanship. Remember, being an informed buyer is the best defense against making a bad deal in the retail arena.

Noting Some Considerations for Your First Guitar

If you're just starting out as a novice guitarist, you may ask the musical question, "What's the minimum I need to spend to avoid winding up with a piece of junk?" That's a good question, because modern manufacturing practices now enable *luthiers* (the fancy term for guitar makers) to turn out some pretty good stuff for around $200 — and even less sometimes.

If you're an adult (that is, someone older than 14), and you're looking to grow with an instrument, plan to spend between $200 and $250 for an acoustic guitar and a little less for an electric. (Electric guitars are a little easier to build than acoustics are, so they usually cost a bit less than comparable acoustics.) Not bad for something that can provide a lifetime of entertainment and help you develop musical skills, is it?

In trying to decide on a prospective guitar, consider the following criteria:

✔ **Appearance:** You must like the way a particular guitar looks, or you're never really happy with it. So use your eye and your sense of taste (and we're referring here to your sense of aesthetics, so please, don't lick the guitar with your tongue) to select possible candidates. A red guitar isn't inherently better or worse than a blue one, but you're perfectly free to base your decision to buy simply on whether you like the look of the guitar.

✔ **Playability:** Just because a guitar is relatively inexpensive doesn't necessarily mean that it's difficult to play (although this correlation was often the case in the past). You should be able to press the strings down to the fretboard with relative ease. And you shouldn't find the up-the-neck frets unduly difficult either, although they're sometimes harder to play than the lower frets.

Here's a way to get some perspective on playability. Go back to that Ferrari — er, more expensive guitar — at the other end of the rack and see how a high-quality guitar plays. (*Hint:* "Like a hot knife through butter" isn't an uncommon reaction when playing a really great guitar.) Then return to the more affordable instrument you're considering. Is the playability wildly different? It shouldn't be, though a more expensive guitar often has better playability than a less-expensive model. If your prospective instrument doesn't feel comfortable to you, move on.

✔ **Intonation:** Besides being relatively easy to play, a good guitar must play in tune. Test the intonation by playing a 12th-fret harmonic on the 1st string (see Chapter 13 for info on how to produce a harmonic) and match that to the fretted note at the 12th fret. Although the notes are of a different tonal quality, the pitch should be exactly the same. Apply this test to all six strings. Listen especially to the 3rd and 6th strings. On a guitar that's not set up correctly, these strings are likely to go out of tune first. If you don't trust your ears to tell the difference, enlist the aid of an experienced guitarist on this issue; it's *crucial.* See Chapter 19 for more information about intonation.

✔ **Solid construction:** If you're checking out an acoustic, rap gently on the top of the instrument (like your doctor does to check your ribs and chest) to make sure it's rattle free. Peer inside the hole, looking for gobs of glue and other evidence of sloppy workmanship. (Rough-sanded braces are a big tip-off to a hastily constructed instrument.) On an electric, test that the metal hardware is all tightly secured and rattle free. Without plugging into an amp, strum the open strings hard and listen for any rattling. Running your left hand along the edge of the neck to check that the frets are smooth and filed correctly is another good test. If you're not sure what you should be feeling, consult an experienced guitarist on this "fret check."

Sifting through Models to Match Your Style

Can you imagine walking into a music store and saying, "I'm a folk player. Do you have a folk bassoon? No, not a rock bassoon or a jazz bassoon — and *please,* not that country bassoon. How about that nice folk bassoon over in the corner?"

Absurd, right? But you're a guitarist, so asking for a type of guitar by musical style is completely legitimate. Ask for a heavy-metal guitar, for example, and the salesperson nods knowingly and leads you to the corner of the store with all the scary-looking stuff (lightning bolts, skulls, and bright colors). If you request a jazz guitar, you and the salesperson trundle off in a different direction (down toward the guys wearing berets and black turtlenecks sporting "Bird lives!" buttons).

Figure 16-1 shows a collection of some popular guitar models. Notice the diversity in shape and design.

Figure 16-1:
Different downstrokes for different folks.

Photographs courtesy of Charvel Guitars, Epiphone Guitar Corp., Fender Musical Instruments Corporation, Gibson Guitar Corp., Guild Guitars, PRS Guitars, and Taylor Guitars

Now, some musical styles do share guitar models. You can play both blues and rock, for example, with equal success on a Fender Stratocaster (or Strat, for short). And a Gibson Les Paul is just as capable of playing a wailing rock lead as a Strat. (As a rule, however, the tone of a Les Paul is going to be different than that of a Strat.) Making your own kind of music on the guitar of your choice is part of the fun.

Following are some popular music styles and classic guitars that most people associate with those styles. (While many of these models are beyond the price range of a first-time buyer, familiarity with them will help you associate models with styles and vice versa. Often, lower-priced guitars are based on the higher-end iconic models.) This list is by no means exhaustive but does include recognized standard bearers of the respective genres:

- ✔ **Acoustic blues:** National Steel, Gibson J-200

- ✔ **Bluegrass:** Martin Dreadnought, Taylor Dreadnought, Collings Dreadnought, Santa Cruz Dreadnought, Gallagher Dreadnought

- ✔ **Classical:** Ramirez, Hopf, Khono, Humphrey, Hernandez, Alvarez

- ✔ **Country:** Fender Telecaster, Gretsch 6120, Fender Stratocaster

- ✔ **Electric blues:** Gibson ES-355, Fender Telecaster, Fender Stratocaster, Gibson Les Paul

- ✔ **Folk:** Dreadnoughts and Grand Concerts by Martin, Taylor, Collings, Larrivée, Lowden, Yamaha, Alvarez, Epiphone, Ibanez, and Guild; Gibson J-200; Ovation Adamas

- ✔ **Heavy metal:** Gibson Les Paul, Explorer, Flying V and SG; Fender Stratocaster; Dean; Ibanez Iceman; Charvel San Dimas; Jackson Soloist

- ✔ **Jazz:** Gibson ES-175, Super 400 L-5, and Johnny Smith; archtops by D'Angelico, D'Aquisto, and Benedetto; Epiphone Emperor Regent; Ibanez signature models

- ✔ **New age, new acoustic:** Taylor Grand Concert, Ovation Balladeer, Takamine nylon-electric

- ✔ **R&B:** Fender Stratocaster, Gibson ES-335

- ✔ **Rock:** Fender Stratocaster, Gibson Les Paul and SG, Ibanez RG and signature series, Paul Reed Smith, Tom Anderson, Ruokangas

Although the preceding list contains guitars that people generally associate with given styles, don't let that limit your creativity. Play the music you want to play on the guitar you want to play it on, no matter what some chart tells you. In other words, after you study this list, take it with a grain of salt and go pick out the guitar you want, play the music you want, and never mind what some chart tells you. These guitars are all super-sweet, and the price tag reflects the quality as well as the heritage of these guitars.

Moving On to Your Second Guitar (and Beyond)

Your toughest decisions in buying a guitar may come not with your first instrument at all but with your second. Admit it — your first time out was probably a blur, but now that you know a little bit about guitar playing and what's available out there, you face perhaps an even more daunting prospect than before: What should you choose as your *next* guitar?

If you haven't already developed gear-lust for a certain model but are hankering for a new toy just the same, consider the following three common approaches to choosing another guitar:

✔ **The contrasting and complementary approach:** If you own an acoustic, you may want to consider getting an electric (or vice versa), because having an array of different guitars in your arsenal is always nice. Diversity is very healthy for a person seeking to bolster a collection.

✔ **The clone approach:** Some people just want to acquire as many, say, Les Pauls as they can in a lifetime: old ones, new ones, red ones, blue ones . . . hey — it's *your* money. Buy as many as you want (and can afford).

✔ **The upgrade approach:** If all you ever want to do is master the Stratocaster, just get a better version of what you had before. That way, you can use the new guitar for important occasions, such as recording and performing, and the old ax for going to the beach.

How much should you spend on your second (or later) instrument? One guideline is to go into the next spending bracket from your old guitar. This way, you don't end up with many similar guitars. Plan on spending about $200 more than the current value (not what you paid) of the guitar you own. By doing so, you ensure that even if you stick with a certain model line, you're getting a guitar that's categorically different from your initial instrument.

When should you stop buying guitars? Why, as soon as you die or the money runs out, of course. Actually, no hard-and-fast rules dictate how many guitars are "enough." These days, however, a reasonably well-appointed guitar arsenal includes a single-coil electric (such as a Fender Strat and/or Telecaster), a humbucker electric (such as a Gibson Les Paul), a semihollow-body electric, a hollow-body jazz (electric), an acoustic steel-string, an acoustic 12-string, and a nylon-string classical. Then maybe you can add one or two more guitars in a given specialty, such as a steel-bodied guitar set up especially for playing slide or a 12-string electric.

When upgrading to a second guitar, the issue again becomes one of *quality*. But this time, instead of just making sure you have an instrument that plays in tune, frets easily, and doesn't collapse like a house of cards if you breathe on it, you also need to *make informed decisions*. Don't worry — that's not as grave as it sounds. Consider for the moment, however, the following four pillars for judging quality in an instrument:

✔ **Construction and body type:** How the guitar is designed and put together

✔ **Materials:** The woods, metals (used in hardware, pickups, electronics), and other substances used

✔ **Workmanship:** The quality of the building

✔ **Appointments:** The aesthetic additions and other doodads

Not sure just what all those terms mean in determining the quality of a guitar? The following sections clue you in.

Construction and body type

How a guitar is built defines what type of guitar it is and (generally) what type of music it's used for. Consider just two examples:

✔ A *solid-body electric guitar* is used for rock. It has no holes in the body — which adds to its *sustain* (the guitar's ability to increase the amount of time a plucked note rings).

✔ An *acoustic archtop* is used for traditional jazz, because it has a carved, contoured top, which produces the mellow tones most associated with that style.

The following sections cover the three most important issues regarding guitar construction: solid versus laminated wood, body caps, and neck construction.

Solid wood versus laminated wood

A solid-wood acoustic guitar is more desirable than a *laminated* acoustic guitar (where, instead of using a solid, thicker piece of top-wood, the guitar maker uses several layers of inexpensive wood pressed together and covered with a veneer). Guitars made completely out of solid wood are more expensive — costing about $500 or more.

The guitar's top is the most critical element in sound production; the back and sides primarily reflect the sound back through the top. So if you can't pick up the tab for an all-solid-wood acoustic guitar, look to various configurations in which the top is solid and various other parts are laminated. A good choice is a solid-top guitar with laminated back and sides, which is much less expensive than an all-solid-wood model.

If you're unsure as to whether a guitar has solid or laminated wood, ask the dealer or consult the manufacturer.

Body caps

In the electric realm, one big determinant of price is whether the top has a cap. A *cap* is a decorative layer of fine wood — usually a variety of *figured* maple (one having a naturally occurring decorative grain pattern) — that sits on top of the body without affecting the sound. Popular cap woods include flame maple and quilted maple. Figured-wood tops usually come with clear, or see-through, finishes to show off the wood's attractive grain pattern.

Neck construction

The following list describes the three most common types of neck construction, from the least expensive to the most expensive:

- ✔ **Bolt-on:** The neck attaches to the back of the guitar with large bolts (although a plate sometimes covers the bolt holes). Fender Stratocasters and Telecasters are examples of guitars with bolt-on necks.

- ✔ **Set-in (or glued-in):** The neck joins the body with an unbroken surface covering the connection, creating a seamless effect from neck to body. The joint is then glued. Gibson Les Pauls and Paul Reed Smiths have set-in necks.

- ✔ **Neck-through-body:** A high-end construction where the neck is one long unit (although usually consisting of several pieces of wood glued together) that doesn't stop at the body but continues all the way through to the tail of the guitar. This type of neck is great for getting maximum sustain. A Jackson Soloist is an example of a guitar with a neck-through-body design.

Just because a construction technique is more advanced or expensive doesn't mean that it's necessarily better than other techniques. Could you "improve" the sound of Jimi Hendrix's Strat by modifying its neck to a glued-in configuration? *Sacrilege!*

Materials: Woods, hardware, and other goodies

A guitar isn't limited by what it's made of any more than a sculpture is. Michelangelo's *David* and your Aunt Agnes's candy dish are both made of marble, but which one would you travel to Florence to see? (Hint: Assume that you don't have an overly developed sweet tooth.) So don't judge a guitar *only* by its materials, but consider that a guitar with better materials (abalone inlays as opposed to plastic ones) tends to have commensurately better workmanship — and is, therefore, a better guitar — than a model that uses inexpensive materials. In the following sections, we note some important guitar materials to consider.

Woods

As you may expect, the more expensive or rare a wood, the more expensive the guitar you construct from that wood. Guitar makers break woods down into categories, and each category has a bearing on the guitar's overall expense.

Following are the three criteria used for classifying wood:

- ✔ **Type:** This category simply determines whether a piece of wood is mahogany, maple, or rosewood. Rosewood tends to be the most expensive wood used in the construction of acoustic-guitar bodies, followed by maple and then mahogany.

- ✔ **Style:** You can classify woods further by looking at the wood's region or grain style. For example, the figured maples, such as quilted and flame, are more expensive than rock or bird's-eye maples.

- ✔ **Grade:** Guitar makers use a grading system, from A to AAA (the highest), to evaluate woods based on grain, color, and consistency. High-quality guitars get the highest-grade wood.

Hardware

In more expensive instruments, you see upgrades on all components, including the *hardware,* or the metal parts of the guitar. Chrome-plated hardware is usually the cheapest, so if you begin looking at more expensive guitars, you start to see gold-plated and black-matte-finished knobs, switches, and tuning machines in place of chrome.

The actual hardware the manufacturer uses — not just the finishes on it — changes, too, on more expensive instruments. High-quality, name-brand hardware often replaces the guitar maker's less prestigious, generic brand of hardware on high-end axes. For example, manufacturers may use a higher-grade product for the tuning machines on an upscale guitar — such as *locking Sperzels* (a popular third-party tuner type and brand), which lock the string in place as opposed to forcing the user to tie the string off at the post.

The bridge is an important upgrade area as well. The so-called *floating bridge* (so designated because you can move it up and down by means of the whammy bar) is a complicated affair of springs, fine-tuning knobs, and anchors. The better floating assemblies, such as the Floyd Rose system or systems manufactured under a Floyd Rose license, operate much more smoothly and reliably than do the simple three-spring varieties found on low-cost guitars. (The strings spring right back to pitch on a Floyd Rose system, even after the most torturous whammy bar abuse.)

Pickups and electronics

Unless a guitar manufacturer is also known for making great pickups, you see more and more use of third-party pickups as you go up the quality ladder. In the electric arena, Seymour Duncan, DiMarzio, Bartolini, Bill Lawrence, Lace and EMG are examples of high-quality pickup brands that guitar makers piggy-back onto their models. Fishman and L.R. Baggs are two popular acoustic pickup systems found on many well-known guitars.

Although they're not known by name brands, the electronics in electric guitars also improve along with the other components as you venture into more expensive territory. You can see a greater variety, for example, in pickup manipulation. Manufacturers can provide circuitry that changes double-coil, or humbucker, pickups into single-coils, enabling them to emulate the behavior of Stratlike pickups. Having one guitar that can imitate the pickup behavior of other guitar types provides you with a tonally versatile instrument. You also see more manipulation in wiring schemes. For example, guitar makers may reverse the *polarity* of a pickup — the direction the signal flows — to make the guitar sound softer and swirlier.

With more expensive guitars, you may also encounter improved volume and tone controls, resulting in better *taper*. Taper is the gradualness or abruptness of change (also called *response*) of a signal's characteristics (in this case, volume and tone) as you turn a knob from its minimum value to its maximum. A knob exhibiting a smoother taper is evidence of a higher grade of electronics. Really cheap guitars give you no sound at all until turned up to 3; then you get a swell of sound from about 4 to about 7 and no change at all between 7 and the knob's maximum value, 10 — or, on those really rare, loud guitars, 11. (And if you don't get that last joke, watch the hilarious rockumentary spoof *This Is Spinal Tap*. It's required viewing for all guitarists.)

Workmanship

For more expensive guitars, you can really bring out the white glove and get fussy. We've seen prospective buyers bring in a dentist's mirror to inspect the interior of an acoustic guitar.

For acoustic guitars in the mid-priced to expensive range, you should expect to find *gapless joints* — solid wood-to-wood connections between components, especially where the neck meets the body. You should also expect clean and glob-free gluing (in the top and back bracing), a smooth and even finish application, and a good setup: the strings at the right height with no buzzing, the neck warp- and twist-free, and the intonation true. (See Chapter 19 for info on intonation.)

Look at the places on a guitar where different surfaces meet — particularly where the neck joins the body and the edge of the fingerboard where the metal frets embed into the fret slots. You should see no trace of excess glue, and the surfaces should be uniformly mated to each other.

You can glean all this information by simply playing the guitar and noting your impressions. Like traveling in a Rolls-Royce or Bentley, playing a quality guitar should be one smooth ride.

Appointments (cosmetic extras)

Appointments are the fancy stuff that have no acoustic or structural effect on the guitar. They exist solely as decorative elements. Some people find fancy appointments showy or pretentious, but we feel that a great guitar is a work of art to behold with the eye as well as the ear. So go for the bling.

Typical appointments include intricate neck inlays (such as abalone figures countersunk into the fretboard), a fancy headstock design, and, on an acoustic guitar, the *rosette*, or decorative design around the sound hole.

One subtle aspect about appointments: You may think that the only difference between two guitars is in the appointments — for example, a fancy inlay job may seem to be the only thing that distinguishes between a certain company's Grand Deluxe and Deluxe models. But the truth is that the more expensive guitar — although nominally the same in materials and construction — often gets the choicest materials and enjoys higher quality-control standards.

This situation is just a Darwinian reality. If 12 pieces of wood, all destined to become guitar tops, come into the factory, slated for six Grand Deluxes and six Deluxes (fictitious titles, by the way, bearing no resemblance to actual guitar models, living or deceased), the six best pieces of wood go to the Grand Deluxes and the six next-best pieces to the Deluxe models. They may all share identical grading, but humans with subjective powers decide which models get which tops.

Before You Buy: Walking through the Buying Process

Buying a guitar is similar to buying a car or house (okay, it's a *little* less monumental than buying a house) in that it's an exciting endeavor and lots of fun, but you must exercise caution and be a savvy customer, too. Only you know the right guitar for you, what the right price is for your budget and commitment level, and whether a deal feels right. Don't deny your natural instincts as a shopper, even if you're new to guitar shopping. Look, listen, consider, go have lunch before the big buy, and talk it over with your sweetie. We provide some helpful guidelines in the following sections.

Keep in mind that you're *shopping*. And the whole shopping experience is no different with guitars than with any other commodity. Do your research and get differing opinions *before* you buy. And trust your instincts.

Choosing between online and brick-and-mortar sellers

With many purchases these days, you face the question, "Do I buy from a store or online?" For a musical instrument, a good rule is this: If you know *exactly* what you want — down to the color and options — you may consider buying an instrument online. You often get the best available price for your chosen instrument by going this route, and you may even avoid paying sales tax (if the music company is out of state), though you may pay shipping. (Some online sellers offer free shipping under certain conditions.) Most online sellers offer a money-back guarantee if you return the instrument quickly, for any reason, no questions asked. That's a hard deal to beat.

Buying sight unseen is common with many products, such as electronic gadgets and computers. But if you can't cotton to buying something as personal as a guitar without falling in love with it first — and you want to "date" your guitar before "marrying" it — you definitely want to stick with the traditional brick-and-mortar storefront approach. A guitar bought from a store usually comes with an official service agreement and unofficial, friendly cooperation from the staff that's worth its weight in gold. Music stores know they're competing with online sellers, and they make up for it in spades with service.

Seeking expert advice

A certain saying goes, "An expert is someone who knows more than you do." If you have such a friend — whose knowledge and experience in guitars exceeds your own — bring the friend along, by all means. This friend not only knows about guitars but also knows *you*. A salesperson doesn't know you, nor does he necessarily have your best interests in mind. But a friend does. And another opinion never hurts, if only to help you articulate your own.

Enlist your guitar teacher (if you have one) to help you navigate through the guitar buyer's jungle, especially if he's been with you awhile and knows your tastes and playing style. Your teacher may know things about you that you may not even realize about yourself — for example, that you've gotten sidetracked in the steel-string section although your principal interests lie in nylon-string guitar music. A good teacher asks questions, listens to your answers, and gently guides you to where *you* want to go.

Another saying, however, goes, "Moe was the smartest of the Three Stooges." If you have a friend who's like Moe — smarter than you in matters of the guitar but otherwise one string short of a set — leave him at home. You don't need a wise guy goofing around (and tweaking the salesperson's nose with a pair of pliers) while you're trying to concentrate.

Involving the salesperson

Dealing with a salesperson doesn't need to be a stressful, adversarial affair, but some people get pretty anxious about the entire situation. Part of that reason is that music store personnel sometimes get a bad rap for being intimidating, aloof, or unknowledgeable (or a combination of all three qualities). But ignore the rumors and negative stereotypes. Bad apples can exist in any industry, but most salespeople in music stores genuinely try to get you the best instrument for your needs. But you can help your chances for a good experience if you establish your priorities before you enter the store, so that you don't come off as vague and unprepared if he asks you questions.

A typical first question from a salesperson may be, "How much do you want to spend?" In essence, the question means "What price range are you looking at so I know which end of the store to take you to?" It's a fair question, and if you can answer directly, you end up saving a lot of time. He may also ask about your playing ability and your style preferences, so be ready to answer those questions, too.

Be prepared to answer the salesperson's questions succinctly — for example, "I prefer Strat-style guitars, although not necessarily by Fender, and I'm an intermediate blues player — not a shredder — and I'd like to keep costs at less than $600." Answers such as these make you sound decisive and thoughtful. The salesperson should have plenty to go on from that kind of information. But if you instead say, "Oh, for the right guitar, price is no object; I like the one that what's-his-name played on last year's Grammy Awards," you're not going to be taken seriously — nor are you likely to end up with the instrument you need.

As the salesperson speaks, listen carefully and ask questions. You're there to observe and absorb, not impress. If you decide you're not ready to buy at this point, tell him that. Thank him for his time and get his card. You're certainly free to go elsewhere and investigate another store. To do so is not only your option — it's also your duty!

Closing the deal

You can often find out the price of an instrument before you walk into the store. Visit the websites of popular online sellers (such as Guitar Center and Sweetwater) to determine the ballpark prices of the models you're interested in. As of this writing, a Gibson Les Paul Standard sells for between $1,860 and $2,600, on average, and a Fender American Standard Stratocaster costs about $1,500. Figure 16-2 shows these two industry stalwarts.

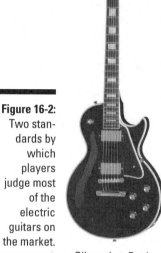 

Figure 16-2:
Two stan-
dards by
which
players
judge most
of the
electric
guitars on
the market.

Gibson Les Paul   Fender Stratocaster

*Photographs courtesy of Gibson Guitar Corp. and Fender Musical
Instruments Corporation*

Remember that the advertised selling price is often the lowest the seller can offer. If you're going to compare online prices to brick-and-mortar prices, make sure your online prices are from reputable and established sellers, and be sympathetic to the slightly higher prices you may find in a store.

 Finally, in deciding where to buy, don't neglect the value of service. Retail stores — unlike online sellers — are in a better position to devote close, personal service to a new guitar customer. Perhaps as a result of facing stiff competition from the booming online biz, many stores are upping their service incentives. Service includes anything from fixing minor problems and making adjustments to providing periodic *setups* (sort of like a tune-up and oil change for your guitar). And, a music store can be a great place to just hang out and talk guitars!

Chapter 17

Eyeing Guitar Amps, Effects, Cases, and Accessories

*A*fter you get your guitar squared away, you need to think about all the little (and not-so-little) items that make life so much easier — if you're a guitarist, that is. Some of the products we describe in this chapter are essential — for example, cases and strings (and amps if you're playing electric) — but you can think of others merely as accessories. We do think that all these items are useful and have some musical or practical application. You find no plugs for bumper stickers and mugs that read "Guitarists are strum-thing special" in these pages — just the short list of stuff that can really help you out.

Getting Wired with Guitar Amplifiers

Strictly speaking, you *can* play an electric guitar without any amplification, but playing that way isn't much fun. Without an amp, you hear the notes buzzing like little musical mosquitoes, but you don't achieve any expression or tone. And you can't possibly rattle the windows and shake the floorboards with your newly learned "Smoke on the Water" riff unless you're wired up and have decibels to burn.

We recommend that you save your most critical purchasing decision for the guitar. But after you break the bank to get that guitar that's just beyond your means, you may as well go right out and exercise some more financial irresponsibility and get a good amp. You can't start to develop a fully mature and individual tone until you have both a quality guitar and a decent amp to run it through. But if you *must* skimp somewhere, we suggest that you skimp on the amp side — at first.

Amps come in two general flavors — practice and performance varieties. The biggest differences between practice amps and performance amps boil down to size, wattage, and cost. Figure 17-1 shows a practice amp and a performance amp.

Figure 17-1: Perfor-mance amps, such as the one on the left, are bigger and more powerful than the practice amp at the right.

a   b

Photos courtesy of Marshall Amplification plc

Starting out with a practice amp

If you have limited funds, start out with a *practice amp* — one that has a decent feature set (tone controls, reverb, and two or more volume controls so you can sculpt your distorted sound) and that delivers a good sound but at low volumes (5 to 25 watts is typical on practice amps). This type of starter amp accustoms you to hearing the electric guitar as it's designed to be heard — through a guitar amp.

Practice amps can run as little as $100 and boast features that appear on their higher-priced performance counterparts. With amplifiers, power — not features — is what drives up the price. Power is expensive to build, requiring heavy-duty transformers, speakers, and cabinetry. For home and casual use, such as jamming with a couple of friends in a garage or basement, 15 or 20 watts is often plenty loud enough, and 5 to 25 watts is sufficient for solo prac-ticing and playing along with your sound system.

On the other hand, features, such as tone controls and effects (like reverb and tremolo), are easier to implement because the manufacturers can stamp them onto a chip and install it on a circuit board. Following are some useful things to look for in a practice amp:

- **Multiple-gain stages:** *Gain* is the technical word for "loudness power," and having two or more separate volume controls on an amp gives you more flexibility in shaping the distorted sound.

- **Three-band EQ:** EQ, or *equalization,* is tone control for bass, mid, and high. An EQ device is a fancy tone control that gives you increased flexibility over the bass, midrange, and treble makeup of your sound.

- **Built-in reverb:** *Reverb* is an echolike effect that makes the guitar sound like it's playing within a given environment — rooms of varying sizes, a concert hall, cathedral, canyon, and so on. (See the "Effects: Pedals and Other Devices" section, later in the chapter, for more information.)

- **Channel switching via footswitch:** *Channel switching* enables you to access different sets of volume and tone control. Some practice amps include it; others don't. (Virtually all performance-based, or high-end, amps do.) Decide whether that feature is important enough to pay for in a practice amp. You can always get your distorted sound through an external effect, such as a stomp box, but that's a little bit more of a hassle. (See the section "Effects: Pedals and Other Devices," later in this chapter, for more information.)

- **Headphone jack:** A *headphone jack* is a very handy thing in a practice amp because it enables you to get a fully amp-treated sound without going through the speaker. Great for late-night practice sessions!

Because of the miniaturization of all things electronic, you can now get full-sounding, authentic guitar sounds from a unit the size of a point-and-shoot camera — as long as you listen to it through headphones or earbuds (meaning it has no speaker or amplifier of its own). Referred to as *personal multi-effects processors,* these strap-on wonders come with belt clips and are battery powered for untethered practicing (great for walking into the bathroom and standing in front of the mirror). And they offer distortion, EQ, reverb, and other effects; numerous *presets* (sounds programmed or set up by the manufacturer); and stereo sound. These units are great for playing in a moving vehicle and can even output a signal suitable for recording or further amplification. They cost about $200 (the Korg Pandora is one example) and are well worth the investment if portability, privacy, and authentic tone are important to you.

Powering up to a performance amp

Practice amps serve a purpose, but they don't hold up if you try to turn them up to performance levels. *Performance,* in this case, means anything from cutting through three friends in a garage jam to making yourself heard over the antics of the overly zealous drummer and bass player at Slippery Sam's Thursday Night Blues Bash.

After you decide to take the plunge into higher-quality amps, you have a galaxy of makes and models from which to choose. Talk to other guitarists and music salespeople, read guitar magazines, and listen to recordings to find out what amps the artists you like use. Your choice of amp is just as personal and individual as that of your guitar. The amp must not only sound good but also look good and *feel* as if it's just the right amp for you. The pursuit of the perfect amp is as elusive as the quest for the perfect guitar. Well, almost.

Performance amps are more powerful than practice amps. More power doesn't just mean a louder amp. Increased power also delivers a cleaner, purer signal at higher volumes. In other words, if two amps of different power are producing the same overall loudness, the more powerful amp yields the cleaner, undistorted signal.

A 50-watt amp is usually more than sufficient for home and normal performing circumstances, such as playing in a five-piece band at a local club or other performance venue. If you play larger venues or play in a genre that requires unusually loud levels — such as heavy metal — go with 100 watts. Some players who desire a squeaky-clean sound and who run in stereo (requiring double the power) may opt for 100 watts regardless, because they can stay cleaner at louder levels.

Many amps can operate at either 100 or 50 watts by enabling you to select the power via a switch. Why would you want to operate at 50 watts when you paid for a 100-watt amp? Because a 50-watt amp breaks up, or distorts, sooner (at a lower level) than a 100-watt one does, and for many types of music (blues, rock, metal), this distortion is desirable.

Once upon a time, all electronic circuits were powered by vacuum tubes — those glass cylinders that glow red in the back of old radios. As technology has developed, solid-state electronics (which consist of transistors and, later, microchips) have replaced tubes, except in guitar amps. The latest generation of amps feature digital technology to *model,* or emulate, a variety of guitar tones and effects. Many argue, however, that tube technology still produces the best tone (warmest and fullest, due in part to the way tubes affect the signal) for guitars because, although they're not as efficient or even as accurate in faithfully reproducing the original signal, tube amps actually deliver the most musical tone. All your favorite guitarists record and play exclusively with tube amps, from the 100-watt Marshall to the Fender Twin Reverb, to the Vox AC30 and the MESA/Boogie Dual Rectifier.

Recording amps

Though high-power amps usually cost more than similarly featured low-power ones, that doesn't mean all low-power amps are inexpensive. Many manufacturers make high-quality, high-priced amps that deliver only low power, and these amps are especially popular for recording because they don't shake the foundations of your house to make music. With *recording amps,* quality, not power, makes them expensive.

As a beginner, you may not appreciate (or care about) the differences between tube and solid-state tone. You can get good-sounding distortion out of a solid-state amp anyway, which is usually cheaper, so you should probably go with a solid-state amp and ignore the whole tone debate. Besides, you may prefer to get your distortion sound from a pedal, and then the whole issue is moot. Look instead for features such as built-in effects (reverb, chorus, and so on) and a headphone jack. Above all, listen to the sound and turn the knobs. If you like what you hear and feel comfortable dialing in the different sounds, the amp is for you.

Effects: Pedals and Other Devices

Electric guitarists seldom just plug into an amp and start playing. Well, they may start out that way, but if you listen to recorded music — and especially any recorded guitar music — you quickly notice a lot more going on than just a "straight" guitar sound. At the very least, you hear some ambient treatment in the form of artificially created echo, or *reverb,* as the effect is known in guitar lingo. You may hear some (intended) distortion, especially in rock and blues music, and you may hear additional effects, such as wah-wah, vibrato, and other electronic manipulations.

Welcome to the wonderful, wacky world of *effects.* Effects are devices that plug in between your guitar and amplifier and enable you to alter your signal in all sorts of creative and unusual ways. Scores and scores of these little devices are available from all different manufacturers and in all price ranges. As you find out in the following sections, you can buy effects as individual units or as an all-in-one box, called a *multi-effects processor.* But whether you go for the package deal or à la carte, effects can spice up the basic sound of your guitar in all sorts of exciting ways.

Most effects come in the form of foot-accessed pedals, also known as *stomp boxes* because they reside on the floor and you activate them by stepping on a footswitch. This setup enables you to selectively turn effects on and off while playing the guitar without interruption. Figure 17-2 shows a typical effects setup with a reasonable number of pedals in the *signal chain* (that is, the path from guitar to amp).

If you plug, say, a reverb device *inline* (that is, between the amp and guitar), you can make your guitar sound as if you're playing in a cathedral. A distortion unit can make your tones sound like those of Jimi Hendrix or Metallica or Nirvana, even at low volumes and with your amp set to a clean sound.

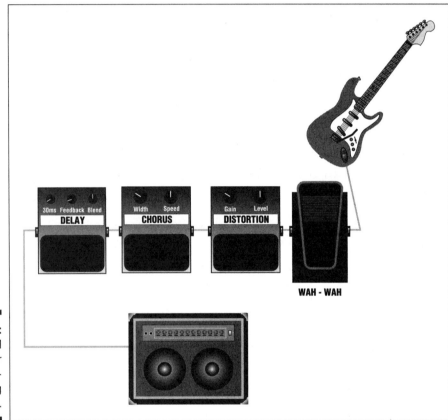

Figure 17-2: A typical setup for a guitarist using effects.

© John Wiley & Sons, Inc.

Investigating individual effects

Dozens of different types of effects are available — more than you could possibly own, not to mention use all at once. The price of these individual units varies, too, with distortion boxes as cheap as $45 and digital reverbs and delays as much as $175 (or more). To help you sort through the myriad of flavors and types of effects, following is a list of some of the most popular ones:

- **Distortion:** This effect simulates the sound of a guitar signal driven too hard for the amplifier; the device overdrives the signal to the point that it breaks up — but in a musically pleasing way. Distortion, to a guitarist, can mean anything from a slightly fat, warm quality to a fuzzy sustain, to screaming chain-saw fuzz, as used by metal and grunge bands.

- **Chorus:** This effect simulates the sound of many guitars playing at once, making the overall sound fatter. Increasing the speed yields a warbling or tremolo-like effect. The Police's "Every Breath You Take" exemplifies the chorus sound.

- **Flanger/Phase shifter:** These two devices produce similar effects that create a whooshy, swirly, underwater sound, heard on early Van Halen albums and in the rhythm guitar sound of many funk songs of the '70s.

- **Pitch shifter:** This device (also known as a *harmonizer*) enables you to play in harmony with yourself by splitting your signal into two paths, the original and a user-defined musical interval, such as a major 3rd (four half steps away); it also provides choruslike effects. A popular fixed-interval pitch shifter is the *octave pedal,* used to great effect by Jimi Hendrix, which produces a pitch one or two (or both) octaves (12 half steps) higher or lower than the original.

- **Digital delay:** This device produces a discrete repetition of your sound, good for echoes, spacious effects, and creating rhythmically timed repeats of your notes. The analog version was a tape-echo device that actually recorded the sound on magnetic tape and played it back moments later. Tape echoes still enjoy some popularity because of their unique, vintage-sounding, tonal quality (which is inferior to the digital version in terms of exact replication of the original signal). Listen to the opening of Guns N' Roses' "Welcome to the Jungle" to hear the sound of digital delay.

- **Wah-wah pedal:** This effects pedal is a type of frequency filter (which varies the bass and treble content of a signal) that imbues the guitar with expressive, voicelike characteristics (it actually sounds as if it's saying "wah"). You control the sound by raising and lowering a foot pedal. This device was made popular by Jimi Hendrix and was a staple of the disco-guitar sound. Eric Clapton also gave the wah a workout on "White Room" during his Cream days.

- **Reverb:** This effect reproduces the natural echo sound produced in environments such as a large room, gymnasium, cathedral, and so on. It's usually included on amps in a limited version (often having only one control), but having it as a separate effect gives you a lot more variety and control.

- **Tremolo:** Like reverb, tremolo was included on many amps from the '50s and '60s (such as the Fender Twin Reverb) and is now available in a pedal. Tremolo is the rapid wavering of the volume (not pitch, like vibrato) that makes your guitar sound as if you're playing it through a slowly moving electric fan. Tommy James and the Shondells' "Crimson and Clover," Green Day's "Boulevard of Broken Dreams," and Pink Floyd's "Money" feature a prominent tremolo effect.

Considering multi-effects processors

Individual pedals are a great convenience because they enable you to buy effects one at a time and use them in a *modular* fashion — you can choose to include them in your chain or not, and you can rearrange their order to create different effects. But many guitarists opt for a *multi-effects processor,* which puts all the individual effects into one housing. Multi-effects processors are *programmable,* meaning that you can store different settings in the effects and recall them with the tap of a foot. Multi-effects processors, like individual pedals, also offer a modular approach to effect ordering, although they accomplish this electronically rather than physically.

Generally, a multi-effects processor can do anything that individual pedals do, so most guitarists who use a lot of effects eventually buy one. You can still use your individual pedals, too, by hooking them up with the multi-effects processor. Most guitarists still keep their individual pedals even after acquiring a multi-effects processor, because the individual pedals are small, simple to operate and convenient. A guitarist may not want to lug the larger, more cumbersome multi-effects processor to a casual jam session when he needs only one or two effects. The price range for guitar multi-effects processors is $120 to $1,500. They can be found in a variety of sizes, including ones that come as apps for a smartphone or other mobile device.

Making a Case for Cases

A guitar case is so important to your guitar that many manufacturers include the case in the price of the guitar. Many manufacturers make cases specially designed for particular models and ship the guitars inside these cases to retailers. This practice makes buying the guitar without the case difficult — and rightly so.

To buy a serious instrument and then try to carry it away from the store without the appropriate, quality protection is a foolish way to save a few bucks. The most important gesture of respect that you can show your instrument is to give it a safe place to sleep.

Cases come in three basic types, which we discuss in the following sections: the hard or hard-shell type, the soft variety, and the gig bag. Each has its advantages, and the protection factor is proportional to cost: The more expensive the case, the better the protection it offers your instrument.

Hard cases

The *hard case* is the most expensive option ($80 to $120 and more) but offers the best insurance against damage to your guitar. It's composed of leather- or nylon-covered wood and can even survive the rigors of airline baggage handlers, providing crush-proof protection to your instrument. They can drop heavy objects on the case and stack it safely under other luggage items without any damage accruing to the precious guitar inside. Some hard cases are made of molded heavy-duty plastic, which makes them resistant to punctures, dents, and scratches, but are lined with fabric-covered padding to provide your guitar a shock-free environment during transport and storage.

The safest thing to do is to go with a hard case, unless you have some really compelling reason not to. If you don't already have a case for your guitar and are thinking of buying one, try to think of any situation where a hard case may *not* be appropriate. If you can't produce a quick and ready response, spring for the hard case and be done with it.

Soft cases

The *soft case* isn't completely soft, being in fact more stiff than truly soft. It usually consists of some pressed-particle material, such as cardboard, and can provide some protection for your instrument — for example, if someone drops a coffee mug on it (an empty coffee mug, that is). But that's about it. You can pick up these cases for about $30.

The soft case is the inexpensive alternative to the hard case because it enables you to transport your instrument without exposing it to the elements and at least prevents an outside intruder from scratching it. But these cases easily buckle if put to any real stress (such as getting caught in an airport conveyer belt) and cave in, fold, and puncture much more easily than a hard case does. In most situations, however, a soft case provides protection against the daily bumps and grinds that would otherwise scratch an unprotected guitar.

Gig bags

The *gig bag* provides almost no protection against shock because it's a form-fitting nylon, leather, or other fabric enclosure — you know, a bag. Gig bags zip shut and are about the consistency of any other soft luggage carrier. They cost anywhere from $25 to $150.

The advantages of gig bags are that they're light, they fit on your shoulder, and they take up no more room than the guitar itself — making them the ideal case if you're taking public transportation or trying to fit your electric guitar into the overhead bin of an airplane.

People who live in big cities and take public transportation favor gig bags. With the gig bag over their shoulder and a luggage cart toting an amp in one hand, they still have a hand free to operate a subway turnstile and hold the poles on a train car. But a gig bag isn't nearly as protective as a soft case, and you can't stack anything heavier than a scarf or a sweater on top of a bagged guitar.

Accessories: Other Essential Stuff to Complete Your Setup

Beyond choosing the principal actors in your setup — guitar, amp, effects, and cases — you still have to decide on a whole cast of supporting characters. These are the little things that, while inexpensive and easily acquired, are vital to keep your main gear happy and healthy. In the following sections, we recommend the indispensable accessories that complete your music-making ensemble.

Strings

You always need to keep extra strings on hand for the simple reason that if you break one, you need to replace it immediately. To do so requires that you carry at least an extra full set because any one of your six strings could break. Unlike car tires, where one spare fits all, guitars use six individually gauged strings. Woe to the guitarists who keep breaking the same string over and over — they're going to have an awful lot of partial sets around! Fortunately, string sets are cheap — about $7 if you buy them in single sets and cheaper still if you buy them in boxes of 12 sets. Or you can buy single strings for about $1.50 apiece.

The higher, thinner strings tend to break more easily than do the lower, thicker ones, so try to carry three spares each of the high E, B, and G strings.

In a pinch, you can substitute the higher adjacent string (a B string for a G, for example), but doing so will cause your playing to sound and feel strange, and the string will be more difficult to tune. So make sure to replace the emergency substitute with the proper string at the very next opportunity (during the drum solo, perhaps). (For more information on strings, including how to change them, see Chapter 18.)

Picks

In your musical career, you're sure to lose, break, toss to adoring fans as souvenirs, and otherwise part company with hundreds of picks, so don't get attached (in a sentimental sense) to them. Treat them as the inexpensive, expendable commodity they are. Stock up by the gross with your favorite color and gauge (thickness) and always carry spares in your wallet, the car, the flaps of your penny loafers and any other, er, convenient place. After you get used to a certain gauge, shape, and make of pick, you don't change around much, even going from electric to acoustic or vice versa. (Check out Chapter 3 for more information on selecting an appropriate gauge. We leave it to you to sort out the color.)

Cables

A *cable,* also known as a *cord* (and not to be confused with a *chord*), is what transports your electronic signal from your guitar to the amp or from your guitar to a pedal. Cables also connect pedals together, if you have more than one. The more pedals you have, the more cables you need to connect everything together. Cables don't have any controls and require no setup — just plug them in and you're done. The only time you have to pay attention to them is when they go bad.

A crackling cable is no fun for either you or your audience. That nasty sound means that the connections inside have become loose or are corroded. It happens to everyone eventually. Keep extra cables on hand of both the long variety (for connecting your guitar to an effect or an amp) and the short (for pedal-to-pedal connections).

Electronic tuners

Although you can tune a guitar to itself, keeping the guitar up to *concert pitch* — the absolute tuning reference of A-440 — is best, especially if you plan to play with other instruments. A guitar is also structurally and acoustically happiest at that tuning. (See Chapter 2 for more information on tuning your guitar.) The best way to keep your guitar at this tuning is to secure a battery-powered electronic tuner and keep it in your guitar case. Electronic tuners can be a plug-in type, which looks like an effects pedal (except that its controls govern tuning parameters rather than tonal ones), or a clip-on variety (sometimes called a *headstock tuner*), which grips the upper part of the headstock, through a spring-loaded clamp, such as those made by D'Addario,

Korg, and Snark. The way you use the tuner depends on the type of guitar you're tuning:

- ✔ **Electric:** If you're using an electric guitar and a non-clip-on tuner, plug it right into the tuner. Plug into the tuner first, and then, from the tuner's output jack, plug into your amp. That way, your tuner stays inline the entire time you play. Turn off the tuner, however, after you're done tuning to preserve the life of its battery. The signal passes through the dormant tuner unaffected.

- ✔ **Acoustic:** If you have an acoustic guitar, you can use the plug-in tuner's built-in microphone for tuning. You don't need to go to great pains to get the microphone to pick up the guitar. Placing the tuner an arm's length away on a tabletop is fine; balancing it on your knee works well, too. If the surrounding atmosphere is quiet enough, you can even keep your tuner on the floor. (But excessive room noise can confuse a tuner.) A wide variety of tuners exist as apps for smartphones and mobile devices. These work very well for acoustic guitars because they use the mobile device's microphone, but they're less successful with electric guitars, especially if ambient (room) noise is present. Clip-on tuners are unaffected by ambient noise, and so are an excellent choice for either acoustic or electric guitars. The best idea is to buy an electronic tuner and keep it with your pedals or inside the guitar case.

Virtually all electronic tuners sold these days are the auto-sensing, chromatic type. *Auto-sensing* means that the tuner listens to your note and tells you what its nearest pitch is (with indicator lights). A meter with a moving needle or an array of indicator lights then tells you whether you're flat or sharp of that note. As you tune the guitar, you see the meter change in the direction of your tuning motions. The word *chromatic* just means that the tuner shows you all the notes in the musical scale (including flats and sharps), not just the notes of the open strings of the guitar. Having all notes available on your tuner is important should you ever decide to tune the guitar differently. (See Chapter 11 for more information on alternate tunings.) The prices of electronic tuners range from about $10 to $200.

Straps

Straps come in all kinds of styles and materials, from nylon to woven fabric to leather. The first rule in choosing a strap is that you get the most comfortable one that you can afford. Wearing a guitar on your shoulder for long periods of time can cause discomfort, and the better the strap is, the more it protects your muscles against strain and fatigue.

Appearance is a close second to comfort as a factor in deciding what strap to buy. You must like the look of your strap, because its function isn't just utilitarian but aesthetic as well. Because it drapes over your shoulder, a strap functions almost like an article of clothing. So try to match the look of your strap to your own look as well as to the look of your guitar.

You can get custom-made straps with your initials embroidered in them, if that's your thing (a must-have if you plan on being a country music matinee idol). Or you can get them in all sorts of motifs, from Southwest patterns to lighting bolts and pentagrams. But if you're looking at strictly the price, a simple, no-frills nylon strap costs as little as $5 and holds your guitar as securely as a $200 one with your name embossed in leather.

For extra insurance, purchase *strap locks,* which secure your strap ends to the guitar by using a two-piece locking mechanism, kind of like what you find on earrings (the pierced kind).

If you own more than one guitar, you're best off with a strap for each type of guitar, electric and acoustic. That way, you don't need to keep adjusting it as you switch from electric to acoustic and back again.

Capos

A *capo* (pronounced *kay*-po) is a spring-loaded, adjustable-tension (or elastic) clamp that wraps around the neck of a guitar and covers all the strings, forcing them all down to the fretboard at a given fret. This device effectively raises the pitch of all the strings by a given number of frets (or half steps). In some cases, you may want to tune your guitar with the capo on, but most of the time, you tune up without it and then place it on the desired fret. Capos enable you to transpose the music you play on your guitar to another key, while you still play the chord fingerings in the original key. (See Chapter 13 for more information on capos.) Figure 17-3 shows a few different capo types you can find at most music stores.

Figure 17-3:
Capos raise
the pitch of
the open
strings.

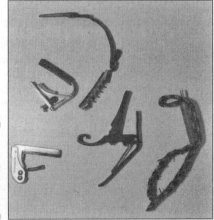

Photograph courtesy of Cherry Lane Music

Capos cost between $5 and $25, with the elastic-band type being the cheapest. The higher-priced clamp and screw-on types are more popular with serious capo users because you can put them on with one hand, and these types of capos generally hold the strings down better than the elastic kinds do. The screw-on type, such as the one made by Shubb, is a particular favorite because you can vary the size and tension of the capo's grip, which enables you to customize the capo size for different parts of the neck. (The lower frets of the neck, toward the headstock, require a smaller capo opening than do the higher frets.)

Other helpful goodies

You can treat yourself to a number of other little doodads and contraptions that make guitar playing a lot more painless and convenient. In no particular order, consider some of the following gizmos, which are often worth their weight in thumbpicks. Figure 17-4 shows these items, which we define in the following list:

- **Batteries:** Tuners, effects pedals, and even some guitars run on batteries. Stock up on a couple of nine-volts and a few AAs and store them in a sealed plastic bag.

- **Bridge pins:** These little plastic pieces wedge your strings into the bridge of your steel-string acoustic guitar. The problem is this: If you lose one (because it goes flying off a dock or into the grass after you yank it out), you can't find anything to substitute for it. Matchsticks are the closest things, but who carries those around these days? The next time you're at the music store buying strings, make sure you also pick up a couple of extra bridge pins.

- **Cloth:** You should always wipe down your guitar after playing to remove body oils that can corrode strings and muck up the finish. Cotton is good, and chamois (pronounced *shammy*) and microfiber are better. At least give your fingerboard a wipe before you put it in the case, and if you're playing with short sleeves, give the top a rubdown, too.

- **Earplugs:** If you play electric guitar and find yourself in a lot of impromptu jam sessions, you should carry earplugs. Your ears are your most precious musical commodities — more important than even your fingers. Don't damage them by exposing them to loud noises in close rehearsal quarters. Buy the kind of earplugs made especially for music listening; they *attenuate* (reduce) frequencies at equal rates across the spectrum. So it's like hearing the original music . . . only softer. Many guitarists are advocates of earplugs, including the Who's Pete Townshend, who claims to have suffered significant hearing loss resulting from long-term exposure to loud music.

- **Peg winder:** This inexpensive ($2) crank turns your tuning keys at about 10 times the rate you can turn them by hand. At no extra charge, these devices include a notched groove that's perfect for removing stuck bridge pins in your steel-string acoustic guitar.

- **Pencil and paper:** Always carry something you can write with and on. That way, you can jot down lyrics, a cool chord that someone shows you, a cheat sheet so you can pick up a chord progression in a jiffy, or even a surreptitious note to another musician. ("Please tell your bass player to turn it down — I've lost three fillings already!")

- **Portable recorder:** Don't miss capturing a once-in-a-lifetime musical moment because you don't have a portable recorder on hand; you never know when inspiration may strike. If you play with other people — especially those who can teach you something — keep the recorder handy so you can preserve licks, riffs, and other cool moves for later study. Digital portable recorders are great because they fit right into your guitar case. After you get good at recording your ideas, you may even consider taking along a four-track recorder (one that enables you to overdub, or add parts to, existing tracks). You can create multipart arrangements with a four-track instead of being limited to only the simple ideas you can capture on a normal stereo recorder. You can get a four-track for as little as $200.

- **Reversible screwdriver:** You can fix everything from a rattling pickup to a loose-set screw in a tuning key with such a handy screwdriver. Get one that has both a Phillips and flat-blade tip.

- **Wire cutters/needle-nose pliers:** Strings are, after all, wires. When you change strings, use wire cutters to trim away any excess and use the pliers for digging out the stubborn remnants of a broken string from a tuning post.

Other doodads you may want to consider throwing in your backpack, gym bag, or all-leather monogrammed accessories case include the following:

- **Tuning fork/pitch pipe:** Having one of these low-tech tuning devices as a spare never hurts in case the battery on your electronic tuner fails or a gravitationally challenged audience member steps on the tuner. Both of these devices are like rowboats in a speedboat and sailboat world: After the gas is gone and the wind stops blowing, you can still function by using your own power.

- **Penlight:** You don't need to wait until night to use a flashlight. Shadows and small sizes pose as much a problem for diagnosing, say, a simple electrical problem as does the complete absence of light. You can hold a penlight between your teeth as you reach into the back of your amp to fix a broken speaker lead.

✔ **Cable tester and volt-ohm meter:** These items cost about $12 and $20, respectively, and earn their keep the first time they diagnose a bad or mis-wired cable. Learn how to use the volt-ohm meter with respect to your equipment — that is, know what power supplies you have and what the appropriate settings are on the meter. You can impress your friends with your "gearhead-geek" aptitude.

✔ **Fuses:** Any new environment can have unpredictable wiring schemes that could cause havoc with your gear — and especially your amp. Your amp's first line of defense is its fuse. If the current in your environment is weird, the fuse blows, and you must have a replacement to get the amp working again.

✔ **Duct tape:** This stuff is the musician's baking soda — an all-purpose utility product that cures a multitude of maladies. You can use duct tape to fix everything from a rattling tailpiece to a broken microphone clip. Even the roll is handy: You can use it to angle your amp up toward the ceiling for better dispersion. Use duct tape to fix your car's upholstery or even patch the holes of your jeans, onstage or off. In some circles, it's even considered fashionable.

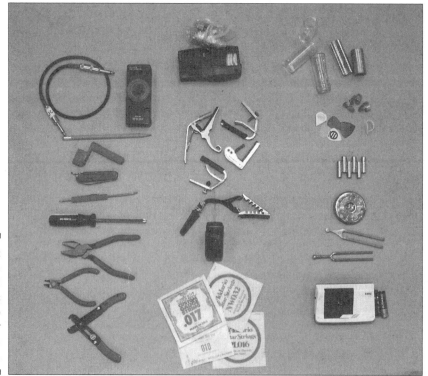

Figure 17-4: Some helpful accessories designed to make guitar life just a little easier.

Photograph courtesy of Cherry Lane Music

Chapter 18

Changing Your Strings

. . . .

. . . .

Many people consider their guitars to be delicate, precious, and fragile instruments: They seem reluctant to tune their strings, let alone change them. Although you should be careful not to drop or scratch your guitar (and setting guitars afire à la Jimi Hendrix generally causes significant damage), you needn't worry about causing damage by changing, tuning, or overtightening guitar strings. The fact is that guitars are incredibly rugged and can deal with hundreds of pounds of string tension while enduring the playing styles of even the most heavy-handed guitarists.

Changing strings isn't something you should be shy about: You can jump into it with both feet. The task is sort of like giving your dog a bath — it's good for the dog, you're glad you did it, and it gives you an opportunity to get closer to man's best friend. Similarly, changing your guitar strings has few drawbacks — it improves the sound of the guitar, helps to prevent broken strings at inopportune moments, and aids you in identifying other maintenance problems. During periodic string changing, for example, you may discover a gouged bridge slot or a loose or rattling tuning post. (We cover these maladies more fully in Chapter 19.)

Surveying String-Changing Strategies

Old guitars improve with age, but old strings just get worse. The first time you play new strings is the best they ever sound. Strings gradually deteriorate until they either break or you can't take the dreary sounds they produce. Old strings sound dull and lifeless, and they lose their *tensility* (their capability to hold tension), becoming brittle. This condition makes the strings feel stiffer and harder to fret, and because the strings no longer stretch to reach the fret, they get tighter, causing your notes to go sharp, particularly up the neck.

You should replace all the strings at once, unless you break one and must replace it quickly. The strings tend to wear at the same rate, so if you replace all the old strings with new ones simultaneously, the strings start the race against time on equal footing.

The following list contains the conditions under which you should probably replace your strings:

- They exhibit visible signs of corrosion or caked-on dirt or grime.
- They don't play in tune, usually fretting sharp, especially in the upper regions of the neck.
- You can't remember the last time you changed them and you have an important gig (and don't want to chance any breakage).

Removing Old Strings

Obviously, to put on a new string, you have to remove the old one. Unless you're really in a hurry (such as when you're in the middle of the first verse, trying to get your new string on and tuned before the guitar solo), you can take off any string by turning the tuning peg to loosen the string so much that you can grab the string from the center and pull it off the post. You don't need to wind it completely off the post by using the peg.

A quicker method is to simply snip off the old string with wire cutters. Snipping off a string may seem weird and brutal, but neither the sudden release of tension nor the cutting itself hurts the guitar. It does a number on the old string, but you don't need to concern yourself with that. (We have it on good authority that guitar strings have no pain receptors.)

The only reason *not* to cut the string is to save it as a spare, in case the new one breaks while putting it on (rare, but it happens). An old B string is better than no B string.

A common misconception is that you should maintain constant string tension on the guitar neck at all times. Therefore, you may hear that you should replace the strings one at a time because removing all the strings is bad for the guitar, but this simply isn't true. Replacing strings one at a time is *convenient* for tuning but is no healthier for the guitar. Guitars are made of tougher stuff than that.

However you remove the old string, after it's off, you're ready to put on a new one. The methods for stringing a guitar diverge slightly, depending on whether you're stringing a steel-string acoustic, a classical, or an electric guitar. The rest of this chapter covers all these methods.

Stringing an Acoustic Guitar

Generally, steel-string acoustic guitars are probably easier to string than classicals or electrics (which we cover in later sections in this chapter). In the following sections, we walk you through the process of changing an acoustic's strings, and we show you how to tune it up.

Changing strings step by step

Following are step-by-step instructions on restringing your acoustic guitar. You have two places to attach your new string: the bridge and the head-stock. Start by attaching the string to the bridge, which is a pretty straight-forward task.

Step 1: Attaching the string to the bridge

Acoustic guitars have a bridge with six holes leading to the inside of the guitar. To attach a new string to the bridge, follow these steps:

1. **Remove the old string (see the earlier section "Removing Old Strings") and pop out the bridge pin.**

   Bridge pins sometimes stick, so you may need to use a table knife to pry it out, but be careful not to ding the wood. A better alternative is the notched edge in a peg winder or needle-nose pliers. (See Chapter 17 for more information on peg winders.)

2. **Place the end of the new string that has a little brass ring (called a** *ball***) inside the hole that held the bridge pin.**

   Just stuff it down the hole a couple of inches. (How far isn't critical, because you're going to pull it up soon.)

3. **Wedge the bridge pin firmly back in the hole with the slot facing forward (toward the nut).**

   The slot provides a channel for the string to get out. Figure 18-1 shows the correct disposition for the new string and the bridge pin.

4. **Pull gently on the string until the ball rests against the bottom of the pin. Keep your thumb or finger on the pin so it doesn't pop out and disappear into the abyss.**

   Be careful not to kink the string as you pull it.

5. **Test the string by gently tugging on it.**

   If you don't feel the string shift, the ball is snug against the bridge pin, and you're ready to secure the string to the tuning post, which is the focus of the following section.

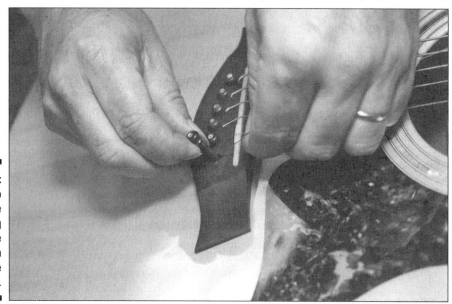

Figure 18-1:
How to place the new string in the bridge and position the bridge pin.

Photograph courtesy of Jon Chappell

Step 2: Securing the string to the tuning post

After securely attaching the string to the bridge pin, you can focus your attention on the headstock. The steps are slightly different for the treble strings (G, B, E) and the bass strings (E, A, D). You wind treble strings clockwise and bass strings counterclockwise.

To attach a treble string to the tuning post, follow these steps:

1. **Pass the string through the hole in the post.**

   Leave enough slack between the bridge pin and the tuning post to enable the string to wrap around the post several times when you tune up.

2. **Kink (or crease) the metal wire toward the inside of the guitar.**

   Figure 18-2 shows how to kink the string to prepare it for winding.

3. **While keeping the string tight against the post with one hand, wind the tuning peg clockwise with the other hand.**

   This step is a bit tricky and requires some manual dexterity (but so does playing the guitar). Keep your eye on the post to ensure that as the string wraps around the post, it winds *down, toward the headstock surface*. Figure 18-3 shows how the strings wrap around the posts. Be sure the strings go into the correct slot in the nut. Don't get discouraged if you can't get your windings to look exactly like the strings shown in Figure 18-3. Getting everything to go smoothly takes a bit of practice.

Figure 18-2:
String kinked to the inside of the head-stock, with slack for winding.

Photograph courtesy of Jon Chappell

Winding the string downward on the post increases what's called the *breaking angle.* The breaking angle is the angle between the post and the nut. A sharper angle brings more tension down onto the nut and creates better *sustain,* the length of time the note continues. To get the maximum angle, wind the string so it sits as low as possible on the post. (This fact is true for all guitars, not just acoustics.)

To attach a bass string, follow the preceding steps, *except* wind the strings *counterclockwise* in Step 3 so the string goes up the middle and goes over the post to the left (as you face the headstock).

If you find that you've left too much slack, unwind the string and start again, kinking the string farther down. If you don't leave enough slack, your winding doesn't go all the way down the post, which may result in slipping if the string doesn't have enough length to grab firmly around the post. Neither situation is tragic. You simply undo what you've done and try again. As may happen in trying to get the two ends of a necktie the same length, you may need a couple tries to get it right.

Figure 18-3:
The treble strings wrap around the posts in a clockwise direction; the bass strings wrap around the posts in a counter-clockwise direction.

Photograph courtesy of Jon Chappell

Tuning up

After you secure the string around the post and start winding it with the tuning key, you can begin to hear the string come up to pitch. As the string tightens, make sure it stays in its correct nut slot. If you're changing strings one at a time, you can just tune the new one to the old ones, which, presumably, are relatively in tune. Check out Chapter 2 for the nuts and bolts (or was that nuts and posts?) of tuning your guitar.

After you get the string to the correct pitch, tug on it (by pulling it out and away from the fingerboard) in various places up and down its length to stretch it out a bit. Doing so can cause the string to go flat — sometimes drastically if you left any loose windings on the post — so tune it back up to pitch by winding the peg. Repeat the tune-stretch process two or three times to help the new strings hold their pitch.

Using a *peg winder* to quickly turn the tuning pegs reduces your string-winding time considerably. A peg winder also features a notch in one side of the sleeve that can help you pop a stuck bridge pin. Just make sure you don't lose the pin when it comes flying out! Chapter 17 has more information on peg winders.

After the string is up to pitch and stretched out, you're ready to remove the excess string that sticks out from the post. You can snip this excess off with wire cutters (if you have them) or bend the string back and forth over the same crease until it breaks off.

Whatever you do, don't leave the straight string length protruding. It could poke you or someone standing next to you (such as the bass player) in the eye or give you a sharp jab in your fingertip.

Stringing a Nylon-String Guitar

Stringing a nylon-string guitar is different from stringing a steel-string acoustic because both the bridge and the posts are different. Nylon-string guitars don't use bridge pins (strings are tied off instead), and their headstocks are slotted and have rollers, as opposed to posts. In the following sections, we describe the steps of changing the strings of a nylon-string guitar, and we explain how to tune it up.

Changing strings step by step

In one sense, nylon strings are easier to deal with than steel strings are, because nylon isn't as springy as steel. Attaching the string to the tuning post, however, can be a bit trickier. As you do with the steel-string acoustic that we talk about earlier in this chapter, begin by securing the bridge end of the string first and then turn your attention to the headstock.

Step 1: Attaching the string to the bridge

Whereas steel-string acoustic strings have a ball at one end, nylon strings have no such ball: Both ends are loose. (Well, you *can* buy ball-ended nylon-string sets, but they're not what you normally use.) You can, therefore, attach either end of the string to the bridge. If the ends look different, however, use the one that looks like the middle of the string, not the one that has the loosely coiled appearance. Just follow these steps:

1. **Remove the old string, as we describe in the section "Removing Old Strings," earlier in this chapter.**

2. **Pass one end of the new string through the hole in the top of the bridge, in the direction away from the soundhole, leaving about 1½ inches sticking out the rear of the hole.**

3. **Secure the string by bringing the short end over the bridge and passing it under the long part of the string, as shown in Figure 18-4a.**

4. **Then pass the short end under, over, and then under itself, on the top of the bridge, as shown in Figure 18-4b.**

You may need a couple tries to get the end at just the right length, where not too much excess is dangling off the top of the bridge. (You can always cut the excess away, too.)

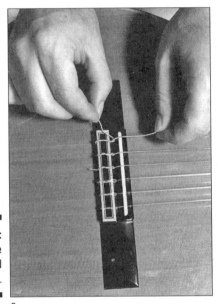

Figure 18-4:
Tying off the
bridge end
of the string.

a

b

Photographs courtesy of Jon Chappell

5. **Pull on the long end of the string with one hand and move the knot with the other to remove excess slack and cause the knot to lie flat against the bridge.**

Step 2: Securing the string to the tuning post

On a nylon-string guitar, the tuning posts (called *rollers*) pass through the headstock sideways instead of going through perpendicularly as on a steel-string acoustic or electric guitar. This configuration is known as a *slotted headstock.*

To attach the string to the tuning post in a slotted headstock, follow these steps:

1. **Pass the string through the hole in the tuning post.**

2. **Bring the end of the string back over the roller toward you; then pass the string under itself in front of the hole.**

Pull up on the string end so the long part of the string (the part attached to the bridge) sits in the U-shaped loop you just formed, as shown in Figure 18-5a.

Make your loop come from the outside (that is, approaching from the left on the lower three bass strings and from the right on the upper three treble strings).

3. **Pass the short end under and over itself, creating two or three wraps.**

Doing so should hold the loose end firmly in place, as shown in Figure 18-5b, and prevent the string from slipping out of the hole.

4. **Wind the peg so the string wraps on top of the loop you just formed, forcing it down against the post.**

5. **Pull the string length taut with one hand and turn the tuning peg with the other hand.**

Wrap the windings to the outside of the hole, away from the center of the guitar.

Figure 18-5:
Creating a
U-shaped
loop with
the short
end of the
string (a).
Creating
wraps to
hold the
short end of
the string in
place (b).

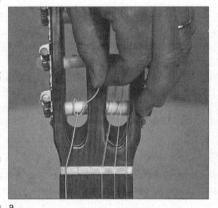
a

b

Photographs courtesy of Jon Chappell

Tuning up

As you continue turning the tuning peg, the string slowly comes nearer to pitch. Nylon strings, like steel strings, require quite a bit of stretching out, so after you get the string initially up to pitch, grab it at various places along its length, pull on it (drawing it away from the fingerboard), and then tune it up again. Repeat this process two or three times to keep the guitar in tune longer.

Snip away the excess after you're done with all six strings. Nylon strings aren't as dangerous as steel strings if any excess protrudes, but the extra string hanging out is unsightly, and besides, classical guitarists are a little fussier about how their instruments look than acoustic guitarists are.

Stringing an Electric Guitar

Generally, electric guitarists need to change their strings more often than do steel-string acoustic or nylon-string guitarists. Because changing strings is so common on electric guitars, builders take a more progressive approach to the hardware, often making changing strings very quick and easy. Of the three types of guitars — steel-string acoustic, nylon-string, and electric — you can change the strings on electric guitars most easily by far. We explain how to change an electric's strings and tune it up in the following sections.

Changing strings step by step

As you would on steel-string acoustic and nylon-string guitars (both of which we cover earlier in this chapter), begin stringing an electric guitar by first securing the string to the bridge and then attaching the string to the headstock. Electric strings are similar to steel-string acoustic strings in that they have ball ends and are made of metal, but electric strings are usually composed of a lighter-gauge wire than steel-string acoustic strings, and the 3rd string is unwound, or plain, whereas a steel-string acoustic guitar's is wound. (A nylon-string's 3rd string usually is unwound but is a thicker nylon string.)

Step 1: Attaching the string to the bridge

Most electric guitars use a simple method for securing the string to the bridge. You pass the string through a hole in the bridge (sometimes reinforced with a collar, or *grommet*) that's smaller than the ball at the end of the string — so the ball holds the string just as the knot at the end of a piece of thread holds a stitch in fabric. On some guitars (such as the Fender Telecaster), the collars anchor right into the body, and the strings pass through the back of the instrument, through a hole in the bridge assembly, and out the top.

Figure 18-6 shows two designs for attaching a string to an electric: from a top-mounted bridge and through the back. The following steps show how to secure the strings to the bridge.

a

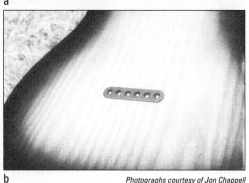

b

Figure 18-6:
Strings pass
through the
bridge in the
direction of
the head-
stock (a).
Strings pass
through the
bridge from
the back
of the
guitar (b).

Photographs courtesy of Jon Chappell

1. **Remove the old string, as we describe in the section "Removing Old Strings," earlier in this chapter.**

2. **Anchor the string at the bridge by passing the string through the hole (from the back or bottom of the guitar) until the ball stops the movement.**

   Then you're ready to focus on the tuning post. You do this on all but a few guitars (such as those fitted with a Floyd Rose mechanism, which we discuss later in this chapter).

Step 2: Securing the string to the tuning post

In most cases, the posts on an electric resemble those of a steel-string acoustic. A post protrudes through the headstock, and you pass your string through the post's hole, kink the string to the inside (toward the center of the headstock), and begin winding while holding the long part of the string with one hand for control. Refer to Figure 18-2 to see how to kink the string to prepare it for winding and about how much slack to leave.

Some electric guitars, notably Fender Stratocasters and Telecasters, feature *string retainers,* which are little rollers or channels screwed into the top of the headstock that pull the top two or four strings down low onto the headstock, sort of like a tent stake. If your guitar has string retainers, make sure you pass the strings under them.

Some tuners feature a *locking* mechanism so you don't need to worry about winding, slack, and all that bother. Inside the post hole is a viselike device that clamps down on the string as it passes through. A *knurled* (ridge-covered) dial underneath the headstock or on top of the post loosens and tightens the vise. Perhaps the best-known company to make this locking device is Sperzel.

Some guitars have tuners with slotted posts instead of a hole. These devices also enable quick string changes, because you simply lay the string in the slot at the top of the post, kink it, and begin winding. You don't even need to leave any slack for winding.

Tuning up

Tuning an electric guitar isn't much different from tuning an acoustic (which we explain how to do earlier in this chapter), except that the strings will slip out of tune more easily and more often, so they'll require more tweaking to get all six strings up to pitch. If you have a floating bridge (described in the following section), tuning a string changes the tension on the bridge, causing all the strings that were formerly in tune to go slightly out of tune, so the process takes even longer. But eventually, all the strings "settle down" and the tuning stabilizes.

Setting up a floating bridge

Rock music in the '80s made extensive use of the whammy bar and *floating bridge* (where the bridge isn't fixed but floats on a spring assembly). Standard floating bridges weren't meant for the kind of abuse that creative guitarists, such as Steve Vai and Joe Satriani, cook up, however, so manufacturers developed better ways to increase the bridges' motion and also to make sure the bridges returned to their original position and the strings remained in tune.

Floyd Rose invented the most successful of these assemblies. Rose used his own patented design to ensure a highly accurate, movable bridge system and *locking nut* (a clamplike device that replaces the standard nut). Other manufacturers, such as Kahler, have developed similar systems.

The Floyd Rose system takes the strings in a top-mounted approach, instead of through the back, but with one notable difference: Guitarists must snip off the ball end before attaching the string so the end can fit in the tiny viselike mechanism that holds the string in place. If you own a Floyd, you must carry a set of spare strings with the balls snipped off or at least have wire cutters always at the ready.

In floating bridge systems that also feature a locking nut, winding the string on the post isn't so critical. After you lock the nut (by using a small hex key or Allen wrench), what you do with the tuning pegs doesn't matter. You then perform all tuning, using small dials, or knobs, on the bridge. These knobs are known as *fine tuners* because their movements are much smaller and more precise than the ones by the tuners on the headstock.

Stringing up and tuning an electric guitar fitted with a floating bridge takes a little longer than it does on a regular electric, but if you plan to do a lot of whammy bar work (necessary for many heavy metal styles), it's well worth the effort.

Chapter 19

Guitar Wellness: Basic Maintenance

. . . .

In This Chapter

▶ Cleaning your guitar

▶ Keeping your guitar protected

▶ Maintaining the proper environment

▶ Trying do-it-yourself adjustments and repairs

▶ Determining the tools you need on hand

▶ Knowing the repairs you shouldn't attempt at home

. . . .

Guitars are surprisingly hardy creatures. You can subject them to a rigorous performing schedule, keep them up all night, and bang on them relentlessly, yet they don't mind a bit. Generally speaking, guitars never wear out, although you may need to replace some parts and perform some tweaks along the way: Unlike your car or body, you don't need to do anything much to a guitar to keep it in excellent health.

If you don't abuse it or subject it to extreme conditions, a guitar not only stays structurally sound for decades, but it also plays in tune and remains comfortable in your hands. In fact, guitars actually *improve* with age and use. We should all be so lucky!

Even so, preventing a guitar from sustaining some injury or needing a few repairs along the way is virtually impossible. You can and should practice good guitar maintenance (with the help of the guidelines in this chapter), and if your guitar does go out of whack, you can perform the repairs yourself in most cases. If you're at all in doubt about your technical abilities, however — or if you're just a plain klutz — consult a qualified repairperson.

Some examples of repairs that you can perform yourself include eliminating rattles, raising and lowering the strings at the bridge, removing dirt and grime, replacing some worn or broken parts, and changing strings. (We devote all of Chapter 18 to changing strings, so turn to that chapter if you just want to replace a broken or worn string.)

Keeping Your Guitar Clean

The simplest type of maintenance is cleaning. You should clean your guitar regularly or, intuitively enough, every time it gets dirty. If a guitar gets dirty, it doesn't exactly come home with mud on its shirt and grass stains on its pants, but it does collect a laundry list of its own washday terrors. The following sections give you the scoop on keeping your guitar clean.

Removing dust, dirt, and grime

Unless you live in a bubble, dust and dirt are part of your environment. Certain objects just seem to attract dust (for example, a windowsill or a tabletop), and guitars definitely attract their fair share. If dust collects under the strings on your headstock and bridge, you can dust them off by using a cloth or a feather duster or a Q-tip (for those hard-to-reach spots). Feather dusters may seem silly things that only uniformed maids in old movies use, but they serve a purpose: They knock the dust off an object without applying pressure (which can scratch a delicate finish). So even if you don't use a feather duster — or if your maid's outfit is at the cleaners — follow the example of old Alice from *The Brady Bunch* and dust lightly.

As dust mixes with the natural moisture content of your hands and fingers (and forearm, if you play in short sleeves, shirtless, or in the raw), that dust becomes grime. Grime can stick to all surfaces, but it's especially noticeable on your strings.

The following sections explain how to clean your guitar's strings, wood and hardware.

The strings

The natural oils from your fingertips coat the strings every time you play. You can't see this oily coating, but it's there, and over time, these oils corrode the string material and create a grimy buildup (which is icky, impedes play, and can actually injure the wood over time). String grime makes the strings go dead sooner and wear out faster than they normally do; if you let the condition go too long, the string grime can even seep into the pores of the fingerboard. Yuck!

The best way to combat the grimy-buildup menace is to wipe down the strings after every playing session, just before you put the guitar back in the case. (Notice that we're assuming that you put the guitar back in the case — another "case" of good preventative maintenance; see Chapter 17.) Chamois is a great material to use to wipe the strings because it doubles as a polishing cloth; a (clean) cotton diaper, however, works well, too (but *no* disposable diapers, please), as does a microfiber cloth. Bandannas may give you that Willie Nelson/Janis Joplin appeal, but they're not made of good absorbent material, so keep your bandanna around your neck or on your head, and don't wipe your guitar with it.

Give the strings a general wipe down and then pinch each string between your thumb and index finger, with the cloth in between, and run your hand up and down the string length. This dries the string all the way around its circumference and shucks off any grunge. That's all you need to do to maintain clean strings and increase their useful life many times over. (And while you're at it, wipe the back of the guitar neck, too.)

The wood

A guitar is mostly wood, and wood likes a good rubdown. (Hey, who doesn't?) If you have a really dusty guitar — for example, one that's been sitting open in a musty attic for a while — blow the excess dust off before you start dusting with a cloth (or feather duster). This simple act may prevent a scratch or abrasion in the finish.

Gently rub the various places on the guitar until it's dust-free. You may need to frequently shake out your dustcloth, so do so outside, or you're going to be wiping sneezes off your guitar as well as the dust. Unless your guitar is *really* dirty — maybe displaying some caked-on gunk that you don't even want to *know* the origin of — dusting is all you need to do to the wood.

If dullness persists or a grimy film is clearly present over the finish, you can rub your guitar down with furniture polish or, better yet, guitar polish. *Guitar polish* is made specifically for the finishes that the manufacturers use on guitars, whereas some furniture polish may contain abrasives. If you're at all in doubt, use the guitar goop that music stores sell. And follow the directions on the bottle.

Although the guitar-goop companies write this information on the label, it bears repeating here: Never put any liquid or spray polish directly onto the guitar surface. Doing so could soak and stain the wood permanently. Pour or spray the substance onto your dustcloth and work it in a bit before putting the cloth to wood.

To dust between the strings in hard-to-reach places, such as the headstock, bridge, and pickup areas, use a small camel's hair paintbrush. Keep the brush in your case.

The hardware

Grimy buildup doesn't really hurt hardware (tuners, bridges, and so on) the way that it can more porous wood, but it sure looks bad — and you don't want to appear on TV with hardware that's duller than a head of brown lettuce.

Rubbing with a dustcloth is all you really need to do for your guitar's hardware, but you can certainly use a mild jewelry or chrome polish if you want — as long as it's not abrasive. Polish not only removes really greasy residue (which a simple wipe won't do) but also brings the hardware to a luster — very important for stage and TV lights.

Many inexpensive hardware components are *dipped,* meaning that they have a thin coating of shiny metal over an otherwise ugly and mottled-looking surface. So you don't want to rub through the coating (which could happen with repeated polishing). And you *certainly* (we hope) don't want to get any liquid polish in the moving parts of a tuning machine.

Don't *ever* touch the pickups of an electric guitar with anything other than a dry cloth or your dusting brush. Pickups are magnetic and abhor liquid as much as the Wicked Witch of the West did. You don't want to risk upsetting a pickup's sensitive magnetic fields with liquid, my pretty.

Caring for the finish

Acoustic guitars have a finish of lacquer or another synthetic coating to protect the wood's surface and give it a shiny appearance. Whether your instrument has a high-gloss finish or the satin variety (more subdued and natural-looking), the plan is the same: Keep the finish dust-free so it stays shiny and transparent for years. Don't subject your guitar to direct sunlight for long periods of time and avoid drastic humidity and temperature changes. (For more on temperature and humidity conditions, see the section "Providing a Healthy Environment," later in this chapter.) Following these simple guidelines helps keep the finish from *checking* (cracking) as it swells and shrinks along with the wood.

If your finish ever cracks because of a ding (a small inadvertent gouge, such as occurs if you bang your guitar into the corner of the table), take it to a repairperson quickly to prevent the crack from spreading like a spider pattern on a windshield.

Protecting Your Guitar

If you play guitar, you certainly don't want to keep it a secret. Well, in the beginning maybe, but after you can play a little bit, you want to bring your music to the people. Unless you plan on doing a lot of entertaining — as in having people come over to your place — you need to take your guitar out into the world. And that requires protection, as you discover in the following sections. Never leave the house without putting the guitar in some kind of protective case.

On the road

Most people don't even think about the guitar's health as they toss their favorite acoustic into the station wagon and head for the beach. But they should. Using a bit of common sense can keep your guitar looking like a guitar instead of a surfboard.

If you're traveling in a car, keep the guitar in the passenger compartment where you can exercise control over the environment. A guitar in a trunk or untreated luggage compartment gets either too hot or too cold in comparison to what the humans are experiencing up front. (Guitars like to listen to the radio, too, as long as it's not playing disco.)

If you must put the guitar in with the spare tire, push it all the way forward so it can benefit from some "environmental osmosis" (meaning that it's not going to get quite as cold or hot next to the climate-controlled passenger cabin as it is at the rear of the car). This practice also helps if, heaven forbid, you're ever rear-ended. You can pay a couple of bucks to have Freddie's Fender Fix-it repair your car, but all the king's horses and all the king's men can't restore the splinters of your priceless acoustic should it absorb the brunt of a bumper-bashing Buick.

 A hardshell case is a better form of protection for a guitar than either a nylon gig bag or a cardboard-like soft case. With a hardshell case, you can stack things on top, whereas other cases require the guitar to be at the top of the heap, which may or may not please an obsessive trunk-packer. (You know, like your old man used to pack before the big family vacation.) See Chapter 17 for more information on cases.

 Nylon gig bags are lightweight and offer almost no protection from a blow, but they do fend off dings. If you know the guitar is never going to leave your shoulder, you can use a gig bag. Gig bags also enable an electric guitar to fit in the overhead compartments of most aircraft. Savvy travelers know what kinds of crafts can accommodate a gig bag and stand in line early to secure a berth for their precious cargo.

In your home

Whether you're going on a long vacation or doing three-to-five in the slammer, you may, at some point, need to store your guitar for a long period of time. Keep the guitar in its case and put the case in a closet or under a bed. Try to keep the guitar in a climate controlled environment rather than a damp basement or uninsulated attic.

If you store the guitar, you can lay it flat or on edge. The exact position makes no difference to the guitar. You don't need to loosen the strings significantly, but dropping them down a half step or so ensures against excess tension on the neck, should it swell or shrink slightly.

Providing a Healthy Environment

Guitars are made under specific temperature and humidity conditions. To keep the guitar playing and sounding as the builder intended, you must maintain an environment within the same approximate range of the original.

If a human is comfortable, a guitar is comfortable. Keep the environment near room temperature (about 72 degrees Fahrenheit) and the relative humidity at about 50 percent, and you're never going to hear your guitar complain (even if you have a talking guitar). Don't go too far with this rule about guitars and humans being comfortable under the same conditions, however. You shouldn't put your guitar in a hot tub even if you offer it a margarita, no matter how comfortable that makes you.

Temperature

A guitar can exist comfortably in a range of temperatures between about 65 and 80 degrees Fahrenheit. For a guitar, heat is worse than cold, so keep the guitar out of the sun and avoid leaving a guitar sitting in a hot car trunk all day.

If your guitar's been cold for several hours because it was riding in the back of the truck that you drove from North Dakota to Minnesota in December, give the guitar time to warm up gradually after you bring it indoors. A good practice is to leave the guitar in its case until the case warms up to room temperature. Avoid exposing the guitar to radical temperature shifts if at all possible to prevent finish checking — the cracking of your finish that results because it can't expand and contract well enough with the wood beneath it.

Humidity

Guitars, whether they're made in Hawaii or Arizona, are all built under humidity-controlled conditions, which stay at about 50 percent. To enable your guitar to maintain the lifestyle that its maker intended for it, you must also maintain that humidity at about 45 to 55 percent. (If you live in a dry or wet climate and compensate with a humidifier or dehumidifier, you should aim for those settings as a healthy human anyway.) Guitars that get too dry crack; guitars that absorb too much moisture swell and buckle.

If you can't afford either a humidifier or dehumidifier, you can achieve good results with the following inexpensive solutions:

✔ **Guitar humidifier:** This item is simply a rubber-enclosed sponge that you saturate with water, squeeze the excess out of, and then clip onto the inside of the soundhole or keep inside the case to raise the humidity level.

✔ **Desiccant:** A desiccant is a powder or crystal substance that usually comes in small packets and draws humidity out of the air, lowering the local relative humidity level. Silicagel is a common brand, and packets often come in the cases of new guitars.

✔ **Hygrometer:** You can buy this inexpensive device at any hardware store; it tells you the relative humidity of a room with a good degree of accuracy (close enough to maintain a healthy guitar anyway). Get the portable kind (as opposed to the wall-hanging variety) so you can transport it if you need to or even keep it inside the guitar case.

Considering Do-It-Yourself Fixes

If you turn on the light in your house and the bulb blows, do you call a handyman? Of course not. You look at the dead bulb to note its wattage, go to the closet, get the right replacement bulb, and in a jiffy, you're bathed in 60-watt luminescence. You suffer no anxiety about performing that "repair," right?

If you can develop this same intuitive approach toward your guitar, you can perform simple adjustments, tweaks, and repairs. Nothing magical goes on in a guitar mechanically. The magic comes in the way that it produces that glorious sound, not in how the tuning machines work or the way the strings attach to the bridge. The following sections describe several adjustments, replacements, and repairs you can perform yourself.

Tightening loose connections

A guitar is a system of moving parts, many of which are mechanical, and as anyone who's ever owned a car can attest, moving things come loose. In guitars, the hardware connections are what typically work themselves loose, such as the nuts on the bridge post or the screws that hold down the pickup covers.

If you hear a rattle, try strumming with one hand to recreate the rattle while touching the various suspects with your other hand. As you touch the offending culprit, the rattle usually stops. Then you can take appropriate measures to tighten up whatever's come loose. (Screws in tuning machines, pickup covers, or jack plates are the most common.) Usually that involves using ordinary tools — screwdrivers, wrenches, chain saws (just kidding) — designed for the appropriate-sized screws, nuts, and so on. Take an inventory of the sizes and shapes of the screws, nuts, and bolts on your guitar and create a miniature tool kit just for fixing your instrument. (For more on this topic, see the section "Gathering the Right Tools," later in this chapter.)

Adjusting the neck and the bridge

Guitars do change over time (such as in going from one season to another), especially if your environment experiences temperature and humidity swings. If the temperature and humidity change frequently, the guitar naturally absorbs or loses moisture, which causes the wood to swell or shrink. This condition is normal and doesn't hurt the guitar.

The problem with this expansion and contraction lies in the fact that the playing and setup tolerances are fairly critical, so a slight bow in the neck results in a guitar that plays buzzy or is suddenly much harder to fret. If this situation occurs, you can often correct the problem through a simple adjustment of the neck and/or bridge. Check out the guidelines in the following sections.

Tightening and loosening the truss rod

The neck of most guitars has what's known as a *truss rod,* which is a one- or two-piece adjustable metal rod that goes down the inside of the center of the neck. You can adjust the truss rod with a nut located at one end. Different manufacturers put them in different places, but they're usually at the headstock, under a cap just behind the nut, or where the neck joins the body, just under the fingerboard. Some older models don't have truss rods or, in the case of old Martin guitars, have truss rods that you can't adjust without taking off the fingerboard. All newer guitars have accessible truss rods.

All guitars come with their particular truss-rod wrench, so if you don't have one for your particular instrument, try to find a replacement immediately. (Try your local guitar store first and, failing that, get in touch with the manufacturer itself.)

The necessary truss-rod adjustment depends on which way the neck bows:

- ✔ If your neck has too much relief, or bows *inward* between the 7th and 12th frets, creating a large gap that makes pressing down the strings difficult, tighten the truss rod by turning the nut clockwise (as you face the nut straight on). Tighten the nut a quarter turn at a time, giving the neck a few minutes to adjust after each turn. (You can play during the adjustment time.)

- ✔ If your neck bows *outward* between the 7th and 12th frets, causing the strings to buzz and *fret out* (that is, come in contact with frets they're not supposed to as you press down the strings), loosen the truss rod with the truss-rod wrench by turning the nut counterclockwise (as you face the nut straight on). Turn the nut a quarter turn at a time, enabling the neck to adjust after each turn.

If you can't correct the problem in a few full turns, stop. You may need a qualified repairperson to investigate. Overtightening or overloosening a truss rod can damage the neck and/or body.

Checking the action

Action is how a guitar plays, specifically the distance of the strings to the fingerboard. If the strings sit too high, they're hard to fret; if they're too low, buzzing occurs. In either case, you have to adjust the action. You usually do this by raising or lowering components of the bridge known as *saddles* (the parts just in front of the bridge where the strings sit). You raise or lower the saddle by turning the hex screws with a tiny hex key (Allen wrench). Turn the screw clockwise to raise the saddle; turn it counterclockwise to lower the saddle. If the saddle has two hex screws, be sure to turn them the same amount so the saddle stays level. (Figure 19-1 shows the saddles' hex screws.)

Adjusting the intonation

Intonation refers to the accuracy of the pitches produced by fretting. For example, if you play the 12th fret, the resulting note should be exactly an octave higher than the open string. If the 12th-fret note is slightly higher than an octave, your string is fretting sharp; if the 12th-fret note is slightly lower than an octave, the string is fretting flat. You can correct a string's intonation by moving the saddle away from the nut if the string frets sharp and toward the nut if the string frets flat. Different bridges have different methods for this, but it's pretty obvious when you look at the bridge assembly carefully.

Photograph courtesy of Jon Chappell

Figure 19-1:
Turn the saddles' hex screws to raise or lower the action.

In one common mechanism (used on Fender Stratocasters and Telecasters), screws at the back of the bridge determine the saddle front-to-back position. Here's how they work:

✔ Turning the screw clockwise (with a simple Phillips or flat-head screwdriver — being careful not to ding the top with the handle as you turn the screw) pulls the saddle back toward the bridge, which corrects a string that frets sharp.

✔ Turning the screw counterclockwise moves the saddle toward the nut, which corrects a string that frets flat.

Keep in mind that adjusting the saddle for a string corrects only that string. You must perform intonation adjustments for each string. So don't invite us to that 38-string guitar's intonation adjustment!

Put on brand-new strings before you adjust the intonation. Old strings often fret sharp and don't give you a true reading of your intonation. (For more information on replacing strings, see Chapter 18.)

Replacing worn-out or broken parts

The following sections list all the parts on your guitar that are most likely to wear out or break and need replacing. You can perform any of these fixes yourself without doing damage to the guitar — even if you screw up.

Tuning machines

Tuning machines consist of a system of gears and shafts, and as the clutch on your car usually does eventually (or the automatic transmission if you never got that whole stick thing), tuners can wear out. Tuning machines deal with a lot of stress and tension, and we don't mean the kind that you endure at your job.

Tuning machines simply screw into the guitar's headstock with wood screws (after you push the post through the hole and fasten the hex nut on top); so if you have a worn or stripped gear, consider replacing the entire machine. If more than one tuner is giving you trouble, consider replacing the entire set. Check that the replacement machine has its screws in the same positions as the original, because you don't want to drill new holes in your headstock. If you're having trouble matching the holes of your new machines with the existing ones already drilled in your headstock, take the guitar to a repairperson.

Strap pins

Strap pins are the little "buttons" that you put through your strap holes to attach the strap to your instrument. The strap pins usually attach to the guitar with ordinary wood screws, and they can sometimes work themselves loose. If simply tightening the wood screw with a screwdriver doesn't do the trick, try applying a little white glue on the screw threads and put it back in. If it's still loose, take the guitar to a repairperson.

Bridge springs

If an electric guitar doesn't have a whammy bar, its bridge affixes directly to the guitar's body. This setup is known as a *fixed bridge.* If the guitar does have a whammy bar, however, it has a floating bridge. A *floating bridge* is held in place by the string tension (which pulls it one way) and a set of metal springs — known as *bridge springs* — which pull in the opposite direction, holding the bridge in balance. You can find the springs (which are about 3 inches long and ¼ inch wide) in the back cavity of the body (see Figure 19-2).

If one of the springs loses tension through age and wear, your guitar will go out of tune when you use the whammy bar. When this happens, replace the springs; change them all at once so they wear evenly. The springs just hook onto little hooks, and with a little tugging and the aid of pliers, you can pop them off and on in no time. You can even tighten the screws on the plate (called the *claw*) where the hooks attach, increasing the spring tension. Don't worry — these springs don't go *sproingggg* and hit you in the eye or go flying off across the room.

Figure 19-2:
The bridge
springs,
shown
through
the guitar's
back cavity.

Photograph courtesy of Jon Chappell

Some people like a loose bridge (which is more responsive but goes out of tune more easily) and some like a tight bridge:

✔ If you like a stiff bridge that stays in tune (and who doesn't!) and you only occasionally use the whammy bar, go for a stiff bridge setup. The more springs, the tighter the bridge; so if you have a two-spring setup, consider switching to a three-spring setup.

✔ If you like to use the bar and you're willing to trade a little tuning trouble for having a bridge with a lot of play, consider a looser setup. Guitarists who like to create *ambient* music (atmospheric music without a defined melody) often do a lot of dips and pulls on the bar, and so prefer flexible bridges.

Crackling controls

Dust and rust (oxidation) pose a potential threat to any electronic connection, and your guitar is no exception. If your pickup selector switch or volume and tone knobs start to make crackling or popping noises through your speaker whenever you're plugged in, or if the signal is weak, inconsistent, or cuts out altogether when the switch and knobs are in certain positions, some foreign matter (however minute) has probably lodged itself in your controls.

Vigorously flick the switch and turn the knobs back and forth around the trouble spot to work out the dust or rub off the little bit of corrosion that may be causing the problem. You may need to perform this action several times on each knob, in different places in the knob's travel. If turning the knobs doesn't do the trick, you may need a repairperson to give your pots (short for *potentiometer,* the variable resistors on your volume and tone controls) a thorough cleaning.

Loose jacks

On electric guitars, you do a lot of plugging and unplugging of your cable, and these actions can eventually loosen the output jack, causing a crackling sound through the speaker. This crackling indicates a disconnected ground wire. Here's the fix: Take off the jack plate or pick guard and locate the detached wire causing the problem.

- If you're handy with a soldering iron, attach the broken wire back to its original lug, and you're done. You may even feel like a real electrician.
- If you're not handy, have a friend who is do the job or take the instrument in to the shop.

Replacement pickups

Replacing your pickups can seem like a daunting task, but it's really a very simple one. Often, the best way to change your sound (assuming that you like the way your guitar plays and looks) is to substitute replacement pickups for the originals — especially if the originals weren't too good to begin with. Here's how:

1. **Purchase pickups of the same size and type as the originals.**

    Doing so ensures that they fit into the existing holes and hook up the same way electrically.

2. **Connect and solder two or three wires.**

    Clear directions come with the new pickups. Follow them!

3. **Seat the pickups in the cavities.**

    You're not dealing with high-voltage electricity either, so you can't hurt yourself or the electronics if you wire something backward.

Again, however, if you don't feel comfortable doing the job yourself, enlist the aid of a handy friend or take your guitar to a repairperson.

Changing your pickups is like changing your car's oil. You can do the job yourself and save money, but you may choose not to because of the hassle.

Gathering the Right Tools

Assemble a permanent tool kit containing all the tools you need for your guitar. Don't "cannibalize" this set if you're doing other household fixes. Buy two sets of tools — one for general use and one that never leaves your guitar case or gig bag. Look at your guitar to determine what kind of tools you may need should something come loose. Determine (through trial-and-error) whether your guitar's screws, bolts, and nuts are metric or not. Here's a list of what you need:

- ✔ **A set of miniature screwdrivers:** A quick inspection of the kinds of screws on an electric guitar reveals different-sized Phillips-head and slotted varieties in several places: the strap pins, the pickup cover, the pickguard, the tuning-machine mounts, the *set screws* (the screws that hold the tuning button to the shaft), the *string retainers* (the metal devices on the headstock — between the tuning posts and the nut — that hold down the strings on Strats and Teles), the volume and tone controls, and the on-the-neck back plates.

- ✔ **A miniature ratchet set:** You can also find several places for nuts: the output jack and the tuning-post *collars* (hex-shaped nuts on top of the headstock that keep the posts from wobbling). A miniature ratchet set gives you better leverage and a better angle than does a small crescent wrench.

- ✔ **Hex keys/Allen wrenches:** The truss rod takes its own tool, usually a hex key, or Allen wrench, which usually comes with the guitar if you buy it new. If your guitar doesn't have one (because it didn't come with the guitar when you bought it or it's gone missing), get the right one for your guitar and keep it in the case at all times.

  Floating bridge systems, including those by Floyd Rose (see Chapter 18), require hex keys to adjust the saddles and other elements of the assembly. Keep these devices on hand in case you break a string.

Tasks That You Shouldn't Try at Home

Some repairs *always* require a qualified repairperson to fix (assuming that anyone can repair them at all). Among such repairs are the following:

- ✔ Fixing finish cracks.

- ✔ Repairing dings and scratches (if they're severe and go through the finish to the wood).

- ✔ Filing worn frets. (If frets start to develop grooves or crevices, they need a pro to file or replace them.)

✔ Fixing pickup failure or *weakening.* (One pickup is seriously out of balance with another, you have possible magnetic damage to the pickup itself, or one of the electronic components in a pickup fails.)

✔ Fixing dirty volume and tone knobs (if vigorous turning back and forth no longer eliminates the crackle such dirt causes).

✔ Solving grounding problems. (You check the cavity and no wires are loose, but you still have inordinate noise problems.)

✔ Fixing severe neck distortion (twisting or excessive bowing in either direction).

✔ Healing certain injuries and breakage (such as the nut, fingerboard, or headstock).

✔ Refinishing or restoring your guitar's wood. (Don't even get near your guitar's finish with a sander or wood chemicals.)

✔ Rewiring your electronics. (Say you decide to replace your five-way with on/off switches, install a coil-tap and phase-reversal switch if any two adjacent pickups are active, plus insert a presence-boost knob in place of the second volume control. . . .)

Huh?! If you understand that last one, you may be beyond *Guitar For Dummies!*

If you have any anxiety about performing *any* repair or maintenance routine, *take the guitar to a repairperson.* A repairperson can tell you whether the problem is something you can fix yourself and maybe even show you how to do it correctly the next time the problem occurs. You're much better off being safe (and spending a couple of bucks) than taking a chance and damaging your guitar.

Part VI
The Part of Tens

For a bonus top ten list, showcasing ten iconic guitar models that have left an indelible mark in the history of guitar music, go to www.dummies.com/extras/guitar.

In this part . . .

✔ Read about ten or so guitarists that you should be acquainted with to expand your musical horizons and give you inspiration.

✔ Discover the signature songs that helped propel these top guitarists to fame and immortality.

✔ Uncover ten great songs that guitarists can use to begin to hone their chops.

Chapter 20

Ten (Or So) Guitarists You Should Know

In This Chapter

▶ Looking at legendary genre masters

▶ Getting to know nontraditional players

Regardless of style, certain guitarists have made their mark on the world of guitar so that any guitarist who comes along after them has a hard time escaping their legacy. We present here, in chronological order, ten (or 12, but who's counting?) guitarists who mattered and why.

Andrés Segovia (1893–1987)

Not only was Andrés Segovia the most famous classical guitarist of all time, but he also literally invented the genre (which we cover in Chapter 14). Before his arrival, the guitar was a lowly instrument of the peasant classes. Segovia began performing Bach pieces and other serious classical music on the guitar (writing many of his own transcriptions), eventually elevating this "parlor" activity to a world-class style. His incredible performing career lasted more than 70 years. His signature pieces include Bach's "Chaconne" and Albeniz's "Granada."

Django Reinhardt (1910–1953)

Born in Belgium, Django Reinhardt was a ferociously virtuosic acoustic guitarist who defined the gypsy jazz guitar sound (flip to Chapter 15 for an introduction to jazz guitar). His blistering single-note runs, vocal-like string bends, and rapid-picked tremolo technique became hallmarks of the style. Reinhardt was centered in Paris for most of his career and made the bulk of his important recordings with his band, the Quintette du Hot Club de France, and with jazz violinist Stephane Grapelli. His stunning instrumental work is all the more amazing when you consider that his left hand had been severely injured in a fire, leaving him the use of just two fingers. His signature tunes include "Minor Swing," "Nuages," and "Djangology."

Charlie Christian (1916–1942)

Charlie Christian invented the art of electric jazz guitar. His fluid solos with Benny Goodman's big band and smaller combos were sophisticated, scintillating, and years ahead of their time. After hours, he used to jam with fellow jazz rebels at Minton's in New York, where his adventurous improvisations helped create the genre known as *bebop*. Christian played the guitar like a horn, incorporating *intervallic* (non-stepwise) motion into his lines. His signature tunes include "I Found a New Baby," "Seven Come Eleven," and "Stardust."

Wes Montgomery (1923–1968)

A legendary jazz player, Wes Montgomery's brand of cool jazz was based on the fact that he used his thumb, instead of a traditional guitar pick, to sound notes. Another of his innovations was the use of *octaves* (that is, two identical notes in different ranges) to create fat, moving, unison lines. He died young, but his proponents still call him one of the all-time jazz greats. His signature tunes include "Four on Six" and "Polka Dots and Moonbeams."

Chet Atkins (1924–2001)

Known as "Mr. Guitar," Chet Atkins is *the* definitive country guitarist. Building on Merle Travis's fast fingerpicking technique (see Chapter 13), Atkins refined the style, adding jazz, classical, and pop nuances to create a truly sophisticated country-guitar approach. He played with Elvis Presley, the Everly Brothers, and countless country stars over the decades. His signature tunes include "Stars and Stripes Forever" and "Yankee Doodle Dixie."

B.B. King (1925–2015)

Although he wasn't the first electric bluesman, B.B. King is easily the most popular: His swinging, high-voltage guitar style complemented charismatic stagemanship and a huge, gospel-fueled voice. Along with his trademark Gibson ES-355 guitar, nicknamed "Lucille," King's minimalist soloing technique and massive finger vibrato cemented his place in the annals of electric blues history. His signature tunes include "Every Day I Have the Blues" and "The Thrill Is Gone." (Check out Chapter 12 for more about blues guitar.)

Chuck Berry (1926–)

Perhaps rock's first real guitar hero, Chuck Berry used fast, rhythmic double-stops to create his signature guitar style. Although some regard him equally for his songwriting and lyric-writing skills, his fire-breathing breaks made his signature tunes "Johnny B. Goode," "Rockin' in the U.S.A.," and "Maybelline" bona fide guitar classics. (Head to Chapter 11 for more about rock guitar.)

Jimi Hendrix (1942–1970)

Considered the greatest rock guitarist of all time, Jimi Hendrix fused R&B, blues, rock, and psychedelia into a mesmerizing sonic soup. His 1967 breakthrough at the Monterey Pop Festival instantly rewrote the rock guitar textbook, especially after he whipped off his Stratocaster and lit it on fire. Young guitarists religiously copy his licks to this day. Hendrix was known for his fiery abandon (even when his guitar wasn't actually on fire) and innovative work with feedback and the whammy bar. His signature tunes include "Purple Haze" and "Little Wing."

Jimmy Page (1944–)

Jimmy Page succeeded Eric Clapton and Jeff Beck in the Yardbirds, but he didn't really find his niche until forming Led Zeppelin, one of the great '70s rock bands — and of all time. Page's forte was the art of recording guitars, layering track upon track to construct thundering avalanches of electrified tone. Yet he could also play sublime acoustic guitar, regularly employing unusual tunings and global influences. In rock circles, his six-string creativity in the studio is unmatched. His signature tunes include "Stairway to Heaven" and "Whole Lotta Love."

Eric Clapton (1945–)

In many ways, Eric Clapton is the father of contemporary rock guitar. Before Jimi Hendrix, Jeff Beck, and Jimmy Page showed up, the Yardbirds-era Clapton was already fusing electric Chicago blues with the fury of rock 'n' roll. He later expanded upon this style in Cream, Blind Faith, and the legendary Derek and the Dominos. Clapton eventually went solo, turning into one of the most popular recording artists of the last 40 years. A true living legend, his signature tunes include "Crossroads" and "Layla."

Stevie Ray Vaughan (1954–1990)

A Texas-born-and-bred rock and blues virtuoso who declined a gig with David Bowie so he could instead record his first solo album, Stevie Ray Vaughan played Texas blues as a high-energy amalgam of B.B. King, Eric Clapton, and Jimi Hendrix. So explosive and pyrotechnic was his playing that people had trouble categorizing him as a blues or a rock player. Vaughan was tragically killed in a helicopter accident leaving from a gig, but every blues guitarist who comes up today has been influenced by him, and his work is the benchmark for modern electric blues playing. His signature tunes include "Pride and Joy," "Texas Flood," and "Love Struck, Baby."

Eddie Van Halen (1955–)

Rock guitar's equivalent to Jackson Pollock, Eddie Van Halen's improvisationally inspired splatter-note approach to metal guitar completely reinvented the style starting in the late '70s. He turned two-handed tapping into a common guitar technique (thanks to his groundbreaking "Eruption"), while pushing the limits of whammy bar and hammer-on expertise. Van Halen is also a master at fusing blues-based rock with modern techniques, and his rhythm playing is one of the best examples of the integrated style (combining low-note riffs with chords and double-stops). A guitar hero in every sense of the term, his signature tunes include "Eruption," "Spanish Fly," and "Panama."

Chapter 21

Ten Great Songs for Beginning Guitarists

. . . .

In This Chapter

▶ Uncovering ten popular songs in various styles and from different eras

▶ Finding the chords and lyrics

▶ Eyeing information and tips for playing the songs

. . . .

*O*ne of the best reasons to pick up the guitar is to play a song that most everyone knows and can sing along with. And by play a song, we mean using the guitar to strum the chords while you, or you and a friend (or you and several friends), sing the words and melody.

Following are ten songs that are ideal for playing and singing, either alone or with other people around to help out. All the songs in this chapter can be played in a number of keys, using just a few simple chords. Determine which key is best for you or your group based on what is most comfortable for the people singing. You may need to experiment to find the right key, but then after you find it, it's just a matter of playing through the song with confidence.

If you need help remembering the words to any of these songs, go on the Internet with a search engine using the word "lyrics" followed by the song's title in the search field to help jog your memory. If you need help with the chords, use an Internet search engine with "chords" and the song title in the search field.

Blowin' in the Wind

Along with rock 'n' roll, the 1950s and '60s popularized folk music, bringing acoustic guitars into the spotlight as performers sang out on topics ranging from love to social protest. Bob Dylan was the most famous of this new era of popular performers known as *singer-songwriters,* and wrote many songs that he himself made popular, or that other artists covered. "Blowin' in the Wind" was a hit for both Dylan and the harmonizing folk trio Peter, Paul & Mary.

The chorus begins with the line "The answer, my friend, is blowin' in the wind," and that's the part where the harmonies come, so make sure someone tries to sing the harmony part if you have more than one person in your group who likes to sing.

Brown Eyed Girl

Written and recorded by Irish rock singer Van Morrison in 1967, "Brown Eyed Girl" remains one of Morrison's most beloved love songs and is a popular song choice for cover bands and karaoke participants. The verses are followed by a vigorous chorus consisting largely of nonsense syllables (a mixture of *sha-la-las* and *la-las* and a couple of *la-dee-dahs*), which is where the harmony vocals come in.

Hang On Sloopy

In this 1965 hit by the McCoys, a boy encourages his girl to keep her grip and assures her that it doesn't matter what her father's occupation is nor that she's from the wrong side of the tracks. "Sloopy" is the official rock song of the state of Ohio and is found in the repertoire of many marching bands. The chorus is jubilantly optimistic, driven by three major chords (the same ones that propel the verses).

House of the Rising Sun

The Animals, the British band, took this traditional folk song — a minor-key cautionary tale about a house of ill repute — electrified it, altered the lyrics, and turned it into a rock classic. The song doesn't contain a chorus, just a succession of verses (including an instrumental, played by the organ), which are all accompanied by an arpeggiated right-hand pattern over simple, first-position chords.

I Saw Her Standing There

Written by John Lennon and Paul McCartney and recorded by the Beatles, "I Saw Her Standing There" was first released as the B-Side of the Beatles' American No. 1 January 1964 single "I Want to Hold Your Hand." It became a chart hit in its own right in February 1964, and has been covered by Bruce Springsteen, Billy Joel, Jerry Lee Lewis, Little Richard, and the cast of *Glee*. Paul McCartney (who sang the original lead vocal when the Beatles did it many decades ago) regularly performs it in his live shows. Female cover versions (with "her" changed to "him" in the lyrics) include those by Tiffany and the Supremes.

I'm a Believer

Many of the Monkees' songs, including their hits, were written by non-band members. "I'm a Believer" reached No. 1 in the United States and was featured in the movie *Shrek* (sung by Eddie Murphy as Donkey). Neil Diamond, a well-known songwriter and singer in his own right, wrote the song, which is a testament to Diamond's songwriting talent because it sounds so quintessentially Monkees. The chorus begins with the line "Then I saw her face," and the next line, "Now I'm a believer," is where the harmony vocals jump in.

Leaving on a Jet Plane

Colorado-based singer-songwriter John Denver (who recorded his own version) wrote this folk favorite. The trio of Peter, Paul & Mary had a hit with it, in 1969, enhancing the arrangement with their signature vocal harmonies on the chorus. (Frank Sinatra, Spanky & Our Gang, Trini Lopez, and the cast of the TV show *Glee* also have covered the song.)

My Girl

"My Girl" was a hit for the Detroit-based Temptations, recording for the Motown label, but it was another Motown star who actually wrote the song, Smokey Robinson (who had his own successful career with his band the Miracles). This song features harmony vocals on the chorus and has a simple but effective guitar lick introducing the verses. If you have more than one guitarist in your midst, having one of you play this infectious guitar melody with the other strumming the chords may be fun.

Stand by Me

Performed by the former lead singer of the Drifters, Ben E. King, who also wrote the song (partnering with the noted songwriting team of Leiber and Stoller), "Stand by Me" was a Top 10 hit in 1969, where it blasted out of every jukebox, transistor radio, and P.A. system in America. It became a Top 10 hit again, in 1986, when it was featured in the Rob Reiner film of the same name.

Twist and Shout

The R&B band the Isley Brothers got to the charts first with this song (where it ranked in the Top 20), but the Beatles produced their own version, which reached No. 2 on the US charts. The song became popular again when it was featured in the films *Ferris Bueller's Day Off* and *Back to School*. Most people are probably more familiar with the Beatles version, where the Fab Four perform their famous harmonies on the *ahs* in the middle and end sections.

Part VII
Appendixes

In this part . . .

- ✔ If you want to move beyond simply reading tab numbers, Appendix A is for you. Find out how to make sense of the various dots, lines, and squiggles that appear in standard music notation. You also see how to find, on your fretboard, any note you may encounter in standard notation.

- ✔ Appendix B shows you, at a glance, how to play 96 of the most widely used chords — a must for any guitarist.

- ✔ In Appendix C, you find useful tips for getting the most out of the online audio tracks and video clips.

Appendix A

How to Read Music

Reading music can seem intimidating at first, but it's not difficult at all. Even little children can do it. This appendix explains the concepts of reading music in the context of a familiar song. After reading this appendix, you can practice your music reading by working on the songs throughout this book, using the standard notation instead of the tab. (If you have trouble getting the durations, you can check them against the audio tracks. And if you have trouble with the pitches, you can refer to the tab.)

The important thing to understand about written music is that it tells you three kinds of information all at the same time: *pitch* (the note's name), *duration* (how long to hold the note), and *expression and articulation* (how you play the note). If you think about how it all fits together, you recognize that our written music system is really pretty ingenious — three kinds of information all at the same time and in such a way that any musician can look at it and play just what the composer intended! Take a closer look at these three kinds of information that written music conveys simultaneously:

- ✔ **Pitch:** This element tells you which notes (or pitches) to play (A, B, C, and so on) by the location of *note heads* (the oval-shaped symbols) on a five-line *staff.* The notes take their names from the first seven letters of the alphabet (A through G), with the pitches getting higher as the letters proceed from A. After G, the next higher note is A again. (If you call it "H," you're sure to get some funny looks.)

- ✔ **Duration:** This element of music tells you how long to hold each note *relative to the pulse,* or *beat.* You may, for example, hold a note for one beat or two beats or only half a beat. The symbols that music scores use for duration are whole notes (𝅝), half notes (𝅗𝅥), quarter notes (♩), eighth notes (♪), 16th notes (𝅘𝅥𝅯), and so on.

- ✔ **Expression and articulation:** These elements tell you *how* to play the notes — loudly or softly, smoothly or detached, with great emotion or with no emotion (that one's rare). These instructions can consist of either little marks written above or below the note heads or little verbal messages written into the music. Often, the words are in Italian (*piano, mezzo-forte, staccato,* and so on) because when composers started adding expression and articulation to their scores, the Italians had the most influence in the music scene. Besides, Italian sounds so much more romantic than English or German.

The Elements of Music Notation

Figure A-1 shows the music for the song "Shine On Harvest Moon" with the various notational elements numbered.

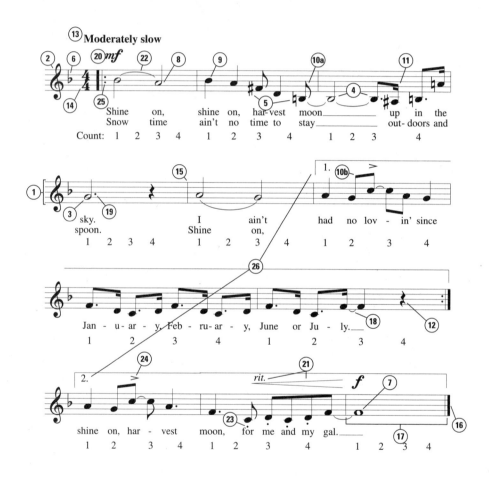

Figure A-1: Music for "Shine On Harvest Moon."

Pitch
1. Staff
2. Clef
3. G note
4. Ledger lines
5. Accidentals
6. Key signature

Rhythm
7. Whole note
8. Half note
9. Quarter note
10. Eighth note
   a. flagged
   b. beamed
11. Sixteenth note
12. Rest
13. Tempo heading
14. Time signature
15. Bar line
16. Double bar
17. Measure
18. Tie
19. Augmentation dot

Expression/Articulation
20. Dynamic marking
21. Crescendo and ritardando
22. Slur
23. Staccato dot
24. Accent
25. Repeat sign
26. Ending brackets

© John Wiley & Sons, Inc.

Review the notational elements in order, referring to the explanations that follow for each number. Numbers 1 to 6 explain the mechanics of reading pitches; 7 to 19 explain the mechanics of reading durations; and 20 to 26 explain expression and articulation markings.

Reading pitch

Table A-1 explains what the various symbols dealing with pitch mean in music notation. Refer to Figure A-1 and this table for the meanings of the symbols. Table A-1 refers to the symbols numbered from 1 to 6 in Figure A-1.

Table A-1		Pitch Symbols and Their Meanings
Number in Figure A-1	*What It's Called*	*What It Means*
1	Staff	Composers write music on a five-line system called a *staff.* In talking about the individual lines of the staff, refer to the bottom line as the *first line.* Between the five lines are four spaces. Refer to the bottom space as the *first space.* You can place note heads on lines or in spaces. As the note heads get higher on the staff, they get correspondingly higher in pitch. The distance from one line to the next higher space (or from one space to the next higher line) is one letter of the alphabet (for example, A to B).
2	Clef	The staff alone doesn't tell you the pitches (letter names) of the various lines and spaces. But a symbol called a *clef,* at the left edge of each staff, identifies a particular note on the staff. From that note, you can determine all the other notes by moving alphabetically up and down the staff (line to space to line, and so on). The clef you use in guitar music is called the *treble clef* (or G clef — see **G note** following).
3	G note	The **clef** you use in guitar music is the *treble clef* (sometimes called the *G clef*), which vaguely resembles an old-fashioned letter *G.* It curls around the second line of the **staff** and indicates that this line is G, and any note on that line is a G note. Some people memorize the letter names of all the lines (E, G, B, D, F, bottom to top) by the mnemonic "Every Good Boy Does Fine." For the spaces (F, A, C, E, bottom to top), they think of the word *face.*

(continued)

Table A-1 *(continued)*

Number in Figure A-1	What It's Called	What It Means
4	Ledger lines	If you want to write notes higher or lower than the **staff,** you can "extend" the staff, above or below, by adding very short additional staff lines called *ledger lines.* The notes (letter names) move up and down alphabetically on the ledger lines just as they do on the normal staff lines.
5	Accidentals (sharps, flats, and naturals)	The seven notes that correspond to the first seven letters of the alphabet (sometimes called *natural* notes) aren't the only notes in our musical system. Five other notes occur in between some of the natural notes. Picture a piano keyboard. The white keys correspond to the seven natural notes, and the black keys are the five extra notes. Because these "black-key" notes don't have names of their own, musicians refer to them by their "white-key" names, along with special suffixes or symbols. To refer to the black key to the *right* of a white key (a half step higher), use the term *sharp.* The musical symbol for a sharp is ♯. So the black key to the right of C, for example, is C-sharp (or C♯). On the guitar, you play a C♯ one fret higher than you play a C. Conversely, to indicate the black key to the *left* of a white key (a half step lower), you use the term *flat.* The musical symbol for a flat is ♭. So the black key to the left of B, for example, is B-flat (or B♭). On the guitar, you play a B♭ one fret lower than B. If you sharp or flat a note, you can undo it (that is, restore it to its natural, "white-key" state) by canceling the sharp or flat with a symbol known as a natural sign (♮). The last note of the first staff of Figure A-1, A-natural, shows this kind of cancellation.
6	Key signature	Sometimes you play a particular pitch (or pitches) as a sharp or flat (see the preceding explanation of **accidentals**) consistently throughout a song. Rather than indicate a flat every time a B occurs, for example, you may see a single flat on the B line just after the **clef.** That indicates that you play *every* B in the song as B♭. Sharps or flats appearing that way are known as a *key signature.* A key signature tells you which notes to sharp or flat throughout a song. If you need to restore one of the affected notes to its natural state, a natural sign (♮) in front of the note indicates that you play the natural note (as in the seventh note of Figure A-1, where the natural sign restores B-flat to B-natural).

Reading duration

A note's shape helps tell how long you need to hold it. Notes can have a hollow note head (as in the case of the whole note and half note) or a solid note head (quarter notes, eighth notes, and 16th notes), and the solid note heads can even have vertical lines (called *stems*) with *flags* (curly lines) dangling off them. If you join together two or more notes, *beams* (horizontal lines between the stems) replace the flags. Table A-2 refers to the symbols numbered from 7 to 19 in Figure A-1.

Table A-2	Duration Symbols and Their Meanings	
Number in Figure A-1	*What It's Called*	*What It Means*
7	Whole note	The longest note is the *whole note,* which has a hollow oval head with no stem.
8	Half note	The *half note* has a hollow oval head with a stem. It lasts half as long as the **whole note.**
9	Quarter note	The *quarter note* has a solid oval head with a stem. It lasts half as long as the **half note.**
10	Eighth note	The *eighth note* has a solid oval head with a stem and a flag (10a) or beam (10b). It lasts half as long as the **quarter note.**
11	16th note	The *16th note* has a solid oval head with a stem and either two flags or two beams. It lasts half as long as the **eighth note.**
12	Rest	Music consists not only of notes but also of silences. What makes music interesting is how the notes and silences interact. Silences in music are indicated by *rests.* The rest in Figure A-1 is a quarter rest, equal in duration to a **quarter note.** Other rests, also equal in duration to their corresponding notes, are the *whole rest* (▬), *half rest* (▬), *eighth rest* (ⁿ) and *16th rest* (ⁿ).
13	Tempo heading	The *tempo heading* tells you how fast or slow the song's beat, or pulse, is. As you listen to music, you (usually) hear an immediately recognizable beat. The beat is what you tap your foot or snap your fingers to.

(continued)

Table A-2 *(continued)*

Number in Figure A-1	What It's Called	What It Means
14	Time signature	Most songs group their beats in twos, threes, or fours. A song's beats may, for example, sound out as "one-two-three-four, one-two-three-four, one-two-three-four" and not as "one-two-three-four-five-six-seven-eight-nine-ten-eleven-twelve." The time signature looks like a fraction (but actually is two numbers sitting one above the other, with no dividing line), and it tells you two things: First, the top number tells you how many beats make up one grouping. In "Shine On Harvest Moon," for example, the top number, 4, tells you that each grouping contains four beats. Second, the bottom number tells you which type of note (quarter note, half note, and so on) gets one beat. In this case, the bottom number, 4, tells you that the quarter note gets one beat. Assigning the quarter note one beat is very common and so is having four beats per grouping. In fact, 4/4 time is sometimes called simply *common time,* and you sometimes indicate it by using the letter *C* instead of the numbers 4/4.
15	Bar line	A *bar line* is a vertical line drawn through the staff after each grouping that the **time signature** indicates. In "Shine On Harvest Moon," a bar line appears after every four beats.
16	Double bar line	A *double bar line* indicates the end of a song.
17	Measure (bar)	The space between two consecutive **bar lines** is known as a *measure,* or *bar.* Each measure consists of the number of beats that the **time signature** indicates (in the case of Figure A-1, four). Those four beats can comprise any combination of note values that add up to four beats. You may have four **quarter notes,** or two **half notes,** or one **whole note,** or one half note and one quarter and two **eighth notes** — or any other combination. You can even use **rests** (silences) as long as everything adds up to four. Check out each measure of "Shine On Harvest Moon" to see various combinations.
18	Tie	A short curved line that connects two notes of the same pitch is known as a tie. A *tie* tells you to not strike the second of the two notes but to sustain the first note for the combined time value of both notes.

Number in Figure A-1	What It's Called	What It Means
19	Augmentation dot (also called a dot)	A *dot* appearing after a note increases that note's time value by half. If a **half note** is equal to two beats, for example, a dotted half note is equal to three — two plus half of two, or two plus one, or three.

Understanding expression, articulation, and other terms and symbols

Expression and *articulation* deal with how you play the music. Table A-3, in conjunction with Figure A-1, tells you about the symbols and terms that deal with these issues. Table A-3 deals with the symbols numbered 20 to 26 in Figure A-1.

Table A-3	Expression, Articulation, and Miscellaneous Symbols	
Number in Figure A-1	**What It's Called**	**What It Means**
20	Dynamic marking	A *dynamic marking* tells you how loudly or softly to play. These markings are usually abbreviations of Italian words. Some of the common markings, from soft to loud, are *pp (pianissimo)*, very soft; *p (piano)*, soft; *mp (mezzo-piano)*, moderately soft; *mf (mezzo-forte)*, moderately loud; *f (forte)*, loud; and *ff (fortissimo)*, very loud.
21	Crescendo and ritardando	The wedge-shaped symbol is known as a *crescendo* and indicates that the music gets gradually louder. If the wedge-shaped symbol goes from open to closed, it indicates a *decrescendo,* or a gradual softening. Often, instead of wedges (or, as some musicians call them, "hairpins"), the abbreviation *cresc.* or *decresc.* appears instead. Another term you can use to indicate a softening of volume is *diminuendo,* abbreviated *dim.* The abbreviation *rit.* (sometimes abbreviated *ritard.)* stands for *ritardando* and indicates a gradual slowing of the tempo. *Rallentando* (abbreviated *rall.*) means the same thing. You can indicate a gradual increase in tempo by using *accel.,* which stands for *accelerando.*
22	Slur	A *slur* is a curved line that connects two notes of different pitch. A slur tells you to connect the notes smoothly, with no break in the sound.

(continued)

Table A-3 *(continued)*

Number in Figure A-1	What It's Called	What It Means
23	Staccato dot	*Staccato dots* above or below notes tell you to play the notes short and detached.
24	Accent	An *accent mark* above or below a note tells you to stress it, or play it louder than normal.
25	Repeat sign	The *repeat sign* tells you to repeat certain measures. The symbol ‖: brackets the repeated section at the beginning (in this case, measure 1), and :‖ brackets it at the end (refer to measure 8 of "Shine On Harvest Moon").
26	Ending brackets	Sometimes a repeated section starts the same both times but ends differently. These different endings are indicated by numbered *ending brackets.* Play the measures under the first ending bracket the first time, but substitute the measures under the second ending bracket the second time. Taking "Shine On Harvest Moon" as an example, you first play measures 1–8; you then play measures 1–5 again, and then 9–11.

Finding Notes on the Guitar

Figures A-2 through A-7 show you how to find the notes in standard notation on each of the six strings of the guitar. By the way, the actual *sounding* pitch of the guitar is an octave (12 half steps) lower than the written pitch. ***Note:*** You sometimes see two notes (for example, F♯/G♭) at the same fret. These notes (known as *enharmonic equivalents*) have the same pitch.

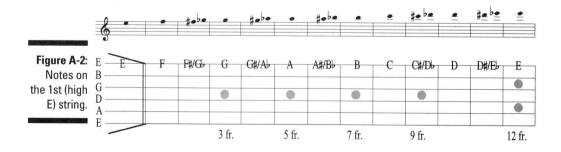

Figure A-2: Notes on the 1st (high E) string.

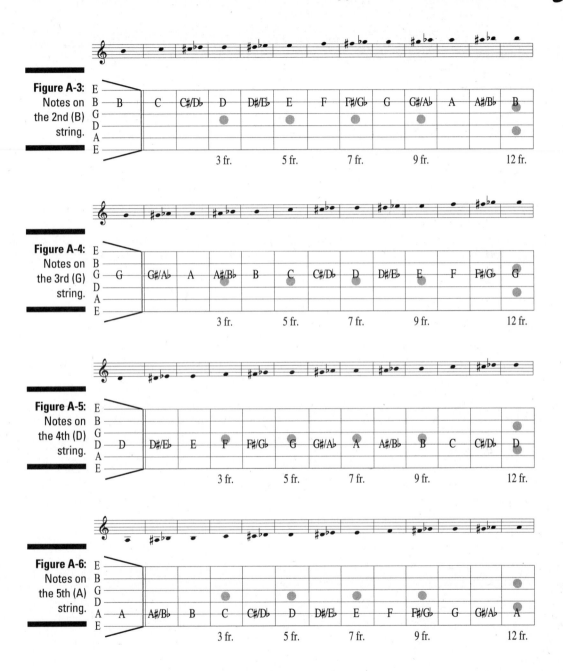

Figure A-3: Notes on the 2nd (B) string.

Figure A-4: Notes on the 3rd (G) string.

Figure A-5: Notes on the 4th (D) string.

Figure A-6: Notes on the 5th (A) string.

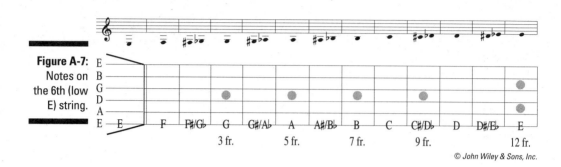

Figure A-7:
Notes on
the 6th (low
E) string.

© John Wiley & Sons, Inc.

Appendix B

96 Common Chords

● ●

*I*n the pages that follow, we include chord diagrams for 96 of the most widely used chords. The chords are arranged in 12 columns from C to B, for all 12 notes of the chromatic scale. Each of the eight rows shows a different quality — major, minor, 7th, minor 7th, and so on. So if you're looking at a piece of music that calls for, say, a Gsus4 chord, go over to the eighth column from the left and then down to the sixth row from the top.

Left-hand fingerings appear immediately below the strings (1 = index, 2 = middle, 3 = ring, and 4 = little). An *O* above a string means to play the open string as part of the chord; an *X* above a string indicates it isn't part of the chord and shouldn't be played. A curved line means to play the dots (fretted notes) immediately below the line with a barre. For a thorough discussion on playing chords, see Chapters 4 and 6.

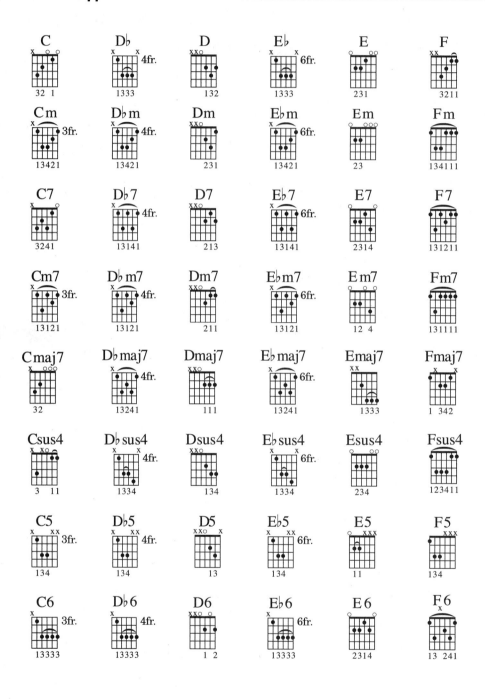

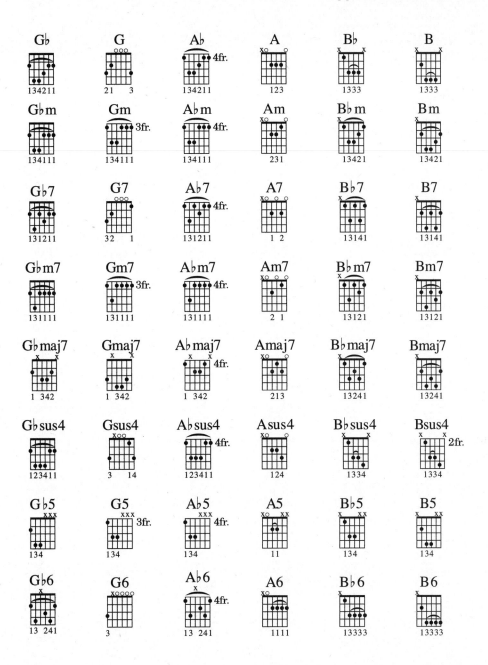

How to Use the Website

. . . .

Note: If you're using a digital or enhanced digital version of this book, go to www.dummies.com/go/guitar for access to the additional content.

Almost every music example in *Guitar For Dummies,* 4th Edition, is performed in an audio track or video clip and appears on the web page that corresponds to this book — more than 160 examples! This makes *Guitar For Dummies,* 4th Edition, a true multimedia experience. You have text explaining the techniques used, graphic representations of the music in two forms — guitar tablature and standard music notation — and audio and video performances of the music, complete with the appropriate tonal treatment (distortion for rock, sparkly acoustic colors for folk, and so on) and the appropriate accompaniment settings.

One fun way to experience *Guitar For Dummies,* 4th Edition, is to just scan the text by music examples, looking at the printed music in the book while listening to or viewing the corresponding performances on the website. When you hear something you like, read the text that goes into detail about that particular piece of music. Or go to a particular chapter that interests you (say, Chapter 11 on rock guitar playing), skip to the appropriate audio tracks and video clips on the website, and see whether you can hack it. A little over your head at this point? Better go to Chapter 9 on barre chords!

Relating the Text to the Website Files

Whenever you see written music in the text and you want to hear what it sounds like or see it performed on the website, refer to the box in the upper-right corner, which tells you the track number and start time (in minutes and seconds) or indicates the video clip number.

If you're searching for an example within an audio track, use the cue button of the *cue/review* function (also known as the *fast forward/rewind* control) of your media player to go to the specific time, indicated in minutes and seconds, within that track. When you get on or near the start time, release the cue button and the example plays.

If you want to play along with the audio track on the website, "cue up" to a spot a few seconds before the start time. Giving yourself a few seconds head start allows you to put down the remote and place your hands in a ready position on the guitar.

Many of the audio tracks and video clips are preceded by a *count-off,* which is a metronome clicking in rhythm before the music begins. This count-off tells you what the *tempo* is, or the speed at which the music is played. It's like having your own conductor going "A-one, and a-two . . ." so you can hit the *downbeat* (your first note of music in time) with the track. Examples in 4/4 time have four beats "in front" (musician lingo for a four-beat count-off before the music begins); examples in 3/4 have three beats in front.

We've recorded some of the examples in what's known as a *stereo split.* In certain pieces, the backing, or accompanying, music appears on the left channel of your playback device, while the featured guitar appears on the right. If you leave your device's *balance control* in its normal position (straight up, or 12:00), you'll hear both the rhythm tracks and the featured guitar equally — one from each channel. By selectively adjusting the balance control you can gradually or drastically reduce the volume of one or the other.

Why would you want to do this? If you've practiced the lead part to a certain example and feel you've got it down good enough to where you want to try it "along with the band," take the balance control and turn or slide it all the way to the left. Now the sound from only the left channel comes out, which is the backing tracks. The count-off clicks are in *both* channels, so you'll always receive your cue to play in time with the music. You can reverse the process and listen to just the lead part, too, which means you play the chords against the recorded lead part. Good, well-rounded guitarists work on both their rhythm *and* their lead playing.

We encourage you to listen to the audio tracks and view the video clips often, even when you don't have a guitar in your hands. Try to get in the habit of following along with the printed music whenever you listen to the audio tracks or view the videos, even if your sight-reading skills aren't quite up to snuff. You absorb more than you expect just by moving your eyes across the page in time to the music, associating sound and sight.

System Requirements

Make sure your computer meets the minimum system requirements shown in the following list. If your computer doesn't match up to most of these requirements, you may have problems using the software and files on the website.

✔ A PC running Microsoft Windows or Linux with kernel 2.4 or later or a Macintosh running Apple OS X or later

✔ An Internet connection

✔ A web browser

What You'll Find on the Website

The following sections are arranged by category and provide a summary of the goodies you'll find on the website. If you need help with listening to or viewing the files appearing on the website, refer to the instructions in the preceding section.

Audio tracks

Here is a list of the audio tracks on the website, along with the figure numbers that they correspond to in the book. Use this as a quick cross-reference to finding more about interesting-sounding tracks. In the Figure Number column, the first number equates to the chapter in which we explain how to play the track. Just flip through the captions and figures in order until you find the track you're interested in playing. To ease matters a bit, the exercises appearing in the text also contain the track numbers (and starting times, if appropriate) to help you find just the track you need.

Track	Start Time	Figure Number	Song Title/Description
1		n/a	Tuning Reference
2	0:00	4-2	Chord progression using A-family chords
	0:16	4-4	Chord progression using D-family chords
	0:43	4-6	Chord progression using G-family chords
	1:10	4-8	Chord progression using C-family chords
3		n/a	"Kumbaya"
4		n/a	"Swing Low, Sweet Chariot"

(continued)

(continues)

Track	Start Time	Figure Number	Song Title/Description
5		n/a	"Auld Lang Syne"
6		n/a	"Michael, Row the Boat Ashore"
7		5-1	Simple melody
8		n/a	"Little Brown Jug"
9		n/a	"On Top of Old Smoky"
10		n/a	"Swanee River" ("Old Folks at Home")
11		n/a	"Home on the Range"
12		n/a	"All Through the Night"
13		n/a	"Over the River and Through the Woods"
14		n/a	"It's Raining, It's Pouring"
15		n/a	"Oh, Susanna"
16		6-6	A 12-bar blues progression in E
17	0:00	7-4a	1-2-3-1 permutation exercise
	0:10	7-4b	1-3-2-4 permutation exercise
	0:20	7-4c	15-14-13 permutation exercise
18		n/a	"Simple Gifts"
19		n/a	"Turkey in the Straw"
20	0:00	8-1	C-major up-the-neck double-stop scale
	0:11	8-2	C-major across-the-neck double-stop scale
21		n/a	"Aura Lee"
22		n/a	"The Streets of Laredo"
23		n/a	"Double-Stop Rock"

Track	Start Time	Figure Number	Song Title/Description
24	0:00	9-2	Progression using E-based major barre chords
	0:13	9-3	Syncopated progression using E-based major barre chords
	0:27	9-4	Progression using major and minor E-based barre chords
	0:40	9-5	Progression using major and dominant 7th E-based barre chords
	0:53	9-6	Progression using major and minor 7th E-based barre chords
25		9-7	Christmas song progression using E-based barre chords
26	0:00	9-11	Progression using A-based major barre chords
	0:12	9-13	Progression using major and minor A-based barre chords
	0:26	9-14	Progression using major, minor, and dominant 7th A-based barre chords
	0:42	9-15	Progression using minor 7th A-based barre chords
	0:55	9-16	Progression using major and minor 7th A-based barre chords
27		9-17	Christmas song progression using A-based barre chords

(continued)

(continues)

Track	Start Time	Figure Number	Song Title/Description
28	0:00	9-20	Power chord progression in D
	0:14	9-21	Heavy-metal power chord progression
29		n/a	"We Wish You a Merry Christmas"
30		n/a	"Three Metal Kings"
31	0:00	10-1a	Open string hammer-on
	0:07	10-1b	Hammer-on from a fretted note
	0:14	10-1c	Double hammer-on
	0:20	10-1d	Double hammer-on using three notes
	0:27	10-2a	Double-stop hammer-on from open strings
	0:34	10-2b	Double-stop hammer-on from 2nd to 4th fret
	0:41	10-2c	Double double-stop hammer-on
	0:47	10-3	Hammer-on from nowhere
32		10-4	Single-note hammer-ons from open strings
33		10-5	Strumming a chord while hammering one of the notes
34	0:00	10-6	Single-note hammer-ons from fretted notes
	0:08	10-7	Double-stop hammer-ons and hammer-on from nowhere

Track	Start Time	Figure Number	Song Title/Description
35	0:00	10-8a	Open string pull-off
	0:07	10-8b	Fretted note pull-off
	0:13	10-8c	Open string double pull-off
	0:20	10-8d	Fretted note double pull-off
	0:27	10-9a	Double-stop pull-off to open strings
	0:34	10-9b	Double-stop pull-off from fretted notes
	0:41	10-9c	Double double-stop pull-off
36	0:00	10-10	Single-note pull-offs to open strings
	0:09	10-11	Strumming a chord while pulling off one of the notes
37	0:00	10-12a	Slide with second note not picked
	0:07	10-12b	Slide with second note picked
	0:12	10-13a	Ascending immediate slide
	0:17	10-13b	Descending immediate slide
38		10-14	Chuck Berry–like slides
39		10-15	Changing positions with slides
40	0:00	10-17a	Immediate bend
	0:06	10-17b	Bend and release
	0:13	10-17c	Prebend and release
41		10-18	3rd-string bending in a rock 'n' roll progression
42		10-19	2nd-string bending in a lead lick

(continued)

(continues)

Track	Start Time	Figure Number	Song Title/Description
43		10-20	Bend and release in a lead lick
44		10-21	Bending in different directions
45		10-22	Intricate bending lick
46		10-23	Double-stop bend and release
47	0:00	10-24a	Narrow vibrato
	0:10	10-24b	Wide vibrato
48	0:00	10-25a	Left-hand muting
	0:08	10-25b	Right-hand muting
49		10-26	Syncopation through muting
50		10-27	Palm muting in a hard-rock riff
51		10-28	Palm muting in a country riff
52		n/a	"The Articulate Blues"
53		11-1	Chuck Berry accompaniment riff
54		11-2	12-bar blues progression in A using double-stops
55		11-4	Box I hammer-ons and pull-offs
56		11-5	Bending in Box I
57		11-6	Double-stop bend in Box I
58		11-7	Box I solo
59		11-9	Typical Box II lick
60		11-11	Typical Box III lick
61		11-12	12-bar solo using Boxes I, II, and III
62	0:00	11-13	Sus chord progression
	0:15	11-14	Add chord progression
63		11-15	Slash chord progression

Track	Start Time	Figure Number	Song Title/Description
64	0:00	11-16	Drop-D tuning phrase
	0:10	11-17	Power chord riff in drop-D tuning
65		11-18	Typical phrase in open-D tuning
66		11-20	Southern-rock lead lick in A
67		n/a	"Chuck's Duck"
68		n/a	"Southern Hospitality"
69		12-2	12-bar blues accompaniment
70		12-3	12-bar blues with boogie-woogie riff
71	0:00	12-6	Box IV riff with triplet feel
	0:10	12-7	Box V lick with slide to Box I
72	0:00	12-9	Box I blues lick
	0:13	12-10	Box II blues lick
	0:23	12-11	Box IV blues lick
73	0:00	12-13	Box I blues lick with major 3rd
	0:10	12-14	Box I double-stop blues lick with major 3rd
74		12-15	Riff showing typical blues phrasing
75	0:00	12-16a	Typical blues move
	0:10	12-16b	Typical blues move
	0:19	12-16c	Typical blues move
	0:29	12-16d	Typical blues move
76		12-18	Steady bass notes with the E blues scale
77	0:00	12-19	Repeated motive at the same pitch
	0:11	12-20	Repeated motive at a different pitch

(continued)

(continues)

Track	Start Time	Figure Number	Song Title/Description
78	0:00	12-21	Alternating between a lead lick and a bass groove
	0:13	12-22	Alternating between a lead lick and a bass lick
	0:26	12-23	Combining fretted notes and open strings
79	0:00	12-24a	Blues turnaround 1
	0:13	12-24b	Blues turnaround 2
	0:26	12-24c	Blues turnaround 3
	0:38	12-24d	Blues turnaround 4
80		n/a	"Chicago Shuffle"
81		n/a	"Mississippi Mud"
82	0:00	13-3	Em arpeggio
	0:07	13-4	Up-and-down Em arpeggio
83	0:00	13-5	Lullaby pattern
	0:10	13-6	Thumb-brush pattern
84	0:00	13-7	Thumb-brush-up pattern
	0:09	13-8	Carter style pattern
85	0:00	13-9a	Travis style, Step 1
	0:08	13-9b	Travis style, Step 2
	0:15	13-9c	Travis style, Step 3
	0:23	13-9d	Travis style pinch
	0:31	13-9e	Travis style roll
86		13-11	"Oh, Susanna" in Travis style
87		13-12	Travis style with open-G tuning
88		n/a	"House of the Rising Sun"
89		n/a	"The Cruel War Is Raging"

Track	Start Time	Figure Number	Song Title/Description
90		n/a	"Gospel Ship"
91		n/a	"All My Trials"
92		n/a	"Freight Train"
93	0:00	14-5	Free-stroke classical exercise
	0:15	14-8	Arpeggio classical exercise
	0:48	14-9	Contrapuntal classical exercise
94		n/a	"Romanza"
95		n/a	"Bourrée in E minor"
96	0:00	15-2	Typical "inside" chord moves
	0:17	15-4	Typical "outside" chord moves
	0:40	15-6	Faking a jazz chord-melody solo
	0:52	15-7	A melody dressed up with altered tones
	1:16	15-8	Approaching target notes from a fret above and below
	1:43	15-9	Playing a melody as arpeggiated chord tones
97		n/a	"Greensleeves"
98		n/a	"Swing Thing"

Video clips

Following is a list of the video clips on the website, along with the figure numbers that they correspond to in the book. Use this list as a way to see how to play figures and other techniques described in the text.

Clip	Figure Number	Description
1	2-1	Tuning using the 5th-fret method
2	n/a	Left-hand fretting
3	n/a	Right-hand position
4	3-9	Playing an E chord
5	4-2	Strumming A-family chords
6	4-4	Strumming D-family chords
7	4-6	Strumming G-family chords
8	4-8	Strumming C-family chords
9	n/a	"Kumbaya"
10	n/a	"Swing Low, Sweet Chariot"
11	n/a	"Auld Lang Syne"
12	n/a	"Michael, Row the Boat Ashore"
13	5-1	Playing a single-note melody
14	5-1	Alternate picking
15	n/a	"Little Brown Jug"
16	n/a	"On Top of Old Smoky"
17	n/a	"Swanee River"
18	6-1	Dominant 7th chords — D7, G7, C7
19	6-4	Minor 7th chords — Dm7, Em7, Am7
20	6-5	Major 7th chords — Cmaj7, Fmaj7, Amaj7, Dmaj7
21	n/a	"Home on the Range"
22	n/a	"All Through the Night"
23	n/a	"Over the River and Through the Woods"
24	n/a	"It's Raining, It's Pouring"
25	n/a	"Oh, Susanna"
26	7-1	One-octave C-major scale in 2nd position
27	7-2	Two-octave C-major scale in 7th position
28	7-3	Two-octave C-major scale with a position shift
29	n/a	"Simple Gifts"
30	n/a	"Turkey in the Straw"
31	8-1	C scale in double-stops moving up neck

Clip	Figure Number	Description
32	8-2	C scale in double-stops moving across neck
33	n/a	"Aura Lee"
34	n/a	"The Streets of Laredo"
35	n/a	"Double-Stop Rock"
36	9-1	Major barre chords based on E
37	9-2	Progressions using E-based major barre chords
38	9-7	Christmas song progression using E-based barre chords
39	9-8	Fingering the A-based major barre chord
40	9-11	Progressions using A-based major barre chords
41	9-17	Chords to "We Wish You a Merry Christmas"
42	9-20	How you use power chords
43	n/a	"We Wish You a Merry Christmas"
44	n/a	"Three Metal Kings"
45	10-1	Playing a hammer-on
46	10-8	Playing pull-offs and double-stop pull-offs
47	10-12	Playing slides
48	10-17	Playing bends
49	10-24	Varying your sound with vibrato
50	10-25	Left- and right-hand muting
51	n/a	"The Articulate Blues"
52	11-5	Lead passage with 3rd- and 2nd-string bends
53	11-7	Solo with slides, bends, pull-offs, and hammer-ons
54	11-12	Solo in three positions
55	11-15	Slash chords with a moving bass line
56	11-20	Country-rock and Southern-rock lead
57	n/a	"Chuck's Duck"
58	n/a	"Southern Hospitality"

(continued)

(continues)

Clip	Figure Number	Description
59	12-3	12-bar blues accompaniment in a triplet feel
60	12-6	Box IV lead lick in a triplet feel
61	12-18	Acoustic blues fingerstyle passage
62	12-21	Alternating between lead lick and bass groove
63	12-24	Four blues turnarounds
64	n/a	"Chicago Shuffle"
65	n/a	"Mississippi Mud"
66	13-3	Playing arpeggio style
67	13-6	Simple thumb-brush
68	13-8	Carter style
69	13-9	Playing the Travis pattern step by step
70	13-12	Travis picking in an open-G tuning
71	n/a	"House of the Rising Sun"
72	n/a	"The Cruel War Is Raging"
73	n/a	"Gospel Ship"
74	n/a	"All My Trials"
75	n/a	Freight Train"
76	14-5	Playing free strokes
77	14-7	Playing rest strokes
78	14-9	Playing counterpoint
79	n/a	"Romanza"
80	n/a	"Bourée in E minor"
81	15-6	Faking a jazz chord-melody solo with three chords
82	15-7	Dressing up a melody with altered notes
83	15-8	Approaching target notes from above and below
84	15-9	Making melodies from arpeggiated chords
85	n/a	"Greensleeves"
86	n/a	"Swing Thing"

Materials for your own music and chords

On the website, you also find, in the form of two PDF files, a sheet of blank music/tab paper and a sheet filled with blank chord diagrams. Print these pages out as you need them so you can write your musical ideas down and preserve them for later recall or posterity.

Troubleshooting

We tried our best to create files that work on most computers with the minimum system requirements. Alas, your computer may differ, and some files may not work properly for some reason.

The two likeliest problems are that you don't have enough memory (RAM) for the programs you want to use or you have other programs running that are affecting the running of a program. If you get an error message such as *Not enough memory,* try one or more of the following suggestions and then try playing the file again:

✔ **Turn off any antivirus software running on your computer.** Installation programs sometimes mimic virus activity and may make your computer incorrectly believe that it's being infected by a virus.

✔ **Close all running programs.** The more programs you have running, the less memory is available to other programs, including media-playing ones. Installation programs typically update files and programs, so if you keep other programs running, installation may not work properly.

✔ **Have your local computer store add more RAM to your computer.** This is, admittedly, a drastic and somewhat expensive step. However, adding more memory can really help the speed of your computer and allow more programs to run at the same time.

Customer Care

If you have trouble with any of the files on the website, please call Wiley Product Technical Support at 800-762-2974. Outside the United States, call 317-572-3993. You can also contact Wiley Product Technical Support at `http://support.wiley.com`.

To place additional orders or to request information about other Wiley products, please call 877-762-2974.

Index

● ●

• E •

• F •

About the Authors

Mark Phillips is a guitarist, arranger, and editor with more than 40 years in the field of music publishing. He earned his bachelor's degree in music theory from Case Western Reserve University, where he received the Carolyn Neff Award for scholastic excellence, and his master's degree in music theory from Northwestern University, where he was elected to Pi Kappa Lambda, the most prestigious U.S. honor society for college and university music students. While working toward a doctorate in music theory at Northwestern, Phillips taught classes in theory, ear-training, sight-singing, counterpoint, and guitar.

During the 1970s and early '80s, Phillips was Director of Popular Music at Warner Bros. Publications, where he edited and arranged the songbooks of such artists as Neil Young, James Taylor, the Eagles, and Led Zeppelin. From 1985 to 2013 he served as Director of Music and Director of Publications at Cherry Lane Music, where he edited or arranged the songbooks of such artists as John Denver, Van Halen, Guns N' Roses, and Metallica, and served as Music Editor of the magazines *Guitar* and *Guitar One.*

Phillips is the author of several books on musical subjects, including *Metallica Riff by Riff, Sight-Sing Any Melody Instantly, Sight-Read Any Rhythm Instantly,* and *How to Read Music.* In his nonmusical life, Phillips is the author/publisher of a series of "fun" high school textbooks, including *The Wizard of Oz Vocabulary Builder, The Pinocchio Intermediate Vocabulary Builder, Tarzan and Jane's Guide to Grammar,* and *Conversations in Early American History.* For the reference value of his numerous publications, he is profiled in *Who's Who in America.*

Jon Chappell is a multistyle guitarist, transcriber, and arranger. He attended Carnegie-Mellon University, where he studied with Carlos Barbosa-Lima, and he then went on to earn his master's degree in composition from DePaul University, where he also taught theory and ear training. He is a competition-winning flatpicker and fingerpicker, specializing in acoustic music.

Chappell was formerly editor-in-chief of *Guitar* magazine, founding editor of *Home Recording Magazine,* and musicologist for *Guitarra,* a classical magazine. He has played and recorded with Pat Benatar, Judy Collins, Graham Nash, and Gunther Schuller. He also has contributed numerous musical pieces to film and TV. Some of them include *Northern Exposure; Walker, Texas Ranger; All My Children;* and the feature film *Bleeding Hearts* directed by actor-dancer Gregory Hines.

In book publishing, Chappell has served as associate music director of Cherry Lane Music where he has transcribed, edited, and arranged the music of Joe Satriani, Steve Vai, Steve Morse, Mike Stern, and Eddie Van Halen, among others. He has more than a dozen method books to his name and is the author of *Rock Guitar For Dummies* (John Wiley & Sons, Inc.), *Blues Guitar For Dummies* (John Wiley & Sons, Inc.), Build Your Own PC Recording Studio (McGraw-Hill), and the textbook *The Recording Guitarist — A Guide for Home and Studio* (Hal Leonard).

Authors' Acknowledgments

The authors gratefully acknowledge the folks at John Wiley & Sons, Inc.: Tracy Boggier, Michelle Hacker, and Chad Sievers. Thanks to Rusty Cutchin of RCM and Brett Parnell for help in the video production. Special thanks also to Woytek and Krystyna Rynczak of W.R. Music Service for the music typesetting.

Publisher's Acknowledgments

Acquisitions Editor: Tracy Boggier, David Lutton

Project Manager: Michelle Hacker

Development and Copy Editor: Chad R. Sievers

Technical Editor: Paul Murin

Art Coordinator: Alicia B. South

Production Editor: Suresh Srinivasan

Cover Photos: Vereshchagin Dmitry/ Shutterstock

Apple & Mac

iPad For Dummies,
6th Edition
978-1-118-72306-7

iPhone For Dummies,
7th Edition
978-1-118-69083-3

Macs All-in-One
For Dummies, 4th Edition
978-1-118-82210-4

OS X Mavericks
For Dummies
978-1-118-69188-5

Blogging & Social Media

Facebook For Dummies,
5th Edition
978-1-118-63312-0

Social Media Engagement
For Dummies
978-1-118-53019-1

WordPress For Dummies,
6th Edition
978-1-118-79161-5

Business

Stock Investing
For Dummies, 4th Edition
978-1-118-37678-2

Investing For Dummies,
6th Edition
978-0-470-90545-6

Personal Finance
For Dummies, 7th Edition
978-1-118-11785-9

QuickBooks 2014
For Dummies
978-1-118-72005-9

Small Business Marketing
Kit For Dummies,
3rd Edition
978-1-118-31183-7

Careers

Job Interviews
For Dummies, 4th Edition
978-1-118-11290-8

Job Searching with Social
Media For Dummies,
2nd Edition
978-1-118-67856-5

Personal Branding
For Dummies
978-1-118-11792-7

Resumes For Dummies,
6th Edition
978-0-470-87361-8

Starting an Etsy Business
For Dummies, 2nd Edition
978-1-118-59024-9

Diet & Nutrition

Belly Fat Diet For Dummies
978-1-118-34585-6

Mediterranean Diet
For Dummies
978-1-118-71525-3

Nutrition For Dummies,
5th Edition
978-0-470-93231-5

Digital Photography

Digital SLR Photography
All-in-One For Dummies,
2nd Edition
978-1-118-59082-9

Digital SLR Video &
Filmmaking For Dummies
978-1-118-36598-4

Photoshop Elements 12
For Dummies
978-1-118-72714-0

Gardening

Herb Gardening
For Dummies, 2nd Edition
978-0-470-61778-6

Gardening with Free-Range
Chickens For Dummies
978-1-118-54754-0

Health

Boosting Your Immunity
For Dummies
978-1-118-40200-9

Diabetes For Dummies,
4th Edition
978-1-118-29447-5

Living Paleo For Dummies
978-1-118-29405-5

Big Data

Big Data For Dummies
978-1-118-50422-2

Data Visualization
For Dummies
978-1-118-50289-1

Hadoop For Dummies
978-1-118-60755-8

Language &
Foreign Language

500 Spanish Verbs
For Dummies
978-1-118-02382-2

English Grammar
For Dummies, 2nd Edition
978-0-470-54664-2

French All-in-One
For Dummies
978-1-118-22815-9

German Essentials
For Dummies
978-1-118-18422-6

Italian For Dummies,
2nd Edition
978-1-118-00465-4

e Available in print and e-book formats.

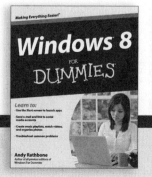

Available wherever books are sold. **For more information or to order direct visit www.dummies.com**

Math & Science

Algebra I For Dummies,
2nd Edition
978-0-470-55964-2

Anatomy and Physiology
For Dummies, 2nd Edition
978-0-470-92326-9

Astronomy For Dummies,
3rd Edition
978-1-118-37697-3

Biology For Dummies,
2nd Edition
978-0-470-59875-7

Chemistry For Dummies,
2nd Edition
978-1-118-00730-3

1001 Algebra II Practice
Problems For Dummies
978-1-118-44662-1

Microsoft Office

Excel 2013 For Dummies
978-1-118-51012-4

Office 2013 All-in-One
For Dummies
978-1-118-51636-2

PowerPoint 2013
For Dummies
978-1-118-50253-2

Word 2013 For Dummies
978-1-118-49123-2

Music

Blues Harmonica
For Dummies
978-1-118-25269-7

Guitar For Dummies,
3rd Edition
978-1-118-11554-1

iPod & iTunes
For Dummies, 10th Edition
978-1-118-50864-0

Programming

Beginning Programming
with C For Dummies
978-1-118-73763-7

Excel VBA Programming
For Dummies, 3rd Edition
978-1-118-49037-2

Java For Dummies,
6th Edition
978-1-118-40780-6

Religion & Inspiration

The Bible For Dummies
978-0-7645-5296-0

Buddhism For Dummies,
2nd Edition
978-1-118-02379-2

Catholicism For Dummies,
2nd Edition
978-1-118-07778-8

Self-Help & Relationships

Beating Sugar Addiction
For Dummies
978-1-118-54645-1

Meditation For Dummies,
3rd Edition
978-1-118-29144-3

Seniors

Laptops For Seniors
For Dummies, 3rd Edition
978-1-118-71105-7

Computers For Seniors
For Dummies, 3rd Edition
978-1-118-11553-4

iPad For Seniors
For Dummies, 6th Edition
978-1-118-72826-0

Social Security
For Dummies
978-1-118-20573-0

Smartphones & Tablets

Android Phones
For Dummies, 2nd Edition
978-1-118-72030-1

Nexus Tablets
For Dummies
978-1-118-77243-0

Samsung Galaxy S 4
For Dummies
978-1-118-64222-1

Samsung Galaxy Tabs
For Dummies
978-1-118-77294-2

Test Prep

ACT For Dummies,
5th Edition
978-1-118-01259-8

ASVAB For Dummies,
3rd Edition
978-0-470-63760-9

GRE For Dummies,
7th Edition
978-0-470-88921-3

Officer Candidate Tests
For Dummies
978-0-470-59876-4

Physician's Assistant Exam
For Dummies
978-1-118-11556-5

Series 7 Exam For Dummies
978-0-470-09932-2

Windows 8

Windows 8.1 All-in-One
For Dummies
978-1-118-82087-2

Windows 8.1 For Dummies
978-1-118-82121-3

Windows 8.1 For Dummies
Book + DVD Bundle
978-1-118-82107-7

e Available in print and e-book formats.

Available wherever books are sold. **For more information or to order direct visit www.dummies.com**

Take Dummies with you everywhere you go!

Whether you are excited about e-books, want more from the web, must have your mobile apps, or are swept up in social media, Dummies makes everything easier.

Visit Us

bit.ly/JE0O

Like Us

on.fb.me/1f1ThNu

Follow Us

bit.ly/ZDytkR

Watch Us

bit.ly/gbOQHn

Join Us

linkd.in/1gurkMm

Pin Us

bit.ly/16caOLd

Circle Us

bit.ly/1aQTuDQ

Shop Us

bit.ly/4dEp9

For Dummies is the global leader in the reference category and one of the most trusted and highly regarded brands in the world. No longer just focused on books, customers now have access to the For Dummies content they need in the format they want. Let us help you develop a solution that will fit your brand and help you connect with your customers.

Advertising & Sponsorships

Connect with an engaged audience on a powerful multimedia site, and position your message alongside expert how-to content.

Targeted ads • Video • Email marketing • Microsites • Sweepstakes sponsorship

21 Million Monthly Page Views & 13 Million Unique Visitors

For Dummies is a registered trademark of John Wiley & Sons, Inc.

Custom Publishing

Reach a global audience in any language by creating a solution that will differentiate you from competitors, amplify your message, and encourage customers to make a buying decision.

Apps • Books • eBooks • Video • Audio • Webinars

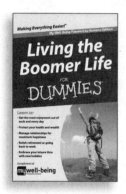   

Brand Licensing & Content

Leverage the strength of the world's most popular reference brand to reach new audiences and channels of distribution.

For more information, visit www.Dummies.com/biz

A Wiley Brand

Dummies products make life easier!

- DIY
- Consumer Electronics
- Crafts
- Software
- Cookware
- Hobbies
- Videos
- Music
- Games
- and More!

For more information, go to **Dummies.com** and search the store by category.

For Dummies is a registered trademark of John Wiley & Sons, Inc.

FOR DUMMIE.

A Wiley Br